THE
ELUSIVE
STATE

THE ELUSIVE STATE

International and Comparative Perspectives

edited by

James A. Caporaso

SAGE PUBLICATIONS
The Publishers of Professional Social Science
Newbury Park   London   New Delhi

For information address:

SAGE Publications, Inc.
2111 West Hillcrest Drive
Newbury Park, California 91320

SAGE Publications Ltd.
28 Banner Street
London EC1Y 8QE
England

SAGE Publications India Pvt. Ltd.
M-32 Market
Greater Kailash I
New Delhi 110 048 India

Printed in the United States of America

Library of Congress Cataloging-in-Publication Data

Main entry under title:

The Elusive state : international and comparative perspective /
   [edited] by James A. Caporaso.
      p.   cm.
   Bibliography: p.
   Includes index.
   ISBN 0-8039-3381-9. — ISBN 0-8039-3382-7 (pbk.)
   1. State, The.   2. Comparative government.   3. International
relations.   I. Caporaso, James A., 1941-
JC325.E48   1989
320.1—dc20   89-34763
                                                                  CIP

FIRST PRINTING, 1989

Contents

1

Introduction: The State in Comparative and International Perspective

JAMES A. CAPORASO

After decades of neglect, the conception of the state is once again a central object of theory and empirical research (see Evans, Rueschemeyer, & Skocpol, 1985; *Daedulus*, 1979; and Carnoy, 1984 for excellent reviews and edited collections). In the Anglo-Saxon world, the reasons for neglect are not hard to find. The philosophy and methodology associated with logical empiricism stressed a decomposable world of atomic facts, each analytically separate from the others. The methodology itself found it difficult to be supportive of more holistic notions, such as political institutions or the state. Pluralism, the reigning version of domestic politics, saw everything as capable of reduction to group process. States, or governments, existed, to be sure, but pluralist theory interpreted them as instruments designed to advance individual and group interests. The pluralist state was primarily passive, reacting to pressures emanating from society. Its dependent role discouraged attention to it as an active agent in the political process.

The resurgence of interest in the state is more difficult to explain. There seems to be no compelling breakthroughs that have stimulated fundamental research. Contemporary research on the state is not of the puzzle-solving, paradigm-elaborating variety. Indeed, one of the most important academic articles on the state was written in 1968 (Nettl, 1968) but attracted very little attention until more than ten years later. Something was not quite yet ripe, and that something probably lay in the political rather than academic world.

If one discounts the cycles of academic fads (from state to government to political system back to the state), it is likely that renewed interest in the state stems from changes that have occurred, and that continue to occur, in and between state and society. The growth of the "public economy"

(Cameron, 1978) has characterized almost all economies of the advanced capitalist world, despite recent privatization movements. Indeed, the very idea of privatization served to highlight the problematic dividing line between public and private power (Maier, 1987). Second, there is the clear role of the state in the process of economic development, either in the form of public ownership of productive capital (state-owned enterprises) or in the sectoral interventions in the economies of countries such as Taiwan and South Korea. The latter role of the state is noteworthy because it extends beyond the standard macroeconomic interventions of the more advanced liberal societies. Third, there has been an unmistakable resurgence of mercantilism in recent years, a pattern that simultaneously involves a utilization of state power and questions liberal-progressive assumptions underlying much of development theory. Finally, the early seventies witnessed some important changes in the "rules of the game" of the international system. These rules, incorporated in the Bretton Woods system, provided the institutional foundations of the international economic system for more than twenty-five years. During this period of time these rules functioned as a proto-state but their very constancy allowed them to be taken for granted. The suspension of many of these rules and the search for alternative institutional frameworks rekindled an interest in structures of rule at the international level.

While these background forces were important in stimulating interest in the state, the central motivation for the special issue of *Comparative Political Studies*,[1] and later this book, was the wide gap separating the perspectives of those working in comparative and international politics. When I wrote the letter of invitation to prospective contributors to the special issue in August 1985, I said the following:

> . . . I have been perplexed at the wide gulf separating the perspectives of comparativists and international relations scholars. This is not the time to go into the respective stereotypes each subcommunity has of the other. It is remarkable that such a gap exists at all; it exists in spite of the fact that many in both groups concede that 'the boundaries between domestic and international politics have crumbled.' If only that were the case for scholars of comparative and international politics.

The State in Domestic and International Politics

Despite numerous conceptual frameworks that would dissolve or dilute the state, the primary political unit of analysis remains the legally sovereign if not operationally autonomous nation-state. The study of comparative politics commences with the idea of domestic society and extends outward to incorporate information about the external environment (which in some cases, e.g., dependency theory, is territorially located within domestic society). The nation-state is generally not only the primary unit of analysis, it is also the foremost unit of action. As Stanley Hoffman put it long ago:

> One of the crucial features and paradoxes of politics today is that whereas internal politics are conditioned and affected by world problems more than ever before, the foreign policies of nations remain largely dictated by the domestic experience and by the nation's image of itself (Hoffman, 1960:4).

The story of the birth of the state in domestic society is often told in terms of a contract among persons in a state of nature. Somehow these persons existed and could contract with one another in the absence of a political mechanism to ensure the minimal level of trust and agreement. Original contractors presumably lifted themselves up by their own bootstraps, effecting a result (trust, submission to a common sovereign) that would seem to be presupposed by the very act of their contracting. But the contract story serves another function apart from the attempt to explain how states came into being. It provides a rational reconstruction of the advantages of the state and society over anarchy and the state of nature.

So the state responds to the predicament of society, or rather presociety—the need for order, elementary property rights—what we might call *primary public goods*. Whether the state responds to societal interests according to the Marxian or pluralist account is an important variation but one that is nevertheless subordinate to a larger societal-centered theme. From here, i.e., from the establishment of these foundations that can be called the *constitution of society*, the role of the state in domestic society is clear: the regulation of the economy, coordination of conflict among groups, the provision of rules and standards of public life, etc.

What about the state in international politics? It is the same state that we deal with in domestic politics, only now it is facing outward and viewed in the context of its interactions with other states. The state is Janus-faced. Viewed from the inside, it provides (at its best admittedly) for stability, order, and security. Substantive agreement is not presupposed but commitment to a common set of procedural norms for resolving disagreements is. Viewed from the outside, the interaction of sovereign states who disagree on substance but do not subscribe to certain procedures for resolving conflict is a recipe for anarchy. Thus, the idea of anarchy, though rightly criticized by recent scholarship (Ashley, 1984; Alker, in press), is often taken as a metaphor for the field of international politics as a whole.

The differences between domestic and international politics, though easy to exaggerate, can be identified on a number of dimensions: the level of decentralization in the system (Hoffman, 1960:1), the physical and social distance among interacting units, the disparate levels of consensus among societal and intersocietal groups, and perhaps most importantly, the degree to which the exercise of organized state power (in violent and nonviolent forms) is contested or noncontested. Domestic units indeed have their problems of order, their secessionist groups, multiple centers of organized violence, while international politics has its elements of order. In fact, as McCamant has argued (1983), in certain areas of the world (e.g., Latin America) during significantly long periods of time, international peace is much more common than domestic peace.

All of the above suggests an alternative view, one not based on the idea that the differences between domestic and international systems are trivial, but that the international system is not simply a dead aggregate of domestic actions projected outward. Instead, the international system has its elements of society, however embryonic its form, however halting and reversible its development. To say that international society constitutes an anarchy may be true in the sense of absence of government; it is, as Nardin argues, far less true of the other senses of anarchy—absence of laws, absence of order (Nardin, 1983:35). In any case, to ignore the societal aspects of the international system is to pass up an important thread for analyzing movement in that system and to represent the laws of balance of power politics as timeless principles "governing" relations among independent sovereign units. It is also to miss an important comparative theme, a theme that enables one to detect similarities and differences at both the domestic and international levels.

Contributions of This Volume

The contributors to this volume were asked to focus on a topic of relevance for the general theme of the state in comparative and international politics. Explicit comparison of the role of the state in comparative and international politics was not the task of individual authors but would, it was hoped, emerge out of the dialogue of the several papers.

The chapter by James Rosenau, "The State in an Era of Cascading Politics: Wavering Concept, Widening Competence, Withering Colossus, or Weathering Change?," provoked the idea of the special issue a number of years ago. Rosenau sees the state as fluid, fragile, and continually contested, ". . . as readily torn down as built up." (p. 17 this volume). At their strongest, states ". . . adapt to the dynamics of history and persist through time." (p. 18). This is in sharp contrast to Krasner's chapter, in which states make their own histories as well as succumb to their constraints.

Consistent with the methodological individualism of American social science, Rosenau wants to "unpack the state" and to treat it as a number of continuous variables. In doing so, he formulates four perspectives on the state: one based on methodology, one on domestic politics, one on interdependence, and one on the adaptive resources available to the state. These are not to be thought of as conceptual frameworks but simply as alternative vantage points that yield somewhat different conclusions. The rest of the article examines the state in light of these four vantage points.

Ted Gurr, in "War, Revolution, and the Growth of the Coercive State," sees states as powerful and resilient institutional structures. According to him:

> . . . these states, typified by the regimes of the United States, France, the Soviet Union, and China, command more resources, absolutely and in proportion to the capabilities of their societies, and have greater capacities to organize and deploy human and material resources in the services of state policies, than any historical political systems, including the largest of empires (pp. 49–50, this volume).

Gurr is centrally interested in the development of the coercive powers of the modern state, as well as their disposition to use these capabilities. In developing his argument, he relies heavily on the historical route to understanding the modern state. Though he recognizes the importance of consensus, ideological integration, legitimacy and community formation in constructing national states, he places special emphasis on the historical development of organized state violence.

The chapter by Stephen Krasner, "Sovereignty: An Institutional Perspective," develops a theoretical framework relevant for understanding state power in a changing, and often challenging, environment. Though fashioned with the institutions of the nation-state in mind, there is little obstacle to applying the framework at the level of international institutions also. As with many others who question the durability of the nation-state in an environment that is rapidly changing, Krasner starts off by noting some of the challenges confronting the state: external economic disturbances, increasing interdependence, and the increasing cost (i.e., in terms of lost opportunities) of autarky in today's world. From these challenges, many have facilely concluded that the state system is increasingly irrelevant or, at the very least, must be supplemented by international and transnational institutions. The last thirty years have seen numerous theses of the "sovereignty at bay" type. But the "necrologists of international relations," as Kal Holsti calls them (Holsti, 1986), have to cope with a state system that not only "persists, survives, and staves off challenges," but one that actually thrives.

Krasner is not among those who jump from state challenge to state obsolescence. Instead, he treats the relationships between environmental challenges and state capacities as hypotheses to be investigated. In this investigation, he finds an institutional framework most helpful. Krasner provides the rudiments of a theory of institutional change that depart from the fluid, efficiency-governed, adaptive model of neoclassical economies. Individuals do not scan the menu of institutional alternatives daily and choose those most efficient for their purposes. There is a great deal of stickiness and irreversibility in institutional choices. Institutions persist not only through inertia and habit but also because past choices limit future ones.

Behind this view of institutions, there is an implicit clash between two fundamentally different views of history. The first view, which has some affinity to deterministic evolutionary theories, is equifinal in structure. Initial conditions and even subsequent choices matter very little since the engine of history lies in the environment and works its logic through the back door. The environment edits and winnows those institutional adaptations that emerge and forces the drift of institutional structures in a certain direction.

The second view has no built-in *telos*, no end state that must result. The historical process, and its outcomes, are much more contingent, depending heavily on variations in starting conditions and subsequent choices. History is not an equifinal process pushing toward a single, adaptive goal state, but rather a tree with a large number of branches, any one of which leads to different options in the future.

In the neoclassical model of institutional change, the long-term consequences of the road not taken are trivial, because all roads lead back to the same place. For economic theory, history is a process with a *telos*, and the core of that *telos* is provided by the idea of efficiency. The institutional theory advanced by Krasner has no such built-in directionality.

The immediate focus of Gregg Kvistad's chapter, "Radicals and the State: The Political Demands on West German Civil Servants," is the *Radikalenerlass*, or the "radicals decree" of the Federal Republic of Germany. This decree, issued in 1972, touched off a debate in West German politics, a debate that reflected both pressures within the contemporary polity and between the present polity and Germany's own past. Though interesting in its own right, Kvistad quickly engages the politics of the radicals decree with the more abstract issue of the role of the state in German politics. He reviews competing conceptions of the state, and finds the *Rechtsstaat* and *Beamtenstaat* useful to his purposes. We can see that these ideas exist as more than conceptual categories, as Hegel's abstract legacy (in the case of the *Rechtsstaat*) to the Federal Republic. Instead, these are ideas that have causal status today, despite their distant beginnings.

Kvistad's conception of the German state as embodying (i.e., attempting to embody) a distinctive concept of the public trust provides an important counterweight to the pure interest conception of politics offered by pluralism and public choice theory. The "holders of the public trust" become, according to the latter view, merely another set of actors in the expanded political-economic marketplace. The point here is not to argue the merits or limits of one or the other approach but simply to note that in one contemporary polity, a competing idea of the state proved to be of consequence.

In "Tactical Advantages Versus Administrative Heterogeneity: The Strengths and the Limits of the French State," David Wilsford examines the operation of the state in one country, France. As with Kvistad's chapter, the generality comes from the reach of the argument and the ways in which ideas deriving from classical political theory connect to modern political practice.

At one level, Wilsford's chapter attempts to formulate an alternative to the model of state domination by sectional interests in society. Kvistad's chapter drew on Hegelian sources for inspiration. Wilsford turns to Rousseau:

> For Rousseau, man's principal problem is his inevitable disunity resulting from society . . . The state then becomes the only means—however imperfect—of overriding the divisive forces of particular wills and instituting a unifying general will (Wilsford, this volume, p. 129).

The idea of the state *overriding* societal preferences sounds strange to the Anglo-Saxon ear. In the United States, the progression from individual preferences to group organization to lobbying and the making of public laws is a natural one. It corresponds to utilitarianism, pluralism, and the view of the state as derivative of societal forces. In the utilitarian state, "the people is my Caesar" may be taken as a motto of the ideology of the state (Harrison, 1983:195), if not its practice. In France, interest groups are viewed with a certain suspicion, and "freedom to associate," taken to be one of the most natural rights in Anglo-Saxon countries, is a freedom circumscribed by state power.

The core of the Wilsford chapter has to do with a certain tension present in all states but more pronounced in France. This is the tension between organized state power on the one hand and bureaucratic fragmentation and societal penetration on the other. The French state has certain tactical advantages against society that flow from its basic structure. Yet divisions within the bureaucracy could allow special societal groups a haven in various bureaucratic locations, a development that could carve the state into numerous self-interested constituencies. Wilsford skillfully examines this tension and provides some comparative insights about France and the United States.

The chapter by Rockman, titled "Minding the State—or a State of Mind? Issues in the Comparative Conceptualization of the State," provides a general theoretical overview of the state in comparative politics, not a small undertaking. Treatment of the state in international relations theory is simpler than in domestic politics, if only because of the strong simplifying assumptions which realism makes. Rockman poses two kinds of questions. First, how are we to understand the resurgence of interest in the state? He finds the answer in a combination of intellectual reasons and developments in the political world: privatization, the argument over the ungovernability of democracies, arguments over the boundaries of the welfare state. His point is not so much that these developments represent radical departures but that they serve to contest the boundaries of state power. Second, he asks how we are to understand an entity that is so diverse and multifunctional as the state. A partial answer is provided in his approach, which is to break down the state into its several purposes and to examine them separately. To those who see the state as a single, organized totality, this approach will not be satisfactory. Yet Rockman's emphasis on the decision-making, production, and intermediary state serves to organize our thinking about the complexity of the state.

Andrew Kirby's chapter, "State, Local State, Context, and Spatiality: A Reappraisal of State Theory," is written from the standpoint of a geographer. After critiquing a number of current approaches, he strives for a new interpretation. As a geographer one might expect him to emphasize the territorial dimension (federalism, centralization of rule). He does highlight the territorial dimension but perhaps not in the expected ways. He introduces the concept of the *local state*. This term does not denote an outlying unit in a federal system but instead the existence of small, spatially organized jurisdictional variations that permit the survival of local traditions, preferences, privilege, and ways of life. Kirby does not see these jurisdictional variations as vestiges of traditionalism or as local obstacles that have not yet yielded to modernity. With Kirby, as with Gurr, Rosenau, and Thomson, the state is not an accomplished fact. There is a continued struggle between centralizing and localizing tendencies.

One of the distinguishing characteristics of the modern state is its legal monopoly of violence. Realist international-relations theory and interdependence theory disagree about many things but the state as a violence monopolist is not one of them. Yet, as Thomson cogently argues in her chapter, "Sovereignty in Historical Perspective: The Evolution of State Control Over Extraterritorial Violence," the acquisition of this legal monopoly is a recent accomplishment, and it did not come easily. The state had competitors: pirates, privateers, mercenaries, and mercantile companies, all coexisting with states in wielding violence.

This is not to say that states were cut off from the violence carried out by other actors. Indeed, sometimes these actors were chartered to perpetrate violence on behalf of the state. However, the ability to control this violence, once in motion, was limited. Also limited was the ability of states to detect the origin of violence and to lay blame on particular countries. This simple inability to distinguish bandits from agents of states produced havoc. In the eighteenth century, the picture was far from one of a world of monopolists of violence operating with exclusive control within a given territorial area. If modern states possess this legal monopoly, it is the result of a conquest. Thomson's chapter demonstrates the fruitfulness of problematizing certain aspects of the state often taken for granted.

Finally, the chapter by Jeremy Paltiel, "China: Mexicanization or Market Reform?," tackles a centrally important issue for socialist economies, viz., the extent and nature of market reform and the impact of such reforms for the economy and society as a whole. Taking the relationship between state and economy as the focal point, Paltiel explores the ways in which the introduction of market reforms in China is related to changes in the state administration and in clientelist alliances between particular social groups and sections of the bureaucracy. The chapter makes considerable advances in drawing out the wider significance of market reforms for the economy, the state, and for property rights.

The idea of the state is so general as to offer pause in using it as an organizing device for a book. In this volume, it has served only as an umbrella concept, as a way of focusing otherwise even more disparate subject matters. At a minimum, the emphasis on the state in comparative and international politics should stimulate curiosity as to why the gap between the two fields is so wide, and it is hoped, to set in motion thinking about how the gap might be narrowed.

Note

1. The articles by Caporaso, Gurr, Krasner, Kvistad, Rosenau, and Wilsford appeared as a special issue of *Comparative Political Studies*, volume 21, number 1, April 1988.

References

Alker, H. R. Jr. (in press). The presumption of anarchy in world politics. In H. R. Alker, Jr. & R. Ashley (Eds.), *Anarchy, power, and community: Understanding international collaboration*. New York: Columbia University Press.

Ashley, R. K. (1984). The poverty of neorealism, *International Organization, 38*(2) Spring, 225-286.

Cameron, D. R. (1978). The expansion of the public economy: A comparative analysis, *American Political Science Review, 72*, 1243-1261.

Carnoy, M. (1984). *The state and political theory*. Princeton, NJ: Princeton University Press.

Daedulus (1979). Special Issue on "The State." 108(4).

Evans, P. B., Rueschemeyer, D., & Skocpol, T. (1985). *Bringing the state back in*. Cambridge: Cambridge University Press.

Harrison, R. (1983). *Bentham*. London: Routledge and Kegan Paul.

Hoffman, S. (Ed.). (1960). *Contemporary theory in international relations*. Westport, CT: Greenwood Press.

Holsti, K. J. (1986). *The necrologists of international relations theory*. (mimeo). Vancouver, B.C.: University of British Columbia.

Maier, Charles S. (1987). Introduction. In Charles J. Maier (Ed.). *Changing boundaries of the political*. Cambridge: Cambridge University Press (pp. 1-24).

McCamant, John F. (1983). Governance without blood. In Michael Stohl & George Lopez (Eds.). *The State as terrorist*. Westport, CT: Greenwood Press (pp. 11-42).

Nardin, T. (1983). *Law, morality, and the relations of states*. Princeton, NJ: Princeton University Press.

Nettl, J. P. (1968). The state as a conceptual variable. *World Politics, 20*, 559-592.

Although the concept of the state is pervaded with ambiguity and, thus, is of questionable utility, the analysis proceeds from the premise that it must be employed inasmuch as so many analysts treat it as useful. At the same time, it is argued that the concept is used in diverse and contradictory ways, including tendencies to treat the state both as increasingly omni-competent and increasingly impotent as an instrument for meeting and resolving collective needs. The analysis also concludes that states are quite resilient and capable of adapting to change under most circumstances.

2

The State in an Era of Cascading Politics: Wavering Concept, Widening Competence, Withering Colossus, or Weathering Change?

JAMES N. ROSENAU

A thousand years scarce serve to form a state;
An hour may lay it in the dust; and when
Can man its shatter'd splendour renovate,
Recall its virtues back and vanquish Time and Fate?
—Byron, from *Childe Harold*, Canto ii, 84

The poet's wisdom is profound. To understand that the state can be on the edge of collapse, that it is as readily torn down as built up, is to grasp an essential truth. It is to see the delicacy and fragility that can prevail behind the coercive controls and authoritative postures of states.

In itself, however, this perspective is not sufficient to the development of deep comprehension. It does not account for the numerous states that have come into existence in recent decades—from 51 signatories to the

---

Author's Note: This is a revised version of a paper presented at the 10th Congress of the International Political Science Association, July 15-20, 1985. I am grateful for the help of James Caporaso, Ivo Duchacek, Hossain Farahani, K. J. Holsti, Jane Jacquette, Gunnar Nielson, and an anonymous reviewer.

United Nations Charter in 1945 to a U.N. membership of 158 in 1984—and the relatively few that have ceased to function. Even as we recognize the fragility of states, in short, so do we also need to grasp how and why most states manage to adapt to the dynamics of history and persist through time.[1]

But what is the *it* that is torn down or built up? What are those phenomena called *states* that manage to adapt? The answer is unclear. As will be seen, the vast literature on the subject contains a wide array of definitions and formulations, many of which are ambiguous and convey the impression that the state is to politics what the hidden hand is (à la Adam Smith) to economics: its activities are often obscure and unobservable, but nonetheless it somehow manages to regulate the course of events in such a way as to produce specifiable outcomes. Thus, few, if any, conceptualizations of the state seem adequate to describe and analyze the phenomena that vary between the edge of collapse and the achievement of coherence.

A clue to an adequate formulation of the concept lies in Byron's insight that the state is susceptible to being reduced to "dust"—that is, whatever *it* may be, the components of the state are subject to fluctuation, to ups and downs, to backing and filling. It follows that the state needs to be conceptualized as a complex of variables and not as a constant. To anticipate and trace a state's movements toward coherence or collapse, it needs to be conceived as a complex of continuous variables that span a wide range of values rather than as a constant that either does or does not exist.

This conclusion runs counter to many formulations, from those of the realists who posit the state in terms of the presence of a force that is exerted in its name to those of a legal or diplomatic nature which, as in the 1933 Montevideo Convention, define states as those political units with four characteristics: "(a) a permanent population, (b) a defined territory, (c) a government, and (d) a capacity to enter relations with other states." Neither the realist nor the legal formulation allows for the kind of variability that underlies Byron's metaphor. The force, properties, and laws of a state can be measured and assessed, to be sure; but the variations that may thereby be traced are hardly descriptive of what *it* is that may turn to dust or range across various degrees of coherence. A population, territory, government, and foreign-relations authority may be prerequisites to the persistence of states, but these are static attributes and not core phenomena subject to variation.

No, the search for an adequate conceptual basis must probe deeper, into those realms where the dynamics of coherence and breakdown are generated. And, upon reflection, such a probe leads quickly to the realization that what can collapse into extinction or cohere into solidity are human relationships, that it is in these relational dynamics that the core phenomena are to be found and the state conceptualized as a complex of master variables.

Thus, at the risk of adding to the morass of formulations, here I have sought to achieve greater precision by defining the core phenomena of states—those authority structures that are as easily torn down as built up—as consisting of the norms governing relationships, the habits of voluntary and coerced compliance, and the practices of cooperation through which large numbers of people form and sustain a collectivity that possesses sovereign authority with respect to them. It is these patterns of compliance and cooperation, as they unfold in response to the application of law and the exercise of force, that fluctuate under changing circumstances. One need only reflect on the brief history of Lebanon to appreciate that variability lies in the norms, habits, and practices through which collectivities cohere, adapt, and remain sovereign within their own space. Indeed, Lebanon poignantly demonstrates the enormous difficulty of fashioning compliance and cooperation patterns that endure. A thousand years may be a poet's license, but such phenomena do not come readily into being and, accordingly, in a world of dynamic change they are continuously subject to coming undone.

For present purposes, therefore, it is the composite of these norms, habits, and practices that I have in mind when I refer hereafter to *the state*. Breaking the composite down into the prime observable, comparable, and variable dimensions of any given state, it is the degree of hierarchy that sets the rulers above the ruled, the degree to which the former enjoy autonomy with respect to the latter, the degree to which the use of coercive force is legal, and the degree to which these relationships are institutionalized that constitute the core variable complex through which the norms, habits, and practices of states can be traced and assessed. Or, to use a term currently in vogue, these are the core components of *statism*, the characteristics that signify the presence of more or less statism whereby societies are managed and economies regulated.

In other words, applying this formulation to the more conventional ways of referring to the state as a constant, the state finds expression in those individuals who act on its behalf, employing its force and applying its laws so as to preserve and enhance the norms, habits, and practices of the collectivity in its entirety (what I also call the *whole system*). Similarly, to distinguish between *strong* and *weak* states is to differentiate not between those that have large and small armies, but rather between those whose norms, habits, and practices facilitate deeply rooted coherence and those whose tendencies favoring the whole system's integrity and sovereignty are superficial.[2]

Given this conception of the state, the purpose of the ensuing analysis is to build on Byron's insight by outlining four different perspectives through which to approach the place of the state in today's world. These perspectives are often competitive, even mutually exclusive, but the goal here is to suggest ways in which they are overlapping and susceptible to synthesis. One of these perspectives is founded on methodological rigor, the second on the salience of domestic politics, the third on the power of global interdependence, and the fourth on the effectiveness of adaptive mechanisms. As will be seen, each perspective highlights a different answer to the question posed in the chapter's subtitle. If methodology seems paramount, then the state emerges as a wavering concept. If the domestic scene is treated as preeminent, the state is posited as having an ever-widening competence. If stress is placed on the consequences of the world's growing interdependence, the state appears as a withering colossus. If adaptive capacities are highlighted, then the state is seen as weathering change.

While a vigorous case can be made for each perspective, to do so, to argue for one as superior to the others, would be to ignore the empirical complexities and philosophical subtleties of life late in the twentieth century. To insist that only the widening-competence perspective is viable would be to downplay the transnationalization of global politics. To argue solely for the withering-colossus perspective would be to dismiss the diverse ways through which societies adapt to the challenges of our time. On the other hand, to rely exclusively on the argument that the state is adaptable and, thus, endlessly able to weather the challenges is to run the risk of treating it as an omnicompetent, predominant actor immune to the precariousness that Byron discerned. Likewise, to argue for abandoning the state as a tool of inquiry on the methodological ground that it is too ambiguous, too susceptible of wavering into reification, would be to risk ignoring the macrophenomena through which societal collectivities conduct their affairs.

In short, the state concept can either serve or undermine our scholarly endeavors. If it is to be serviceable as a means of achieving clarity on the many macroproblems that presently crowd the world's agenda, we need to recognize its multiple meanings and uses. Whatever definition of the state one may prefer, approaching it in the context of synthesizing several contradictory perspectives seems imperative as a prerequisite to cogent analysis.

The State and Its Chains

There is a compelling reason to view the task of sorting out and integrating these perspectives as urgent: a number of global trends (summarized below) may be converging to foster a worldwide crisis of authority which, in turn, may throw the world's images of political institutions and its conceptions of political processes into flux. Redefinitions of political life may develop and, along with them, respecifications of the norms, habits, and practices that comprise the state may evolve. Hence, it is a time for intellectual leadership, for political scientists to pave the way for new understandings of politics that are consistent with the emergent patterns and that, thus, shape how the world's politicians, journalists, and publics perceive the processes in which they participate. In the absence of such leadership, global political institutions may change faster than the world's capacity to comprehend them, and at that point orderly mechanisms for resolving conflict will surely be more unobtainable than ever.

Efforts to rethink what the state encompasses are urgent and important, all the more so because our initial reactions to the quickened pace of change are hardly encouraging. Political scientists have not been oblivious to the dynamics transforming world politics. On the contrary, these dynamics have fomented a resurgence of interest in the state and in restoring it as a prime analytic concept (e.g., see Matthews & Pentland, 1984; and Roder, 1985). Unfortunately, however, the resuscitation of the state concept has led, not to shared conceptual consensus, but to a multiplicity of surprisingly weak, discrepant, and vague formulations. It is almost as if an absence of clarity on the uses and limits of the concept has facilitated a headlong surge to embrace the state as a master variable. The result, it might be said, reversing and paraphrasing Rousseau, is that the state is in chains, but virtually everywhere it is thought to be free.

If this is the case, as argued below, then it is here, in the headlong surge to restore the state as a prime concept, that the greatest urgency lies: such a surge can set back inquiry for decades if we frame and pass on ill-defined abstractions that lead our successors to futile pursuits of an elusive reality, rather than to systematic empirical analyses. Freud is alleged to have done this to many generations of psychologists, each of which chased after ids, egos, and superegos without concern for the empirical foundation of their work. It is estimated that psychology was thus set back by some forty years. It is hoped that we can avoid this fate by exercising care in how we conceptualize the key actors and processes comprising the era of cascading politics that is now emerging.

To appreciate the strengths and weaknesses of the wavering, widening, withering, and weathering perspectives, it is useful to summarize the changing patterns of global life that may be altering the norms, undermining the habits, and constraining the practices of whole systems and, thus, possibly, drawing the chains around the state ever tighter. At the microlevel, the chains have been forged by a tendency on the part of people everywhere to replace their links to whole systems (e.g., societies and states) with greater attachments to subsystems (e.g., ethnic, racial, religious, and class groups).[3] This mounting *subgroupism* is conceived to derive largely from the inability of whole systems to confront and solve the big issues of our time and the resulting sense people have of having lost control over their own lives. Eckstein (1979:17) notes that this "lack of a sense of wholeness in contemporary developed states" was in earlier times "supplied by God, by the idea of Empire, by the belief in the natural order"—by, in effect, "majestic words for convention"—but that "now we have nothing left that is majestic but the state," and it has been "overtaken by history."

At the macrolevel, too, the chains may be tightening around the state. Through the diverse processes of aggregation whereby microconcerns are converted into macrophenomena, the advent of a pervasive subgroupism may be strengthening the authority structures to be found in all walks of contemporary life, thereby creating in every realm of society "a special world within an increasingly hollow framework of national states" (Eckstein, 1979:17). No less important, macrolevel changes appear to have been fostered by dynamic technologies that have shrunk physical and social distances and thereby transformed economies and sociopolitical structures such that events and trends in one part of the world are increasingly shaped by developments in other parts. The consequence of interest rates in the United States for people elsewhere, the capacity of the IMF to require Third World countries to adopt new and more stringent domestic policies, the advent of religious leaderships as prime political actors in Poland and Iran, the growing vulnerability of national embassies and commercial aircraft to capture and destruction, the opening up of space to military and industrial uses—these are but a few of the transnationalizing patterns that seem to be shrinking the world and rendering long-standing legal and geographical boundaries ever more tenuous.

Among the broad consequences of these global dynamics, three possibilities seem especially noteworthy here: (1) the legitimacy and authority of whole systems may be undergoing progressive diminution, thereby rendering governments less effective and encouraging further the trend toward subgroupism; (2) the distinction between foreign and domestic affairs may become increasingly obscure; and (3) the resulting tensions between and within subsystems may, in a number of ways, have become inextricably woven into a worldwide crisis of authority that, in turn, is marked by emergent structures and an overall pattern that I have labeled *cascading inter-dependence*. Hypotheses pertaining to the overall pattern and the various ways in which changes have cascaded across the global landscape are elaborated at length elsewhere (Rosenau, 1984, 1985, 1986), but their implications for the state need to be highlighted for present purposes.

However the state may be conceptualized, there are important ways in which the era of cascading interdependence appears to have narrowed its scope, lessened its autonomy, and constricted its capacity to adapt. Its scope seems narrowed by virtue of the fact that domestic problems now have a large international component—those associated with managing the national economy are conspicuous examples—with the result that long-established norms, habits, and practices are less and less sufficient as a basis for governments to resolve such problems on their own. Similarly, the autonomous capacity of states to be effective at home can be seen as increasingly dependent on either favorable circumstances abroad or the cooperation of foreign actors. Presumably, too, this diminished effectiveness has been exacerbated by the greater coherence of subgroups and their intensified readiness to press nonnegotiable demands, a process that can infuse stalemate and paralysis into governments and further constrains the norms, habits, and practices from which they derive their legitimacy.

There may be, moreover, a momentum built into the proliferation of the constraints immobilizing states. Each new evidence of lessened autonomy, reduced legitimacy, and diminished effectiveness can enlarge the readiness of subnational and supranational actors to ignore or challenge established lines of authority and evolve their own codes of conduct. The recent domestic histories of Lebanon, Poland, and Argentina, and the recent international roles played by Libya and Iran, are perhaps best viewed not as anomalies, but as exemplaries of the breakdown of traditional norms and the authority crises into which states and the state system have entered.

To be sure, most states still possess the means of coercion needed to repress rebellion and contain authority crises. But the maintenance of public order is not the same as framing effective policies and creatively adapting to change. Declaring martial law can keep people off the streets and out of meeting halls, but such actions cannot lower trade deficits or enhance agricultural production. Domestic tranquility, in short, can be enforced, but successful problem solving cannot. Indeed, often the enforcement of tranquility can diminish a state's capacity to cope with its internal and external challenges, as the regime in Poland and the military in Argentina recently found out.

The State as a Wavering Concept

To a considerable degree, our perspective on both the current circumstances constraining the state and its adequacy as an analytic tool is
rooted in the values and subjective purposes that drive our uses of the concept. Those whose values lead them to assume microsimilarities and to focus
on macrophenomena—such as realists who stress power and Marxists who
emphasize class conflict—are inclined to posit states as the primary actors
in world politics and to see them as ever capable of making the adjustments
necessary to maintain their primacy. For such analysts, there are no
methodological problems: the state is a given, a reality so significant as
to be self-evident. On the other hand, those whose values preoccupy them
with microdifferences as well as macropatterns—such as behavioralists who
concentrate on decision making and sociologists attentive to opinion
formation—are predisposed to attach relevance to substate and individual
actors and, thus, to see the primacy of states as problematic. It follows that,
for these analysts, the study of the state is plagued with methodological
difficulties: rather than a given, the state looms as an ambiguous abstraction, virtually an all-purpose residual category for analyzing those macroprocesses that cannot be readily explained through the observation and
cumulation of microphenomena.

As one who has long argued for theoretical syntheses of macro- and micro-
variables (Rosenau, 1986), my values lead me neither to dismiss the structures and processes of whole-system collectivities as too ambiguous nor
to accept the premise that a rigorous empirical approach to them is unnecessary. Rather, I argue that macro whole systems (of which the state
is one type) are as subject to systematic observation as their micro counterparts. Admittedly, developing such an argument has not been easy. The
state seems to waver so widely across the conceptual map of the discipline
that the strict empiricist in me balks at attempting to operationalize its
variables and thereby analyzing it in the context of a scientific methodology.
Yet, obviously, such an attitude is inconsistent with the urgency of the
aforementioned need to rethink the foundations of political life in the wan-
ing years of the twentieth century. This is a time for creative theorizing
and not conceptual debunking, and, thus, in preparing this analysis I quelled
my balkiness and returned to the concept of the state after a long absence.

This positive spirit did not yield immediate results, however. Long baffled
by the concept of the state, and chagrined that so many competent analysts
have no trouble with it, I spent many hours reading a number of recent
works on the subject, Marxist as well as non-Marxist, and I also went back

to some earlier, more traditional literature addressed to it.[4] To a large extent, however, I remain disconcerted by the wavering, multiple uses and elusive formulations of the concept, not to mention intimidated by an inability to reconcile such unqualified observers as those who assert that " 'the state' is not a thing . . . it does not, as such, exist," with those who argue that "nothing is more real in this world of ours than states."[5] Nonexistent? Nothing more real? But the words used to describe them bring to mind vague and ambiguous pictures. They convey images of an amorphous entity that wields great power. States intrude, protect, resist, assert, or otherwise engage in a wide range of actions that (usually) evoke compliance or (occasionally) defiance. Sometimes the entity is posited as a regime, at other times as a socioeconomic class, or as a government, or as a set of values. And whichever of these specifications are used, often the entity is conceived as having individuals that act on its behalf, but even more often its actions are not attributed to a concrete source. As such, its actions are either autonomous or dependent and, somehow, they result from thoughts, plans, expectations, calculations, and/or perceptions that articulate enduring concerns and widely shared values.

Most of all, it is puzzling why such profound ambiguities have not led analysts to consider abandoning the state concept. For a discipline deeply committed to dealing with observables, it seems only logical that the elusive characteristics of the state would encourage practitioners to turn elsewhere for their conceptual equipment. Yet, not only has this not happened, but the exact opposite trend has marked the discipline in recent years.[6] Despite its methodological problems, and notwithstanding the degree to which the scope, autonomy, and effectiveness of whole systems may have diminished, the state has become increasingly attractive as an analytic concept. Or, put more negatively, "The state, a concept that many of us thought had been polished off a quarter of a century ago, has now risen from the grave to haunt us once again" (Easton, 1981:303). Indeed, inquiries along this line have been elevated to "a statist approach" (Krasner, 1978, 1984; Lentner, 1984) in which a central process is that of "statization" (Clark & Dear, 1984:60). While chains may be tightening around the state, it is nonetheless widely regarded as worthy of restoration.

Why? A number of factors appear to have sustained the upsurge of efforts to reinstate the concept to a preeminent analytic position. One is that the diminished effectiveness of whole systems has highlighted their importance and the cruciality of social mechanisms for achieving cooperation on a huge, society-wide scale.[7] With much energy in the Third World being devoted to shoring up the states whose habits of cooperation and practices of compliance had originally been artificially induced by the dictates of colonialism, and with technology in the First and Second Worlds hastening the dynamics of change, the capacities of whole systems have been thrown in doubt, with the result that attention has focused increasingly on their delicacy and fragility. Under these circumstances it is hardly surprising that the state has reemerged as a master concept: the vast and rapid change has created a need for a baseline, for some conceptual means of identifying the constancies of whole systems, those enduring norms, habits, and practices through which the structures and processes of all-embracing collectivities preserve and/or promote their coherence and move toward their goals. Moreover, if it is the case, as Eckstein (1979) cogently argues, that only whole systems can effect the redistribution of resources that appear to be required by the challenges of an ever more interdependent world, the appeal of the state becomes all the more compelling. It offers the formal regulations, the "ordering device" (Eckstein, 1979:6), through which the processes of redistribution can be initiated and sustained by politicians and explored and grasped by students of politics.

A second factor underlying the revival of the state concept involves a deep disillusion with systems analysis. In both its cybernetic and structural-functionalist forms, the systems concept was brought onto the social scientific scene by the behavioralist movement of the 1950s and it quickly replaced the state as the prime means for examining how national societies managed their problems and moved toward their goals. At that time the state had been unquestioningly accepted as the political actor possessed of ultimate authority and, thus, capable of coping with any problem; but Easton's *The Political System* (1953), with its appeal for empirical theory and its denunciation of hyperfactualism, led the way in galvanizing several generations of political scientists into research that treated the state as a vague abstraction and sought instead to probe more precisely the dynamics whereby societal systems do or do not cope with internal and external challenges to their coherence and aspirations. The advent of systems analysis, of conceptual equipment that seemed capable of carrying explanation well beyond the limits imposed by the amorphousness of the state concept, was a liberating breakthrough of heady proportions for the 1950s-1960s generations.

With hindsight, however, it is clear that the resulting expectations greatly exceeded the potentials of systems analysis. The comparative approach, in which diverse systems were contrasted in terms of common structures and functions, posed as many problems as it solved and certainly did not yield findings anywhere near as exhilarating as had been anticipated. Likewise, the stress on modernization and democratic development in the Third World facilitated by systems analysis and adopted as public policy in foreign aid programs did not precipitate trends toward either modernization or democracy anywhere near those that had been forecast. On the contrary, as the problems of the Third World deepened and its polities became more authoritarian in the 1970s, disillusionment with the systems concept followed for a number of analysts.

So the baby went out with the bath water and the bathing enterprise turned back to pre-1950s conceptual equipment for its cleansing needs. In the words of the overall theme of the 1981 Annual Meeting of the American Political Science Association, the task became that of "Restoring the State to Political Science."

Skocpol (1982:2-3) suggests a third explanation for the renaissance of the state as an analytic concept, namely, the shifting structures of world politics. Some of the very changes that are here seen as sources of cascading interdependence and, thus, as lessening the utility of the state as an organizing concept, she sees as conducive to greater reliance on it: "the Pax Americana of the period after World War II" encouraged Western social scientists to focus on modernization and to treat "spontaneous, socioeconomic and cultural processes . . . [as] the primary loci of change," all of which enabled them "to keep their eyes averted from the explanatory centrality of states as potent and autonomous organizational actors." According to Skocpol, the 1970s were a conceptual turning point not only because of the slow and erratic pace of the knowledge generated by the "structural-functional theories predominant in political science and sociology in the United States during the 1950s and 1960s," but even more because the American Century came to an abrupt end in the 1970s, rendering the United States and British economies "beleaguered . . . in a world of competing national states. It is probably not surprising that, at this juncture, it became theoretically fashionable to begin to speak of 'the state' as an actor and as a society-shaping institutional structure." As Skocpol sees it, the more the United States and Great Britain appeared like other "state-societies in an uncertain, competitive, and interdependent world of many such entities," the more did a "paradigmatic shift . . . [get] underway in the social sciences, a shift that involves a fundamental rethinking of the role of states in relation to societies and economies."

Krasner (1984) offers a somewhat different explanation for the resurgence of interest in the state as "the master noun of modern political discourse." Agreeing that vast changes have marked recent decades of global politics and that these include the rapid decline of American power, he sees the changes as highlighting the constraints at work in world affairs and, as if the operation of constraints somehow is not a form of behavior, as thus requiring the development of the analytic equipment inherent in the concept of the state:

> The more comfortable and familiar world of the 1950s and 1960s is gone. American global hegemony has eroded. "Enlighted" policies have not ended social ills. Economic problems do not respond to conventional solutions. Third World countries will not follow the path trod by the United States. Institutional arrangements that seemed to be part of the basic nature of things have come undone. In such a world the attention of scholars will turn from behavior within a given set of institutional constraints to the constraints themselves . . . "The state" will once again become a major concern of scholarly discourse (Krasner, 1984:243-244).

Whatever the full array of reasons for the resurgence of the state concept,[8] the result is a bewildering hodge-podge of definitions and formulations that waver across a broad conceptual spectrum. Long ago, MacIver discerned seven uses of the concept in the traditional literature (1926:3-4) and another observer claims to have identified 145 separate definitions of the state (Titus, 1931:45). More recently, Clark and Dear (1984:15) have identified no less than 18 different theories of the state and Deutsch has noted 12 types of states, at least 5 of which are "observable in history" (1986:12), while Jessop (1977:354-357) has elaborated 6 different conceptions in the classical Marxist literature alone, Wolfe (1977, as summarized in Clark & Dear, 1984:32) has delineated 7 different forms of the state in the history of just one country (the United States), and Benjamin and Duvall (1982) have examined 5 distinct forms of the phenomena encompassed by the concept. In none of these diverse formulations, however, have the key variables been operationalized in such a way as to clearly specify the empirical phenomena it embraces and, consequently, ambiguity is pervasive in all the formulations.

Indeed, for some analysts, a lack of operational indicators is not troublesome. They view the very abstractness of the concept as bringing together "a complex of disparate components" and, thus, allowing "us to organize our thoughts about the entity [i.e., the state], *even though it may exist in somewhat incoherent and fragmented form much of the time*" (Lentner, 1984:373, italics added). Only behavioral scientists who abhor ambiguous and reified entities that obscure the complexity of social processes are distressed by the incoherence and, thus, inclined to view the state as a fictional abstraction that confounds rather than clarifies inquiry. Those who have returned to the state concept, on the other hand, not only are undisturbed by the ambiguity inherent in their conceptualizations, but they are even inclined to see some virtue in it. As Benjamin and Duvall put it, *"fortunately* this position [of the behavioralists] is no longer ascendant in political science" (1982:6, italics added).

Fortunately? Yes, fortunately, in that the readiness to accept abstract, nonoperational conceptions of the state enables one to focus on, or waver among, notions of the state as—to cite Benjamin and Duvall's five meanings (1982:6-13)—an actor, as a set of organizing principles (or structures) for governance, as a set of social relations (or ruling class) governing society, as a set of norms that sustain the institutional-legal order of a society, and/or as those values that form the dominant normative order in society. To be sure, no self-respecting analyst would indiscriminately shift back and forth among these diverse conceptions. Yet, in the absence of a commitment to methodological rigor, all too many do so. Their broad normative concern for macroprocesses impels them unknowingly to waver among such diverse formulations, with the result that "much of the confusion surrounding debates and discussion over the state develops from authors shifting from one conception to another without explicitly realizing or noting it" (Benjamin & Duvall, 1982:13).

In short, the restoration of the state concept has not been accompanied by comparable efforts to recast it in precise terms. For many analysts, the concept still seems to be a residual category used to explain that which is otherwise inexplicable in macropolitics. All too often it takes them back to billiard balls, to unitary actors, to reified collectivities. It obscures their perception of how decision making, bureaucratic politics, and aroused publics affect the conduct of whole-system affairs. It inclines them to assume, rather than probe, the processes of aggregation and adaptation through which structures are transformed. It encourages them to underestimate the delicacy of system-subsystem relations by collecting all authority under the rubric of sovereignty instead of focusing attention on the conditions whereby authority is created, legitimacy sustained, and compliance achieved. It tends to deny them an ability to discern unintended consequences and to distinguish between manifest and latent functions. It predisposes them to rely on intuition rather than observation, to accept anthromorphism in place of empiricism, to use what Eckstein (1979:15) calls "a profoundly flawed" methodology—"the formal-legal mode of study." Moreover, "The very casualness of [such usages] is particularly disturbing . . . because we have thereby skirted the meticulous scrutiny of new terms now becoming customary in social science" (Easton, 1981:321).

And perhaps most serious of all, the ambiguity of the concept tends to discourage formulations in which the state is seen as a variable, as a collective entity and/or process that systematically varies either as a consequence of antecedent internal or external variables or as source of subsequent internal or external variables. Rather, no matter the level at which the state is conceptualized, a tendency to treat it as a constant, as an unvarying actor in a world of change, persists. More accurately, even when the state is seen as having undergone change, the change is posited as contextual background, and analysis then focuses on the new constant into which history has transformed it. Likewise, myriad are the studies that allow for shifts in particular elements or dimensions of states—such as their purposes and policies—but usually these fluctuations are not then linked back to corresponding adjustments by the whole systems in which they occur. The state itself, in other words, remains fixed even as it may be a site or agent of change. In this whole-system sense, the literature on the state is not rich with propositions that depict variability and invite empirical tests.

What does one do when confronted with a wavering concept that serves more as a residual category than as an inclusive theoretical tool? One could, along with Burton (1968:27-39), differentiate between states and systems, positing the former as serving the latter; but this solution hardly renders states into concrete empirical entities. Or one could, along with Easton (1981:322), issue an eloquent and revived plea for abandoning the concept, hoping that "the historic pressures toward more rigorous analysis, together with the current imperatives of applied research, will force those who are today flirting with the idea of the state to pause long enough to question its theoretical adequacy and its operational potential for continued empirical and theoretical research of the highest quality."

Such a hope, however, strikes me as wishful thinking. The normal line of reasoning on the need for empirical rigor simply does not apply to the state. The resurgence of the concept has been so powerful that cogent efforts to elaborate the pervasive ambiguities and weaknesses inherent in the concept tend to fall on deaf ears. Even analysts who do not hesitate to acknowledge its many flaws and diverse meanings—and many do indicate a keen awareness of the problem—continue to rely on the state as the centerpiece of their formulations (e.g., Bull, 1979; Haass, 1979). As implied above, for example, Benjamin and Duvall (1982) offer a devastating critique of the ambiguity and multiple uses of the concept, but instead of developing precise analytic equipment, they settle for cautioning against its misuse, reject three of its five meanings, and then proceed to differentiate between the other two by referring to State 1 and State 2 in their subsequent chapters. The power of the state as a label was apparently just too great: they could not resist retaining it even though using very different designations for their two meanings would enable their readers to differentiate more clearly between States 1 and 2 as they proceed through the manuscript.

In short, the reality of our analytic world is that the state is deeply embedded in our terminology and is unlikely to yield to efforts to replace it. It may be a fictional abstraction, but as such it is a serious fiction and, like all fictions that are so serious as to create their own reality, cannot be ignored.

If the rule of abandoning ambiguous conceptual equipment is thus inapplicable to the state, how does one proceed? I propose here to suspend antipathy to the concept and proceed as if the norms, habits, and practices conceived to comprise states can be specified in reasonable ways that allow for the framing of hypotheses that are testable and the derivation of variables that are operationally measurable. That is, despite the regrettable tendencies associated with the state as a residual, wavering category, I presume there are no inherent reasons why any of these dimensions of the state cannot be developed in terms of independent and dependent variables and precise indicators that trace their interactive variation. The norms, habits, and practices of states are not disembodied values that somehow prevail. They get articulated, enacted, transmitted, and revised through time by succeeding generations, and they are, thus, subject to empirical observation and evaluation if the analyst is ready to treat them for what they are, concrete patterns frequently and varyingly reiterated through specifiable deeds and words. Such patterns acquire a life of their own as successive generations are guided by them, but this is not to say they are beyond observation. If they have any meaning as embodiments of the state, they are bound to surface in recognizable and repeated forms of action.

I do not mean to imply that operationalizing this conception of the state is easy. On the contrary, the more abstract the norms, habits, and practices ascribed to it, the more does the state concept require analysts to make simplifying assumptions about the behaviors that are expressive of it, a process that is bound to seem distortive of the deeper dynamics that may be at work. Difficult as it may be, however, such dynamics can be rendered operational, if not in a fully satisfying way, at least in ways that contest ambiguity and allow for the teasing out of researchable propositions founded on hypothesized variability.

In short, the state need not be incompatible with the basic premises of empirical inquiry. It need not be a license to loose, unverifiable analysis. Those who use the concept need not waver across the conceptual landscape, if they remain sensitive to the fundamental canons of systematic observation.

Widening Competence or Withering Colossus?

Whatever the level of abstraction at which one may prefer to cast the state, its expanded role in domestic affairs and its diminished place in global affairs can be confusing. It requires one to entertain the possibility that the capabilities of states are *both* expanding and contracting, a perspective that seems bound to confound debate and foster misunderstanding. Yet such is the argument here, and it is precisely the simultaneity of states undergoing expanded and contracted capabilities that leads the analysis to conclude with an emphasis on the adaptive processes through which they cope with change.

It is not difficult to highlight the expanding competence of states. A large empirical literature has become available that depicts their extensive control over welfare programs and the domestic economy—what one observer calls "the new transparence of the state's impact on daily life" (Berger, 1979:30). And the evidence is substantial that societies have been changed in numerous ways through the conscious, programmatic policies of states (e.g., Wilensky, 1975). To a large extent, in other words, the state has become so dominant in the economic life of whole systems, be they organized along socialist or capitalist lines, that it appears to have a free hand in the conduct of public affairs. From this perspective, no chains are visible and, instead, the state seems omnicompetent. Indeed,

> the active penetration of society and economy by agents of the state is as extensive as at any previous period in the several-centuries history of the modern state, including the so-called "age of absolutism." This situation is widely recognized and is true of virtually all countries. "Statism" is pervasive. (Duvall & Freeman, 1981:100)

Nor is it sufficient to note the manifest ways in which state power seems so extensive:

> At the most general level, it is apparent that the state intervenes in virtually all aspects of everyday life . . . However, at a deeper level, there lies an uneasy suspicion held by many, radicals *and* conservatives, that the state does more than simply supply a range of public goods and services. There is an increasingly popular sentiment that it purposely controls, and even forms the

fundamental processes and structures of society, such as patterns of social
welfare, income distribution, and power. (Clark & Dear, 1984:1; italics in
the original)

The pervasiveness of the state in domestic affairs is especially conspicuous
in the present era because its activities are no less extensive in capitalist
as in socialist systems. So fully has the state become involved in the economic
growth of capitalist societies that it has become obsolete to speak of the
marketplace as the prime determinant of the course of the economy. Markets
still allocate values in important ways, but through techniques of demand
management and production stimulation, the state is also a key determinant:
its actions shape saving, investment, and consumption patterns as well as
the financing (even, in some cases, ownership) of new industrial sectors
and the preserving of old sectors. "Indeed, capital accumulation is so directly
and thoroughly affected by the state that it becomes increasingly difficult
conceptually to distinguish the 'public' from the 'private' in analyzing the
dynamics of accumulation. The capitalist spheres of production and exchange
and the capitalist state are inextricably bound together" (Duvall & Freeman,
1981:100).

Nor has the state's widening competence been confined to the domestic
economy. Modern technology has enlarged its power to maintain order,
mobilize consent, control opposition, and otherwise shape the social and
political lives of its members. Most notably, the microelectronic revolution has enhanced the capacity of whole systems to keep tabs on their farflung
memberships through the computer and to influence their orientations
through the television screen.

In sum, while the year 1984 fell far short of Orwell's prediction, there
are substantial indications that the last years of the twentieth century are
and will continue to be marked by states increasingly able and inclined to
intrude into their domestic arenas. Yet, despite the pervasiveness of statism,
widened competencies and expanded power bases do not necessarily result
in greater control and dominance. It remains questionable whether state
power is sufficient to resolve the major problems endemic to the complexity of the postindustrial era. Neither the concentration nor the expansion
of the resources presently available to the state enables it to end poverty,
eradicate unemployment, stabilize agriculture, eliminate pollution, or overcome the many other obstacles to a better quality of life within their jurisdictions. As already implied, there are numerous dynamics underlying the persistence of these intractable problems, and collectively they point to the
conclusion that the state has not and will not become the unchallengeable
colossus that it once was.[9] It may even be a withering colossus as some

of the trend lines describing its staying power move more in the direction of exemplifying Byron's insight than toward affirming Orwell's prediction.

The demands and challenges driving these trend lines originate both at home and abroad. Among the domestic sources eroding the state's competence, two are particularly noteworthy. One is the aforementioned proliferation of subgroupism, which has emboldened new publics to contest state policies and thereby lessen the legitimacy of whole-system actions. The other is a deepening of analytic skills on the part of individual citizens. The very facets of the microelectronic revolution that have widened the competence of states have also enlarged the competence of its members to articulate their interests, press their demands, redirect their support, or otherwise participate in public affairs. As elaborated elsewhere (Rosenau, 1984), moreover, the enhancement of these citizen skills and motives is worldwide in scope, embracing the Third World urban poor as well as the First World sophisticate. Even citizens of closed systems have evidenced greater involvement in the course of distant events and an improved capacity for piecing together alternative interpretations of them from the meager information they receive (Burns, 1983). Taken together, the combination of a more aggressive subgroupism and a more skillful citizenry has fragmented states and made them increasingly vulnerable to stalemate and paralysis insofar as their ability to address and resolve whole-system problems are concerned. Even military dictatorships have lately failed to withstand the withering of state power and, equally noteworthy, the militaries in stalemated countries such as Argentina, Brazil, Peru, and Uruguay appear to have withdrawn from power out of an appreciation of the intractability of domestic problems and a fear of taking the onus for failing to solve them.

But the main inroads into the power and legitimacy of the modern state come from abroad, from the previously noted dynamics that underlie the emergence of cascading interdependence on a global scale. There seem to be just too many ways in which the life of communities has become inextricably linked to external trends and institutions for the state to retain intact the norms, habits, and practices necessary to the resolution of its domestic problems. Even if subgroupism were to give way to broad and solid national consensuses, it is doubtful whether states would have access to all the levers necessary to initiate and shape desirable outcomes to their internal problems. Indeed, and ironically, the external linkages withering the state's scope and authority in domestic affairs can also be a source of its widening competence in such matters. The shrinking economic, social, and political distances that have transnationalized global affairs and made them ever more complex and interdependent have so greatly increased the vulnerability of domestic economies to external influences as to render domestic market forces decreasingly capable of sustaining stability and progress. So, in order to cope minimally with the internationalization of their market and banking systems, states have had to develop institutions and adopt policies that extend their competence to intervene in the flow of goods, services, and money at home. In so doing, however, those very same institutions and policies have become dependent on the course of events abroad whose vagaries they are designed to manage. Thus, for example, the widened competence of states inherent in new policies that impose austerity measures and travel restrictions stem to a large degree from their withering ability to withstand the encroachments of a shrinking world.

Stated differently, an inverse relationship between internal controls and external vulnerabilities appear to have emerged as a prime parameter within which the modern state must function. And since the trend line for the future seems likely to involve an ever growing vulnerability to global events and processes, the controls exercised by the state at home appear destined to undergo a corresponding expansion. Even the attempt of the Reagan administration to diminish the state's role in the domestic marketplace may prove to be an exception that eventually conforms to this rule. That diminution through lowered tax rates and relaxed regulatory mechanisms led to a volatile currency, the influx of foreign capital, huge trade deficits, and, thus, to an ever increasing involvement in the international marketplace, seems likely, in turn, to result in an eventual return to and a greater reliance on domestic controls.[10]

The close and complex connection between the state's widening domestic competence and its withering ability to remain in control of its own destiny is also evident in the transnational flows of people and knowledge that have accompanied the emergence of a global capitalist economy. As labor migrations from the Third to the First World swell, as technology transfers in the opposite direction expand, and as the gap between computer generations in the First and Second Worlds grows, the state has had to become increasingly attentive to the controls through which immigration policies, industrial peace, and high-tech facilities are maintained. Efforts to manage the flow of Latins into the United States and Turks into West Germany are among the more obvious instances of how states have become more active and manifest on the domestic scene. Similarly, the consequences of technology transfers to the Third World for labor in obsolete First World industries have added to the appearance of widened state competence even as they have also revealed yet another way in which the state has become linked into the global system. The Thatcher government's attempt to break the power of the unions in Britain's coal industry is illustrative in this regard.

To be sure, there is a positive side to the price states have to pay for their greater involvement in world affairs. As demonstrated by recent U.S. experience, for example, the dynamics of interdependence can lead to high interest rates and huge budget deficits, but so do they allow states to promote inflows of foreign capital, economic recovery, and other benefits to offset their diminished control over the course of domestic affairs. Stated differently, while greater interdependence has not eradicated the ability of states to shape and reshape their cost-benefit ratios, in important respects it has limited their choices in this regard, rendering each benefit more difficult to realize and each cost more resistant to reversal.

In short, there is no clear-cut answer to the question of whether the state's competence is widening or withering. More accurately, both are the case, with the widening and withering processes being functions of each other. The forecasts of those analysts who see a long-run future in which the state is replaced by new forms of whole-system organization founded on new norms, habits, and practices seem headed for negation, as do the predictions of those who anticipate the state becoming ever more colossal in the life of whole systems. Rather, given the continuing need for whole-system institutions that concentrate authority and mobilize collective action, the foreseeable future is likely to be one of states limping along, muddling through as it were, buffeted by internal and external forces that leave the norms, habits, and practices relevant to their capacities for cooperation hovering endlessly on the brink of transformation and yet managing to persist through time, sometimes resisting the tides of change and sometimes astride them, but with few exceptions somehow retaining sufficient legitimacy to sustain their essential structures and undertake collective action. While Byron's insight highlights the ever-present possibility of collapse, the likelihood is that most states will correct for the tendencies in this direction and fluctuate around levels of survival that fall short of total immobilization and extinction.

If this is so, if the competence of states is both widening and withering, analysis must turn to the question of how they will weather the dynamics of change that lie ahead. Faced with increased demands from within their borders and growing challenges from abroad, how will they cope? Through what dynamics are they likely to remain viable as whole-system collectivities?

The Adaptation of States

The answer to the foregoing questions lies in viewing the state as an adaptive entity and its activities as a politics of adaptation.[11] Such a perspective treats the cooperative norms, habits, and practices that sustain whole systems as the essential structures of a state. These structures are posited as endlessly fluctuating in response to internal dynamics and external challenges, any or all of which can intensity or lessen the readiness of the collectivity's members to adhere to the norms, habits, and practices through which their state retains its legitimacy, capabilities, and sovereignty. Normally the apparatus and institutions of the state are able to keep the fluctuations in its essential structures—such as the viability of its economy, the cohesiveness of its society, and the decisiveness of its polity—within acceptable limits that enable it to persist through time. Since nothing less than survival is at stake, all states set aside resources for—and assign personnel to—assuring that their essential structures remain intact. As a result, all states evolve mechanisms and institutions that routinely contain the fluctuations in their essential structures. The compromise, the policy reversal, the expedient concession, the scapegoat, the symbolic gesture, the alleged enemy, and the postponed goal are but a few of the mechanisms utilized widely to avoid excessive jolts to essential structures. As for the potential of a slow, long-term erosion of their competence posed by the challenges of subgroupism, states have developed a variety of coping mechanisms embedded in such processes as consociationalism, neocorporatism, and federalism.

Notwithstanding, their adaptive mechanisms and institutions, however, states can conform to Byron's forecast. They can act maladaptively as well as adaptively, and then can be unable to prevent such actions leading them ever closer to extinction. That is, states are always on the edge of collapse in the sense that their essential structures are rooted in human orientations and relationships that are susceptible to variation and, thus, can, under certain circumstances, fluctuate beyond the limits necessary to their maintenance. As recent developments in Afghanistan, Lebanon, and Poland clearly demonstrate, the internal and external challenges to the modern state can undermine the relationships and habits of compliance on which it is founded to the point where its existence becomes problematic.

Keeping the fluctuations of a state's essential structures within acceptable limits entails the maintenance of some form of balance—or, better, a range of balances—between the challenges from abroad and the demands from at home. As developed at much greater length elsewhere (Rosenau,

1981:63-79), the internal-external balance is conceived to approximate any of four generic types. If those who act on behalf of the state give higher priority to the conditions abroad than those at home as threats that might undermine the norms, habits, and practices of citizens, as is the case in East European states today, then the internal-external balance amounts to that of acquiescent adaptation. If, on the other hand, internal challenges are treated as predominant, as has long been true of South Africa, intransigent adaptation is the basic mode through which the state seeks to keep its essential structures within acceptable limits. Preservation adaptation results when both the internal and external challenges are experienced as extensive and defined as equally important, an orientation which tends to characterize most states late in the twentieth century. Promotive adaptation persists when those who act for the state treat both the internal and external demands as minimal and, thus, pursue policies that advance their own conception of the state's interests, a form of balance that often marks the conduct of revolutionary regimes (e.g., present-day Iran). Table 2.1 presents a summary of these four basic modes of adaptation.

Since states are usually able to keep the fluctuations in their essential structures within acceptable limits, their mode of adaptation tends to be enduring, measurable more in terms of eras than months or years. The norms, habits, and practices through which people orient themselves toward sovereign authority are too fundamental, and the resulting internal-external balances too deeply rooted in their culture, for the essential economic, societal, and political structures to fluctuate widely and extremely in response to day-to-day events. The external environments of states (such as the Soviet Union bordering Poland) tend to constitute conditions that are normally presumed to be given, just as the basic nature of their internal arrangements (such as the relative strength of the church and army in Poland) usually tend to be taken for granted—with the result that only under extraordinary circumstances are the norms, habits, and practices flowing from these presumptions subject to profound alteration.

This is not to say, however, that the adaptive perspective is marked by a conservative bias. Quite to the contrary, the notion of an enduring internal-external balance is an empirical observation and, thus, as will be seen, the adaptation model allows for disturbances that are so dislocating as to foster transformations from any of the four adaptive modes to any of the other three.

At least five advantages flow from positing any state as an adaptive entity in this way. Least important, and yet worthy of mention, is the terminological advantage offered by the adaptation framework. Labels may not facilitate

TABLE 2.1   The Nature of Decision Making in Different Patterns of Adaptation

Patterns of adaptations	*Demands and changes emanating from a society's external environment*	*Demands and changes emanating from the essential structures of a society*
Acquiescent	+	−
Intransigent	−	+
Promotive	−	−
Preservative	+	+

+ officials responsive to changes and demands, either because the changes and demands are intense or because their intensity is perceived to be increasing.

− officials unresponsive to changes and demands either because the changes and demands are not sufficiently intense or because their intensity is perceived to be decreasing.

comprehension, but they do serve to orient us toward our subject matter, perhaps excluding much that seems irrelevant and narrowing our focus on the dynamics we seek to explain. Viewed in this way, the adaptation framework allows for a richer way of classifying states in this era of cascading interdependence. Or at least it yields labels that highlight the persistent tensions between internal demands and external challenges. Instead of clustering states by their capabilities (say, as superpowers, middle powers, and small powers), by the degree and nature of their industrialization (say, as First, Second, and Third World states), or by their regional location (say, as African, Asian, or Western states), treating them as adaptive entities allows for categorizing them in terms of their way of coping with the dynamics of change (say, as acquiescent, intransigent, promotive, and preservative states).

Secondly, the adaptation perspective offers a useful means of addressing the problem of measurement and the task of subjecting states to empirical observation. As previously indicated, the norms, habits, and practices through which individuals and groups orient themselves toward sovereign authority are pervasive, and expressions of them are manifest in a wide variety of behaviors. Thus, they lend themselves to operationalization and to a careful tracing of their fluctuations. Statements of leaders and/or newspaper editorials, for example, can be content analyzed for shifts in the norms that sustain the legitimacy of states, just as changes in the habits and practices expressive of the legitimacy sentiments of citizens and organizations can be assessed through operationalized formulations in which various forms of compliance and protest are systematically measured. In so doing, moreover, such operational indicators can be readily expanded to include the priorities people attach to diverse internal and external threats to the state's coherence and unity.

This is not, again, to imply that one can expect to be free of difficulty in operationalizing the core phenomena of states. Obviously, such is not the case, since these phenomena are deeply embedded in the behavior through which public affairs are conducted from one day to the next. Yet, they do surface in a variety of concrete, observable forms, and thereby make it possible to treat the state empirically and not as a residual category or mystical entity.[12]

A third advantage of the adaptation approach is that it provides a means for anticipating and tracing those instances when Byron's forecast proves sound and a state collapses "in the dust." Whatever might be the legal definition of states, empirically they cease to exist when the fluctuations in their essential structures persistently exceed acceptable limits. Under these circumstances, the norms, habits, and practices of compliance are no longer evident and the state can be said to have disappeared and collapsed into its environment as those who were its members are observed directing their legitimacy sentiments toward new entities. Modern-day Lebanon is a quintessential example of a state following this pattern and moving toward total demise.

Fourth, the adaptation framework is well suited to analyzing the dynamics whereby states are able to cope with cascading changes that render the fluctuations in their essential structures as more than routine and pose the danger of moving them beyond acceptable limits. As previously noted, these structures are so essential and so deeply rooted that historically their fluctuations have been mild and easily handled. As the pace of global change has accelerated in recent decades, however, so have the internal and external demands on states intensified and fostered ever wider fluctuations in their essential structures. Yet, only rarely have these swings approached extinction. Such an outcome is always possible, but it rarely occurs. Why? Why is the Lebanese pattern more an exception than a rule? Because as a last resort under conditions of cascading change—or at least as the danger of demise looms on the horizon—states have both the option and the capacity to redress their fundamental internal-external balance, a process that amounts to what I have labelled an "adaptive transformation."[13]

Stated differently, although each of the aforementioned four basic modes of adaptation are so deeply embedded in the fundamental norms, habits, and practices through which people orient themselves toward sovereign authority that a state's adaptive mode tends to be enduring, it is the very nature of cascading interdependence that even the most enduring internal-external balances are subjected to intense assaults from a variety of directions. The austerity programs demanded by the IMF and the autonomy demanded by ethnic groups are but the more obvious features of the current world scene that can undermine the habitual ways of maintaining a state's internal-external balance. The probability of states undergoing adaptive transformation, in other words, would appear to be growing in proportion to the rising tide of subgroupism, the diminished effectiveness of governments, and the increasing dependence of whole systems on their international environments. That is, if confronted with the possibility of their essential structures fluctuating beyond the limits necessary to their maintenance, states seem likely to redress their internal-external balances as a means of weathering change and avoiding the fate Byron forecast. As the President of South Africa, P. W. Botha, has often said, reducing this same point to a terse phrase, "Adapt or die."

But adaptive transformations occur not only to avoid total collapse. Typically, they unfold when long-standing institutions at home and/or established circumstances abroad undergo profound alterations, which do not threaten the state's existence but do initiate shifts in the configuration—or relative importance—of the individual, governmental, societal, and systemic variables that have sustained the existing mode of adaptation. As illustrated by the recent histories of Iran and Libya, for example, changes which bring new individuals, groups, and/or regimes to power can result in reinterpreted mandates that lead to revised priorities among their commitments to internal and external stimuli. Similarly, as two decades of developments in the energy field have so clearly demonstrated, the discovery of new resources and sharp changes in the price of existing resources can transform systemic variables in such a way as to foster new internal-external balances, just as the discovery and organization of new common values among publics (as happened with Solidarity in Poland) can significantly shift the salience of societal variables. Indeed, it can readily be argued that most adaptive transformations occur, not as a response to the threat of extinction, but as a result of deep structural changes, which are rare in the history of national collectivities precisely because they give rise to new conceptions of the interplay between internal and external challenges.

A measure of the depth of these structural changes is provided by comparing the columns of Table 2.2, which summarize in a dichotomous format the configuration of individual, governmental, societal, and systemic variables that, by definition, must prevail for each of the four types of adaptation to persist, and noting what new priorities have to attach to each of the variable clusters if each adaptive mode is to undergo transformation to any of the other three. Twelve basic transformations are theoretically possible in this context, but as indicated in Table 2.3, the structural alterations they require are so great as to be empirically improbable in many instances. The crude probability estimates in the cells of Table 2.3 were derived by juxtaposing the relevant rankings from Table 2.2 that converge in each cell of Table 2.3. Such a procedure leads readily not only to the interpretation that some of the twelve possible transformations are likely to occur more than others, but also that more than a few of them involve a convergence of social and technological forces that is extremely unlikely.

Stated differently, since they call into question nothing less than the fundamental institutions that sustain collectivities and the basic orientations whereby people attach legitimacy to them, adaptive transformations seem likely to be marked by volatility and upheaval on the rare occasions when they do occur. Once the practices of compliance are free of their habitual foundations, demands are likely to grow and authority relationships are likely to become ever more fragile as the state seeks to keep the fluctuations within acceptable limits or, failing that, to develop a new internal-external balance in response to the dynamics of change.

That eras of adaptive transformation are pervaded by swelling demands and volatile relationships is implicit in the conditions that have to develop for six of the twelve possible transformations in Table 2.3 to unfold. Indeed, as elaborated elsewhere (Rosenau, 1981:83-87), the volatility and violence that attaches to these six possible transformations is likely to be so extensive that the probability of their occurring is virtually nil. In the case of a Type 1 transformation, for example, to replace an orientation of acquiescence to demands from abroad with intransigent postures toward them is to reverse the internal-external balance so totally that the agents

TABLE 2.2   The Relative Potencies of Four Clusters of Independent Variables as Sources of Four Types of National Adaptation

Relative potency of variable clusters	Acquiescent adaptation	Intransigent adaptation	Promotive adaptation	Preservative adaptation
HIGH	systemic	societal	individual	systemic societal governmental
LOW	societal individual governmental	systemic individual governmental	systemic societal governmental	individual

TABLE 2.3 Estimated Probability of Occurrence of the Twelve Types of Adaptive Transformation

| Transformation from: | Acquiescent adaptation | Transformation to: | | |
		Intransigent adaptation	Promotive adaptation	Preservative adaptation
Acquiescent adaptation	—	1 nil	2 low	3 high
Intransigent adaptation	4 nil	—	5 nil	6 high
Promotive adaptation	7 nil	8 nil	—	9 high
Preservative adaptation	10 low	11 nil	12 low	—

of the states are likely either to use force to prevent the reversal (as happened with martial law in Poland) or to be forcibly ousted and succeeded by new agents committed to the new adaptive mode (as happened with the advent of Khomeini in Iran). Only adaptive transformations to the preservative mode from any of the other three (Types 3, 6, and 9 in Table 2.3), the earlier analysis suggests, are capable of occurring without violence, albeit in each case new agents of the state are likely to come to power before the transformation is completed (as happened with the fall of the Marcos regime in the Philippines).

In short, states do possess mechanisms for weathering change and coping with the explosive dynamics of cascading interdependence. That these dynamics are simultaneously widening their role in domestic affairs and withering their autonomy with respect to foreign affairs points to the conclusion that in the long run all states will probably undergo transformation to preservative adaptation, to a form of balance in which the dynamics of cascading change are both absorbed and contained through a readiness to acknowledge that the state's internal and external conditions are equally relevant to its welfare and progress.

This is not a trivial conclusion. Assuming it is essentially correct, it means that what now appears as the chaos of our time will prove to be its stability. That is, for example, transformations to preservative adaptation will enable states with international debt problems to yield to pressures for domestic austerity programs without severely dislocating the norms, habits, and practices of compliance through which their coherence is sustained. Protests against the stringency of IMF demands may be vigorous and raucous, but in the end, states will go along and their publics will make the necessary adjustments.

Toward Synthesis

A final advantage of the adaptation framework remains to be noted. Namely, it offers a means of synthesizing the diverse perspectives on the state noted at the outset. As indicated above, the conception of states as adaptive entities enables the analyst to account for how they weather change and in so doing to take the waver out of the concept by highlighting operational measures for tracing their fluctuating responses to new domestic demands and new structures abroad. As for the withering and widening perspectives, these too fit readily into the adaptation framework. Contradictory as they may be, the strains toward the contraction and expansion of the competence of states are brought into juxtaposition by viewing them as expressive of fluctuations in the internal-external balances that mark the persistence of states through time. Indeed, by treating domestic and foreign challenges as components of an overall balancing mechanism, the adaptation model calls attention to the probability that the competence of modern states will simultaneously undergo widening and withering as the dynamics of interdependence grow and cascade across the global landscape.

Notes

1. For a cogent analysis in which the allegedly weak states of Africa are found to have considerable staying power, see Jackson and Rosberg (1982).
2. For an elaborate formulation of the distinction between the power of whole systems and the strengths and weaknesses of states, see Buzan (1983:65-69, 118-120).
3. For an extensive discussion of the diverse subsystems available for people to redirect their attachments, see Nielsson (1985). An incisive analysis of the powerful appeal inherent in subgroups can be found in Connor (1979).
4. The earlier literature included Avineri (1972), Cassirer (1946), Laski (1935), Lindsay (1947), MacIver (1926, 1947), Maritain (1951), and Watkins (1934). Among the more recent, neoMarxist works examined were Block (1977), Brucan (1980), Clarke (1983), Delaroix (1980), Guliasi (1983), Jessop (1982, 1983), Miliband (1974), and Poulantzas (1978), while the nonMarxist materials consisted of Andrews (1975), Badie and Birnbaum (1983), Bull (1979), Buzan (1983), Carnoy (1984), Clark and Dear (1984), Connolly (1984), Cornford (1975), Cox (1981), d'Entreves (1967), Dyson (1980), Fallers (1974), Haass (1979), Held (1983), Matthews and Pentland (1984), Poggie (1978), Roder (1985), and Skocpol (1979).

5. The first observation is from Miliband (1974:46) and the second from Ogg and Ray (1925), as quoted affirmingly in Lentner (1984:368).

6. For an exception which posits a trend toward the disuse of the state as a tool of analysis, see Cassese (1986:24). For another exception in which the word "state" is "avoided scrupulously" because "clarity of expression demands this abstinence," see Easton (1953:108).

7. For a cogent analysis of newly emergent mechanisms for large-scale cooperation, see Keohane (1984).

8. Four additional reasons—"Marxism revived, a longing for traditional, strong authority, economic liberalism, and policy analysis"—can be found in Easton (1981:304-307), and still another in Walker (1984:531): "It is no accident that the reassertion of the centrality of the state in world politics should be accompanied by a growing literature expressing concern about the inadequacy of our understanding of change in world politics."

9. For an analysis which highlights the limits of state power, see Biersteker (1980).

10. For a formal economic analysis that leads to the same expectation, see Schott (1984).

11. For a full presentation of the adaptation model, see Rosenau (1981). Somewhat similar models organized around the concept of "adjustment" and "conduit" can be found, respectively, in Ikenberry (1984) and Lake (1980). Deutsch (1986:213) offers still another formulation based on the "adaptive learning state."

12. For an extended discussion of the problems—and the possibilities—inherent in operationalizing the key variables in the adaptation framework, see Rosenau (1981:88-101).

13. The distinction between the fluctuations in a state's internal-external balance and the transformation of that balance is the difference between perturbations within a given set of priorities and an alteration of the priorities themselves. Any domestic and foreign policy issue on the state's agenda can give rise to momentary increases, decreases, and/or pauses in the readiness of its members to attach weight to the relative importance of internal and external challenges, but such fluctuations always occur in the context of a priority between the two sets of challenges. Transformations, on the other hand, become manifest as the momentary shifts all ensue in the same direction and result in a new context that either evens off the weight attached to the two sets of challenges or replaces one set with the other as more compelling.

References

Andrews, Bruce (1975). Social rules and the state as a social actor. *World Politics, 27* (July), 521-540.

Avineri, Schlomo (1972). *Hegel's theory of the modern state*. Cambridge: Cambridge University Press.

Badie, Bertrand, & Birnbaum, Pierre (1983). *The sociology of the state*. Chicago: University of Chicago Press.

Benjamin, Roger, & Duvall, Raymond D. (1982). *The capitalist state in context*. (mimeo). Minneapolis, MN: University of Minnesota.

Berger, Suzanne (1979). Politics and antipolitics in western Europe in the seventies. *Daedalus, 108* (Winter), 27-50.

Biersteker, Thomas J. (1980). The illusion of state power: Transnational corporations and the neutralization of host-country legislation. *Journal of Peace Research, 17* (September), 207-222.

Block, Fred (1977). The ruling class does not rule: Note on the Marxist theory of the state. *Socialist Revolution, 7* (May-June), 6-28.

Brucan, Silviu (1980). The state and the world system. *International Social Science Journal, 32*(4), 752-770.

Bull, Hedley (1979). The state's positive role in world affairs. *Daedalus, 108* (Fall), 111-123.

Burns, J. F. (1983, Sept. 4). Kremlin hints at concern over domestic reaction. *New York Times*, p. 18.

Burton, J. W. (1968). *Systems, states, diplomacy and rules.* Cambridge: Cambridge University Press.

Buzan, Barry (1983). *People, states and fear: The national security problem in international relations.* Chapel Hill: University of North Carolina Press.

Carnoy, Martin (1984). *The state and political theory.* Princeton, NJ: Princeton University Press.

Cassese, Sabino (1986). The rise and decline of the notion of state. *International Political Science Review, 7,* 120-130.

Cassirer, Ernst (1946). *The myth of the state.* New Haven, CT: Yale University Press.

Clark, Gordon L., & Dear, Michael (1984). *State apparatus: Structures and language of legitimacy.* Boston: Allen & Unwin.

Clarke, Simon (1983). State, class struggle, and the reproduction of capital. *Kapitalistate,* 113-130.

Connolly, William, (Ed.). (1984). *Legitimacy and the state.* New York: New York University Press.

Connor, Walker (1979). Nation-building or nation-destroying? *World Politics, 24* (April), 319-356.

Cornford, James (Ed.). (1975). *The failure of the state: On the distribution of political and economic power in Europe.* Totowa, NJ: Rowman & Littlefield.

Cox, Robert W. (1981). Social forces, states, and world orders: Beyond international relations theory. *Millenium: Journal of International Studies, 10* (Summer), 126-155.

Delacroix, Jacques (1980). The distributive state in the world system. *Studies in comparative international development,* (Fall), 3-21.

D'Entreves, Alexander Passerin (1967). *The notion of the state: An introduction to political theory.* Oxford: Oxford University Press.

Deutsch, Karl W. (1986). State functions and the future of the state. *International Political Science Review, 7,* 209-222.

Duvall, Raymond D., & Freeman, John R. (1981). The state and dependent capitalism. *International Studies Quarterly, 25* (March), 99-118.

Dyson, Kenneth H. F. (1980). *The state tradition in western Europe.* New York: Oxford University Press.

Easton, David (1953). *The political system: An inquiry into the state of political science.* New York: Alfred A. Knopf.

_____ (1981). The political system besieged by the state. *Political Theory, 9* (August), 303-325.

Eckstein, Harry (1979). On the 'science' of the state. *Daedalus, 108* (Fall), 1-20.

Fallers, Lloyd A. (1974). *The social anthropology of the nation-state.* Chicago: Aldine Publishing Co.

Guliasi, Les (1983). On the concept of state autonomy. *Kapitalistate,* 165-170.

Haass, Richard (1979). The primacy of the state...or revising the revisionists. *Daedalus, 108* (Fall), 125-138.

Held, David, et al., (Eds.). (1983). *States and societies.* New York: New York University Press.

Ikenberry, John (1984). *The state and strategies of international adjustment.* Paper presented at the annual meeting of the American Political Science Association (August 30), (mimeo).

Jackson, R. H. & Rosberg, C. G. (1982). Why Africa's weak states persist: The empirical and the juridical in statehood. *World Politics, 35* (October), 1-24.

Jessop, R. (1977). Recent theories of the capitalist state. *Cambridge Journal of Econometrics, 1,* 353-373.

_____ (1982). *The capitalist state: Marxist theories and methods.* Oxford: Marin Robinson & Co.

_____ (1983). Accumulation strategies, state forms, and hegemonic projects. *Kapitalistate,* 89-112.

Keohane, Robert O. (1984). *After hegemony: Cooperation and discord in the world political economy.* Princeton: Princeton University Press.

Krasner, Stephen D. (1978). *Defending the national interest: Raw materials investments and United States foreign policy.* Princeton, NJ: Princeton University Press.

_____ (1984). Approaches to the state: Alternative conceptions and historical dynamics. *Comparative Politics, 16* (January), 223-246.

Lake, David A. (1980). *The state as conduit.* Paper presented at the annual meeting of the American Political Science Association (August 30-September 2), (mimeo).

Laski, Harold J. (1935). *The state in theory and practice.* New York: The Viking Press.

Lentner, Howard H. (1984). The concept of the state: A response to Stephen Krasner. *Comparative Politics, 16,* (April), 367-376.

Lindsay, A. D. (1947). *The modern democratic state,* (Vol. 1). New York: Oxford University Press.

MacIver, R. M. (1926). *The modern state.* Oxford: Oxford University Press.

_____ (1947). *The web of government.* New York: Free Press (revised ed., 1965).

Maritain, Jacques (1951). *Man and the state.* Chicago: University of Chicago Press.

Matthews, Robert O., & Pentland, Charles (Eds.). (1984). The nation-state revisited. *International Journal, 39*(3), (Summer), 505-654.

Miliband, Ralph (1974). *The state in capitalist society.* London: Quartet Books.

Nielsson, Gunnar P. (1985). States and 'nation-groups': A global taxonomy. In Edward A. Tiriyakian & Ronald Rogoski (Eds.), *New nationalisms of the developed west.* Boston: Allen & Unwin, 27-56.

Ogg, Frederic, & Ray, P. Norman (1925). *Introduction to American government,* 2nd ed. New York: Century Co.

Poggi, Gianfranco (1978). *The development of the modern state: A sociological introduction.* Stanford, CA: Stanford University Press.

Poulantzas, Nicos (1978). *State, power, socialism.* London: NLB.

Roder, Karl-Heinz (Ed.). (1985). The future of the state. *International Political Science Review, 6*(1), 9-132.

Rosenau, James N. (1981). *The study of political adaptation.* New York: Nichols Publishing Company.

_____ (1984). A pre-theory revisited: World politics in an era of cascading interdependence," *International Studies Quarterly, 28* (September), 245-305.

_____ (1985). *Micro sources of macro global change.* Los Angeles: Institute for Transnational Studies.

_____ (1986). *Patterned chaos in global life: Structure and process in the two worlds of world politics*. Los Angeles: Institute for Transnational Studies.

Schott, Kerry (1984). *Policy, power and order: The persistence of economic problems in capitalist states*. New Haven, CT: Yale University Press.

Skocpol, Theda (1979). *States and social revolutions: A comparative analysis of France, Russia, and China*. Cambridge: Cambridge University Press.

_____ (1982). Bringing the state back in: A report on current comparative research on the relationship between states and social structures. *Items, 36*, (1-2), 1-8.

Titus, C. H. (1931). A nomenclature in political science. *American Political Science Review, 25*, 45-60.

Walker, R. B. J. (1984). The territorial state and the theme of Gulliver. *International Journal, 39* (Summer), 529-552.

Watkins, Frederick M. (1934). *The state as a concept in political science*. New York: Harper & Brothers.

Wilensky, Harold (1975). *The welfare state and inequality: Structural and ideological roots of public expenditures*. Berkeley, CA: University of California Press.

Wolfe, Alan (1977). *The limits of legitimacy: Political contradictions of contemporary capitalism*. New York: Free Press.

Modern states are powerful, resilient institutions, the most durable of which have established and consolidated their rule through conquest, revolution, and war. Successful involvement in violent conflict leads to the development of militarized and police states and reinforces elite political cultures that favor the use of coercion in future disputes. If warfare has unfavorable outcomes, elites will prefer noncoercive strategies in the future. From these and other propositions are derived models of the processes by which garrison states emerge and persist in autocracies and democracies. States with high material capabilities are more likely to become garrison states than weaker states, which tend to avoid international conflict and to rely on accommodation in internal conflicts. States with low political capabilities are susceptible to revolutionary overthrow and the establishment of revolutionary garrison states. The role of diversion of domestic conflicts to the external environment also is considered. One general conclusion is that only homogeneous democracies with low power capabilities and limited alliance obligations are unlikely to develop the institutions and political culture of militarized and police states.

3

War, Revolution, and the Growth of the Coercive State

TED ROBERT GURR

Introduction: The Bases of State Power

The late twentieth-century state, James Rosenau to the contrary, is an extraordinarily powerful and resilient set of institutions. The largest members of this political species, which populate most of the northern part of the globe, are the most powerful human agencies ever devised. I use *power* in a precise sense: these states, typified by the regimes of the United States,

Author's Note: The essential ideas of this paper were presented at a Roundtable on "The Garrison State as Amplifier of International Conflict," American Political Science Meetings, Washington, D.C., August 1986. My ideas on the sources of international conflict have been substantially influenced by a seminar on conflict behavior, which I have taught jointly with Manus Midlarsky at the University of Colorado. James Caporaso offered useful comments on an earlier version. Hayward Alker (1988) has urged me to break away from pessimistic realist assumptions.

France, the Soviet Union, and China, command more resources, absolutely and in proportion to the capabilities of their societies, and have greater capacities to organize and deploy human and material resources in the service of state policies than any historical political systems, including the largest of empires. The point can be substantiated by reference to data on the proportional size of the public sector, which in Western democracies has grown to approximately half of total national productivity, and the size and technical proficiency of military establishments.[1]

The material bases of the modern state's power have been conceptualized, and measured, in terms of the national territory's raw materials, population, energy and steel production, and military establishment. The analysis of the changing distribution of capabilities among states has been central to the empirical study of the causes of war.[2] The state's growing capacity to raise manpower and money is a recurring issue in the comparative study of national development (see the contributions to Tilly, 1975). The political bases of state power are equally or more important but less readily indexed. The logic I follow is that capabilities, as conceptualized by Singer, Bremer, and Stuckey (1972) represent the potential for or "necessary conditions" of state power. The three political bases of state power identified below are, by extension, conditions that determine the extent to which the state apparatus and rulers are able to recruit, extract, and organize human and material resources, then use them coherently (efficiently over time) in the service of the state's interests.[3] (1) Internal divisions along lines of communal and class cleavage almost always are a source of resistance to state efforts to mobilize human and material resources. The reduction and management of those divisions, by whatever combination of coercion and compromise, is a necessary political condition for optimum mobilization of national resources. (2) A second political basis of state power is the extent of the state's *legitimacy*: I use the term to denote people's acceptance of rulers' right to make binding decisions. Legitimacy determines the extent of voluntary compliance with state policies aimed at mobilizing and using resources. (3) The third basis is the capacity of the state apparatus to reach prompt and relevant decisions under both routine and crisis conditions. *Decisional efficacy*, as Eckstein denotes this property (1971), is essential for coherent use of mobilized resources in the pursuit of the state's objectives.[4]

International bases of state power also bear mentioning. To a variable but usually limited extent states can enhance their capabilities by drawing on external resources from other states: money, human skills, military aid. Considerably more important is the operation of the international capitalist system, which over time has contributed enormously to the material resources available to states at the core.[5] Whereas the world capitalist system has been of greatest benefit to states at the core, weaker states (not all of which are on the economic periphery) have gained most from the political infrastructure of the international system. By *infrastructure*, I mean the organization of states into regional groups, blocs, and alliances in which weaker members are propped up by the military, diplomatic, and material support of neighboring states and bloc leaders (on the persistence of weak African states, see Jackson and Rosberg 1982).

Coercion and the Growth of State Power

The assertions of the above three paragraphs may be debatable but are not at issue in this chapter. They are treated as assumptions, which provide the foundation for a closer theoretical examination of the sources of states' coercive capacities. The first premise of the specific argument is that the means of state coercion and the disposition of rulers to use them are grounded in the historical experiences of each successful state. Recurring deadly conflicts have accompanied the establishment and expansion of powers of most contemporary states. The states that dominate the modern global system and set the standards to which emerging nationalist elites aspire are those that have most effectively organized and deployed the means of coercion in the face of internal and external challenges. This is not to assert that the modern state rules necessarily or exclusively by force. Internal political consensus and acceptance of a state's claims to legitimacy are vitally important mechanisms of rule: consent freely given is cheaper and more reliable than consent given under duress. A similar principle operates in the international arena: negotiation, compromise, and respect for international standards of conduct are preferred, because they are usually less costly and more predictable, as alternatives to warfare.

The fact remains that force—the threat and use of deadly violence—is and always has been the *ultima ratio regnum*. All the durable states of the modern world established and consolidated rule over their national territories by the successful use of force: by revolution, by suppressing rebellions and secessions, by forcibly subordinating and integrating, in diverse combinations and sequences, neighboring peoples, reluctant aborigines, ethnic minorities, lords and merchants, peasants and laborers, kulaks and capitalists. Most of the durable states also have aggressively projected and defended their interests vis à vis bordering states in wars and lesser militarized disputes. Those with few wars, notably in Latin America, have benefited from the policing role of larger powers. The fact that some durable states, like those of Sweden and Switzerland, rarely make use of coercion in contemporary domestic or international disputes does not contradict the general assertion: historically these states relied on force to establish their internal authority and international legitimacy, and each maintains a substantial military establishment to give credibility to contemporary policies of neutrality.

One specific consequence of recurring involvement in war, internal or external, is the development of specialized organizations ready to fight future wars. A fateful threshold was passed when the states of early modern Europe began to establish standing armies and navies to replace the feudal levies, mercenaries, volunteers and privateers upon whom earlier monarchs had relied. A permanent military establishment was not enough to guarantee a state's survival in the international competition that reduced the number of European polities from c. 500 proto-states in 1500 (Tilly 1975:17-46) to less than 20 national states and empires in 1900 but it most certainly helped, especially for the states that took the lead in the development of new military tactics and weaponry (see McNeil 1982). In the exemplary case of Prussia, the quality of arms and armies was instrumental in transforming a small, resource-poor, peripheral state into the organizing force of Germanic Europe.

There have been parallel though less widely recognized processes in the development of agencies of internal security. European states began to establish specialized police forces in the late eighteenth and early nineteenth centuries: rural forces in response to rebellions, for example, by the British in Ireland, urban ones in response to the growing disorder of expanding cities (see Bayley 1975; Gurr 1976: 118-123). The last century has witnessed the development of new and more specialized agencies aimed at controlling political opposition, including paramilitary units, security services and secret police. The circumstances of their establishment and their size and scope are telling indicators of a state's concern about and capacity for maintaining internal order. A systematic comparative history of such agencies remains to be written.

Secret police are a particularly notorious species of internal security agencies, notorious because they have been widely used by authoritarian states as the instruments of massive political repression and murder. Typically secret police have been established during episodes of intense political conflict and have continued to operate afterwards under the direct control of the central organs of the state. The *Shutzstaffeln* (SS) is an example of such an agency: it was formed in 1925 as an instrument of Hitler's struggle for political power and after the Nazi victory was employed to consolidate and extend it. From 1932 on, Himmler and the leaders of the SS sections helped both to define and execute the coercive policies of the Nazi state: suppressing Communist and Socialist opposition, eliminating potential opponents in occupied areas, forceable resettlement of "slave" people, reprisals, and implementation of the Final Solution (Koehl, 1983). The secret police of Czarist Russia was founded in 1881 during a period of revolutionary activity. Later known as the *Okhrana*, it used surveillance, agents provocateur, and systematic campaigns of arrest, exile, and execution against revolutionaries and other political dissidents. It was also the inspiration for and direct ancestor of the Soviet secret police agencies: in December 1917, six weeks after the Bolshevik revolution, the *Cheka*, later known as OGPU, was established to deal with counterrevolutionaries. The Okrana's extensive files on dissidents, revolutionaries, and collaborators continued to be used by the Cheka under the direction of the same official, one Zheeben (Ivianski, 1980:59). The Cheka practiced revolutionary counterterror during the Civil War, OGPU provided the armed force and executioners for Stalin's forced collectivization of the peasantry in 1930-1932 (Conquest, 1986), and its successor, the NKVD, carried out the 1936-1938 purges in which more than half a million political activists died (Gouldner, 1977, 1978).

War and revolutionary conflicts leave legacies other than armies and secret police. The general principle is that elites who have secured state power and maintained their positions by violent means are disposed to respond violently to future challenges. The rational basis of their calculations is easily specified: successful use of coercion enhances their assessment of its future utility. Probably of equal importance is a normative factor that gets less attention in the literature: elites who are successful in the violent pursuit and defense of power become habituated to the political uses of violence, and their acceptance of coercive violence becomes part of the elite political culture or myth of their cadre and successors.

There is a great deal of scattered evidence, some direct and some inferential, about the circumstances in which rulers and functionaries have become habituated to political murder. Studies of the bureaucrats, physicians, guards and others who implemented the Nazis' Final Solution are particularly detailed and instructive.[6] We can infer that the recurring episodes of mass murder in Stalin's Russia were a reflection of Stalin's own disregard for the lives of any who stood in the way of his policies, imprinted on the operating code of security agencies and the political belief structures of a

generation of Soviet leaders. From a different century and a different con-
tinent, we have testimony that the traditional rulers of Baganda and the Zulu
(under the Paramount Chief Shaka) repeatedly committed large-scale,
ritualistic political murders, in Walter's interpretation (1969) for the purpose of demonstrating their absolute power. Part of the explanation may
lie in the fact that these rulers also were leaders in their people's recurring
wars with neighbors and, thus, were habituated to violence. This is another
subject that awaits comparative social research: the circumstances in which
elite and mass political cultures accept and celebrate what an American
historian has called *patriotic gore*.

The general arguments developed above can be stated in these
propositions:

Proposition 1: States involved in recurring episodes of violent conflict tend (a)
    to develop and maintain institutions specialized in the exercise of coercion;
    and (b) to develop elite political cultures that sanction the use of coercion
    in response to challenges and perceived threats.

Proposition 2: To the extent that coercive strategies lead to conflict outcomes
    favorable for the political elite, their preference for those strategies in future
    conflict situations is reinforced. To the extent that coercive strategies have
    unfavorable outcomes, political elites will prefer noncoercive strategies in
    future conflicts.

These propositions are general ones, applicable to both domestic and international conflict. The next section derives some implications of the propositions for different types of states in different conflict situations.

The Emergence of Militarized and Police States

National population, resources, and productivity provide the foundation
of state power, whereas effective national power depends on the state's
capacity to mobilize, organize, and deploy those resources efficiently in
the service of its objectives. Under what circumstances have ruling elites
chosen to concentrate national and political resources in the means of coercion? The broad outline of the answer follows from the preceding propositions: states that have repeatedly faced and successfully responded to
domestic and international conflicts are most likely to have developed the
characteristics of *garrison states*. Lasswell defined the garrison state as one
dominated by specialists in the management of violence. He anticipated that

democracies as well as autocracies, armed with the instruments of modern science and technology, could become predominantly concerned with—one might say fixated on—the expectation of violent challenges and the need to contain and respond to them (Lasswell, 1962:51-54).

I intend the garrison-state concept to designate states that maintain large-scale military and/or internal security establishments and whose elite political culture sanctions the use of extreme coercion. Such states are not necessarily dominated by Lasswell's specialists in violence. In democratic garrison states, as he recognizes, the specialists in violence may be subordinated to elected officials who have broader interests. Or, in Fitch's interpretation of the garrison-state concept, "effective power would be concentrated in the hands of a loosely knit elite of civilianized military officers and militarized civilians, with increasing integration of corollary skill elites . . . ." (Fitch, 1985:32). In my conceptualization the distinction between civilian and military elites is not consequential: the garrison state is characterized by a high concentration of coercive power and a disposition, by those at the center of the state apparatus, to use it.

Lasswell also distinguishes military and police states (1962:53) but does not elaborate on the distinction. It is crucial to my conception of the origins and character of garrison state. The militarized state, the term used here, maintains a large military establishment and is ruled by an elite whose policy agenda is dominated by preparations for war and national defense. The police state maintains a large internal security establishment and is ruled by an elite that relies primarily on coercion to control domestic opposition and implement state policies. Clearly the extent of militarization and reliance on coercion to maintain internal order are variables that can be treated as such in empirical analysis. This paper is concerned with the conditions of the more extreme manifestations of the phenomena: the emergence of a persisting pattern of garrison-state institutions and attitudes. Therefore, my propositions refer to the categorical types, though most of them can also be rephrased in probabilistic terms.

Another qualification: Some contemporary states have both sets of traits, but that does not justify treating all garrison states as similar. Whereas the United States and the USSR are both militarized states, the former has no semblance of the Soviet Union's internal security apparatus nor the elite preoccupation with suppressing dissent. The Third World affords many examples of police states whose elites, armies, and security establishments are almost entirely fixated on internal order: Chile under Pinochet and Zaire under Mobutu are archetypical.

The historical dynamics by which militarized and police states have evolved also differ. Propositions 3 and 4 are probabilistic statements which follow from general propositions 1 and 2:

> *Proposition 3:* Frequent involvement in violent international conflict, and relative success in those conflicts, leads to the development of militarized states.
>
> *Proposition 4:* Frequent success in the use of state-organized violence for national consolidation and the suppression of internal challenges leads to the development of police states.

These propositions implicitly raise the question of what happens to states that are unsuccessful in the use of coercion against opponents. The historical answer is that many of them did not survive. Losers in international war were absorbed into empires, suffered territorial and material losses, or were forced into a subordinate relationship with the winner. Contemporary political elites are well aware of these historical possibilities and tend to respond to challenges in keeping with their capabilities. With regard to war, weak states—those with limited power capabilities—tend to avoid involvement except when acting in consort with powerful allies (see Bueno de Mesquita, 1981). A proposition and corollary follow from the arguments:

> *Proposition 5:* States with limited power capabilities tend to avoid involvement in war.
>
> *Corollary 5a:* States with limited power capabilities tend not to become militarized states.

Apparent exceptions to the corollary, which in fact support it, are Israel and Vietnam. Both Israel and the revolutionary government of North Vietnam faced tremendous international pressures during their formative years as states. Both had the political capacities for maximum mobilization of their limited resources to confront external challenges, and both succeeded.[7] In each case, the legacy of winning was the creation of a potent though very expensive military establishment and a strong disposition among the political elite (and in Israel, the general public) to employ force in future international disputes. In both respects, these two states are anomalies among the small states of the global system. One also can speculate that they will retain the characteristics of military states only in the face of external challenges: the costs and risks of chronic belligerence for small states are too great to be sustained over the longer run.

The consequences of failure to suppress internal challenges are more diverse. States that have failed to win civil wars have disintegrated into several still weaker states. States that have been too weak to counteract revolutionary challenges generally come under new management. Typically their new revolutionary elites are committed to strengthening the state apparatus. In three social revolutions studied by Skocpol (1979), she attributes the state-strengthening impulse to international competition. In four "revolutions from above" examined by Trimberger (1978) the new military-bureaucratic elites were concerned with establishing stable and powerful nation-states based on autonomous industrial development. The arguments developed above suggest that another dynamic also is at work, surely a more immediate one: new revolutionary elites are preoccupied first and foremost with securing their power against counterrevolutionaries and would-be separatists. They cannot be expected to have any inhibitions about using violence for that purpose. And the means for doing so are readily available: the revolutionary fighters and zealots become the cadre of new or transformed agencies of state security. In Conquest's account (1986) of the forced collectivization of the Soviet peasantry, for example, one finds many references to revolutionary veterans, a dozen years after 1917, serving as OGPU and militia officers.

Thus, in the aftermath of revolutionary seizures of power, the apparatus of control and internal security is customarily the first part of the state to be built up, and postrevolutionary states are highly likely to take on the characteristics of police states. Most of the successful revolutionary struggles of this century, right or left, have spawned police states whose security agencies inherited the men, mission, and means of the revolution: the Soviet Union, Fascist Italy, Nazi Germany, Falangist Spain, Communist China, Castro's Cuba, Vietnam, Kampuchea under the Khmer Rouge, revolutionary Iran. Among the handful of apparent exceptions are wars of revolutionary independence, as in Indonesia and Algeria. The lack of counterrevolutionary resistance after independence may explain why institutionalized police states did not emerge in these countries. The argument can be summarized in another proposition:

Proposition 6: Postrevolutionary states that face internal resistance in the immediate aftermath of revolution tend to become police states.

Postrevolutionary states also are highly likely to become institutionalized autocracies. The term is not a synonym for *police state*. The institutions and practices of a police state are inconsistent with plural democracy and consistent with autocracy, but not all autocracies base their political authority primarily on coercion. The contemporary regimes of Singapore, Burma,

Malawi, Saudi Arabia, Tunisia, and Hungary, among others, sharply restrict political participation and opposition but have enough popular support that police-state tactics are ordinarily unnecessary.

Democracies and the Uses of Coercion

In the face of widespread and persistent opposition, autocracies can and do develop into police states. Leftist opposition in Argentina during the 1960s provided the *causus belli* for the police-state tactics exemplified by the "dirty war" in which at least 9000 civilians were murdered by death squads and military executioners between 1976 and 1980. Plural democracies also sometimes employ police-state tactics against extreme opposition;[8] but do not become full-fledged police states unless and until they undergo a shift to autocratic rule. Such transitions occurred in Uruguay and Chile in 1973. In Uruguay democratic rule was suspended so that security forces could have a free hand to deal with the Tupamaro revolutionaries. In Chile a long-lived democratic regime was overthrown by the military, which quickly developed a full-fledged security apparatus to suppress the leftists who had supported the democratically elected Allende regime (see Duff & McCamant 1976:183-200).

In general, plural democracies make little use of police-state tactics because historically they have been relatively successful in using noncoercive means to defuse and deflect challenges. The argument derives from my observations about the historical sequences of conflict and political reform in Western societies and from evidence about contemporary responses to protest by democratic and autocratic regimes. Regimes, like protestors and rebels, develop repertoires of action for use in conflict situations and a set of normative beliefs about which kinds of actions are most appropriate in which circumstances. The elites of democratic states have developed and employ a complex repertoire of noncoercive responses to challenges: increased channels of political participation, redistribution, symbolic and substantive shifts in public policy, cooptation of opposition leaders, diversion of affect and attention onto external targets. Also included in the repertoire are coercive means, but the popular and elite political culture of durable democracies emphasize norms of compromise and responsiveness. Officials who use or condone violence against domestic oppositions risk the loss of legitimacy and office as a consequence. Practical as well as normative considerations play a part. Both European and Third-World democracies such as India have track records of using reforms, concessions, and diversion to defuse opposition, which gives their elites confidence about their successful use in future conflicts.[9]

This proposition and corollary are the counterpart to propositions about reliance on coercion by the elites of garrison states:

> *Proposition 7:* Frequent success in the use of reforms, concessions and displacement to manage internal challenges leads to the development of the institutions and norms of democratic rule.
>
> *Corollary 7a:* Democratic states are unlikely to rely mainly on coercion in response to internal challenges.

Models and Linkages

The foregoing arguments are summarized and extended in the accompanying figures. They show the predominant sequences by which militarized and police states emerge and are reinforced in three types of political systems, given different levels of national capability. Let me comment briefly on the models, with particular attention to what they imply about the enduring question of the linkages between domestic and external conflict.

War and the Militarized State

The paths to the development of militarized states in autocracies (Figure 3.1) and democracies (Figure 3.2) are identical. For states with high power capabilities—population, resources, productivity—war and lesser international disputes are likely to have favorable outcomes, which enhances the bellicose state's effective power and reinforces its militarization. Powerful states also are more likely than weak states to use their power actively in the pursuit of state objectives, which in turn increases the likelihood that they will face future challenges from other states whose interests are threatened. A series of positive feedback effects thus enhances the war-proneness of most global and regional powers, whether autocratic or democratic in their political organization. Weak states, by contrast, are less likely to be successful in international conflicts, therefore tend to avoid it and are less likely to develop the traits of militarized states.

Internal Conflict and Revolution

Institutionalized autocracies and democracies have evolved distinct modes of response to violent internal challenges: the former rely more on systematic

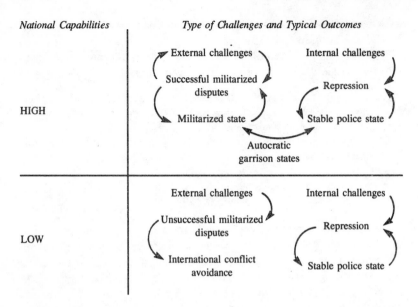

Figure 3.1 The Emergence and Persistence of Garrison States in Institutionalized Autocracies

coercion (the police state models in Figure 3.1), the latter on conflict-management techniques denoted *compromise* in Figure 3.2. Both of these tend to be stable, conflict-dampening systems. The most numerous exceptions to these patterns are found in states with limited political capacities for control, organization, and mobilization. Such states are characterized in various ways in the literature: they do not penetrate or effectively control their societies; political competition in them is uninstitutionalized or *anocratic*, the style of governance is *personalist* or *Praetorian*. By any label, they have limited political capabilities either to wage war or to control internal challenges. They rely mainly on coercion in response to internal challenges, as shown in Figure 3.3, but coercion so sporadically and inconsistently applied that it often stimulates still greater challenges. Such states have chronically unstable coercive rule, characterized by positive feedback loops between repression and challenges.

These politically weak states are particularly susceptible to revolutionary takeovers by successful challengers. When revolutionary victory is won after a protracted war that hardens the attitudes and military capabilities of the new leaders, very different patterns of conflict behavior emerge in them. Domestically they rapidly develop the traits of stable police states,

National Capabilities Type of Challenges and Typical Outcomes

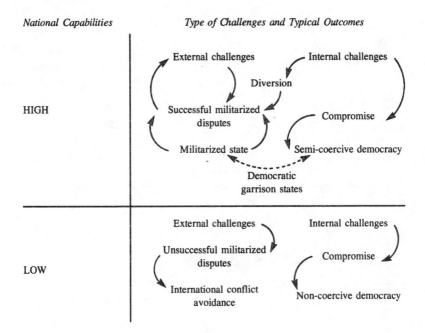

Figure 3.2 The Emergence and Persistence of Garrison States in Institutionalized Democracies

though often at horrific cost to people who have opposed the revolution.[10] Successful revolutions also breed external challenges, by revolutionaries who seek to export their revolution and foreign opponents seeking to overthrow or preempt them. With the exception of Zambia, every successful mass revolution since 1970 has precipitated new militarized international conflicts: Kampuchea, Vietnam, Nicaragua, Iran.[11] Thus, postrevolutionary regimes rapidly acquire both facets of the garrison state. Their leaders continue to rely on the coercive strategies that brought them to power, using revolutionary fighters as the backbone of new armies to oppose foreign enemies and new agencies of internal control. These regimes become, in other words, revolutionary garrison states.

Linkages

The postrevolutionary states exhibit in striking degree the reinforcing connections between internal and external coercion. The disposition of revolutionary elites to rely on force readily generalizes from the revolutionary

Type of Challenges and Typical Outcomes

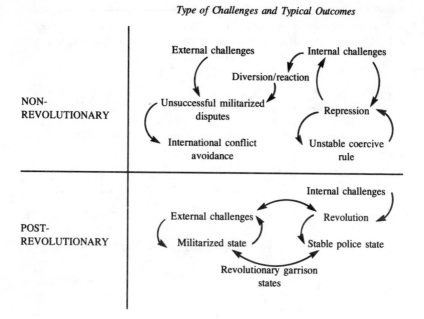

Figure 3.3 The Emergence and Persistence of Garrison States in Regimes with Low Political Capabilities

to the postrevolutionary situation and from internal to external conflict: violence is justified against all enemies of the revolution. The organizational consequences are parallel, in fact often overlapping: the personnel and agencies of warfare and internal security are interchangeable, though functional specialization between them develops more or less quickly.

The question is whether there is similar but more subtle generalization in other kinds of political systems. I suggest that there are strong linkages of this sort in the militarized autocracies and somewhat weaker ones in militarized democracies. Such linkages are not a consequence of institutional interchangeability, because these kinds of states have sharply differentiated institutions of warfare and internal control. Rather the linkage is to be found primarily in the dispositions and decisional calculus of rulers and leaders. In powerful autocracies the normative disposition to rely on coercion, and estimates of its utility, are reinforced by both domestic and international experience.

In powerful democracies I postulate a weaker tendency whereby elites who become convinced of the efficacy of force in the international arena also place considerable value on it in some kinds of domestic dispute. I would expect this disposition to be activated in several kinds of circumstances. First, the elites of democratic garrison states will be particularly sensitive to internal challenges that threaten to weaken the country's international position. Therefore, internal support for a country's foreign opponents and opposition to militarization are particularly likely to trigger coercive elite responses, not solely or necessarily because of the objective extent of threat but because coercion is assumed, by bellicose elites, to be an appropriate response to any threat to the state's international position. Second, elites of democratic garrison states are more likely to employ coercion against domestic opponents in the aftermath of successful wars than at other times because they are heady with victory. To be precise, the successful use of international coercion increases confidence in its domestic utility and decreases, at least temporarily, normative restraints on the domestic uses of coercion. Both tendencies are checked by the operating norms of democracy: state elites themselves and the public generally prefer compromise over coercion. It is this countervailing tendency, inherent in the democratic ethos and the operation of competitive politics, that makes the linkage between international and domestic coercion weaker in democracies than in autocracies. Evidence that may be relevant to this hypothesis is Stohl's finding (1976) that the twentieth-century wars fought by the United States were usually followed by periods and episodes of repression. He attributes this to the reaction of political and economic elites to the upward mobility of subordinate groups during wartime. My argument suggest an alternative (though not mutually exclusive) interpretation, and also implies that postwar repression in democracies is a pattern that should be most pronounced following successful wars in powerful democratic garrison states.

Diversion

Diversion, a term used by Hazelwood (1975), is the deliberate projection or extension of internal conflicts onto the external environment.[12] It has often been evoked in the literature as a common, even primary connections between domestic and international conflict. Until recently cross-national statistical studies concluded that diversion is not a strong force (see Stohl 1980) despite suggestive case- and country-study evidence of its occurrence. A major recent contribution is Russett's study (in press) of major powers' participation in international disputes since 1853. The results show, among other things, a recurring connection in democratic countries, but not others, between short-term economic decline, increasing protest and repression, and participation in international disputes. In the United States there is a pronounced association between low economic growth, electoral pressure (an impending national election), and American involvement in international conflict. Russett's conclusion from his extensive evidence is that in democracies, "participation in international conflict becomes an alternative state policy for dealing with protest especially if repression fails."

In the context of the propositions developed in this paper, my hypothesis is that diversion of internal conflict is common only in states (a) in which rulers are directly threatened by popular discontent and (b) in which the international costs of diversion are likely to be less than the internal gains. There are two kinds of political systems in which these conditions commonly coincide: in weak regimes with low political capabilities and in militarized democracies. In weak regimes, which are chronically subject to potentially revolutionary challenges, diversion of public attention and disaffection by a carefully chosen foreign adventure is potentially less costly than revolution. This is, nonetheless, risky business because foreign disputes may escalate in unpredictable ways, as they have for Libya under Gadhafi. If unsuccessful they add to pressures for revolutionary change. Diversion for these regimes is only likely to be chosen because its potential gains— displacing threatening discontents, mobilizing popular support—outweigh, in the short run, its potential costs. This argument is represented graphically in the diversion/reaction linkage shown in Figure 3.3. Postrevolutionary regimes may also benefit from the internal solidarity that comes from foreign conflict, but they seldom need to provoke fights for that purpose. Their external enemies usually are quite real and threatening.

The calculus of elites in powerful militarized democracies will be rather different: diversion is likely to appear to be high in potential gains, both domestically and internationally, and low in potential costs. These states are confident of their military capacity and of the likelihood of winning a limited dispute, and well aware of the electoral advantages of uniting public opinion behind a winning team. Institutionalized autocracies have less to gain politically from diversion because their rulers do not need electoral validation and rely mainly on coercion to minimize internal challenges. The weak democracies are far less likely to choose diversion because their elites have little to gain domestically or politically from them. Thus, a diversion linkage is shown for powerful democracies in Figure 3.2 but not for autocracies or weak democracies.

No type of regime is likely to risk a major international conflict as a diversion mechanism because full-scale war has high potential costs, even for powerful states. Thus, evidence of diversion is likely only with regard to limited international disputes. This is in fact what Hazelwood (1975) found using crude aggregate data: domestic conflict (across all countries) predicted less intense conflict better than more intense conflict.

Conclusions

I have developed some general propositions about the consequences of states' uses of extreme coercion in domestic and international disputes. Some of the propositions refer to generic processes about what political elites learn about the utilities of violence. Others refer to the conditioning effects of their countries' power capabilities and types of political system. The arguments appear to be internally consistent and not wildly at odds with comparative evidence on the emergence of variants of the garrison state. Throughout, I have been more concerned about the logical consistency of the theory and models than the evidence, in the expectation that the argument will provoke the kinds of empirical research needed to validate and qualify it.

The general propositions and models have other important implications that have not yet been developed. It can be demonstrated, for example, that given these assumptions, there are tendencies in the international system that lead to the continued expansion of garrison-state phenomena. Only homogenous democracies with low power capabilities and limited alliance obligations are insulated from the development of the institutions and political culture of militarized and police states. The argument also implies that chronic international conflict undermines the maintenance of noncoercive means of managing internal conflict both in specific countries and in the international system as a whole. There may be idealistic paths to a national and global future with diminished reliance on violence for the management of conflict, but they do not follow from the realistic propositions and models advanced here.

Notes

1. In four Western European countries for which time-series data are available, budgeted central government expenditures as a percent of GNP increased from an average of 6.4%

in 1875 to 11.2% in 1925 and 44.1% in 1982 (from Gurr & King, 1987:26). In research thus far unpublished, I have documented a tenfold growth in the size of armies relative to total population in France and England from 1066 to World War II. A detailed historical account of the growth of military capabilities among European states since the medieval epoch is McNeil (1982).

2. See Waltz (1979) and Gilpin (1981). The seminal empirical study on capabilities and war is Singer, Bremer, and Stuckey (1972). Zinnes (1980) reviews the empirical evidence to 1979. Major recent studies which have used this operational approach to capabilities in studies of the onset of war are Organski and Kugler (1980) and Bueno de Mesquita (1981).

3. This kind of political or functional approach to assessing state power has been developed, inter alia, by Organski and Kugler (1980:33-38, 66-103), Snider (1986), and Gurr (1988). Most would regard it as complementary to, rather than as an alternative to, the material capabilities approach.

4. Most of the new literature on the autonomous state attributes a single objective or interest to the state. Buchanan (1975) and Levi (1981), among many others, impute to officials a desire to maximize resources. Nordlinger (1986) argues that the common denominator of state interest is the enhancement of state autonomy. Categories and hierarchies of state interests are postulated in Gurr and King 1987, chap. 1, distinguishing among short-term and long-term, and primary and expedient, interests of elected and administrative officials.

5. To sketch an argument very briefly, my assumption here is neomercantilist rather than Wallerstinian: successful states at the center of expanding networks of trade and industrial production have generally promoted that expansion and have benefited as a consequence from growing tax revenues and cheaper and more abundant commodities and manufactured goods— commodities and goods that have public as well as private uses.

6. See, for example, Sereny's (1974) portrait of the commandant of the Treblinka Extermination Camp, Lifton's (1986) study of Nazi physicians who murdered in the name of science, and analyses by Charny (1982) and Kelman (1973) of the psychological processes by which ordinary people can become guiltless agents of mass murder.

7. On the relative capabilities of these two states and their opponents see Organski and Kugler (1980:74-103, passim). In the late 1970s both devoted more than 20% of their GNP to military purposes, compared with 12.2% for the USSR and 5.1% for the United States, and a median international value of 3.0% (Taylor & Jodice, 1983:24-26).

8. Examples are the tactics used by American police agencies against armed black militants in the 1968-1972 period and the West German responses to the Baader-Meinhof revolutionary terrorists and their successors.

9. This argument deserves more detailed development than I can give it here. Some evidence and interpretations which support it are summarized in several of my recent essays (Gurr 1979, 1980, 1986).

10. In a comparative study of genocides and politicides since 1945, we find that 12 of 42 were carried out by new elites in the immediate aftermath of revolutionary seizures of power (Harff & Gurr, 1988). The mass political murders in Pol Pot's Kampuchea are an extreme example of a common phenomenon.

11. Zeev Maoz reports evidence that this kind of phenomena has been pervasive in the international system since 1816. He finds that "revolutionary states (whether new entrants into the club of nations or existing states that have undergone revolutionary regime change) tend to be involved in a relatively large number of international disputes in the initial period following independence or the regime change" by comparison with other states, including those that have undergone evolutionary change (personal correspondence, 30 March 87).

12. The term is used in preference to *displacement* because the latter implies an unconscious psychological process. I regard *diversion*, when it happens, as a deliberate policy choice of national elites.

References

Alker, H. R., Jr. (1988) Emancipatory empiricism: Towards the renewal of empirical peace research. In P. Wallensteen (Ed.) *Peace research*. Boulder, CO: Westview Press.

Bayley, J. D. (1975). The police and political development in Europe. In C. Tilly (Ed.) *The formation of national states in western Europe*, pp. 328-379. Princeton, NJ: Princeton University Press.

Buchanan, J. (1975). *The limits of liberty: Between anarchy and leviathan*. Chicago: University of Chicago Press.

Bueno de Mesquita, B. (1981). *The war trap*. New Haven, CT: Yale University Press.

Charny, I. W. (1982). *How can we commit the unthinkable? Genocide: The human cancer*. Boulder, CO: Westview Press.

Conquest, R. (1986). *The harvest of sorrow: Soviet collectivization and the terror-famine*. New York: Oxford University Press.

Duff, E. A. & McCamant, J. F. (1976). *Violence and repression in Latin America: A quantitative and historical analysis*. New York: Free Press.

Eckstein, H. (1971). *The evaluation of political performance: Problems and dimensions*. Beverly Hills, CA: Sage Professional Papers in Comparative Politics 01-017.

Fitch, J. S. (1985). The garrison state in America: A content analysis of trends in the expectation of violence. *Journal of Peace Research, 22*, 32-45.

Gilpin, R. (1981). *War and change in world politics*. Cambridge: Cambridge University Press.

Gouldner, A. W. (1977-78). Stalinism: a study of internal colonialism. *Telos, 34* (Winter 1977-78), 5-48.

Gurr, T. R. (1976). *Rogues, rebels and reformers: A political history of urban crime and conflict*. Beverly Hills, CA: Sage.

_____ (1979). Alternatives to violence in a democratic society. In H. D. Graham & T. R. Gurr (Eds.), *Violence in America: Historical and comparative perspectives*. Beverly Hills, CA: Sage.

_____ (1980). On the outcomes of violent conflict. In T. R. Gurr (Ed.), *Handbook of political conflict: Theory and research*. New York: Free Press.

_____ (1986). The political origins of state violence and terror: A theoretical analysis. In M. Stohl & G. A. Lopez (Eds.), *Government violence and repression: An agenda for research*. New York: Greenwood Press.

_____ (1988). The political dimension of national capabilities: Concepts and measurement. *International Interactions, 14*, 133-139.

Gurr, T. R. and King, D. S. (1987). *The state and the city*. London: Macmillan. Chicago: University of Chicago Press.

Harff, B. & Gurr, T. R. (1988). Toward empirical theory of genocides and politicides: Identification and measurement of cases since 1945. *International Studies Quarterly, 32*(3), 359-371.

Hazelwood, L. A. (1975). Diversion mechanisms and encapsulation processes: The domestic conflict-foreign conflict hypothesis reconsidered. In P. J. McGowan (Ed.), *Sage International Yearbook of Foreign Policy Studies, 3*. Beverly Hills, CA: Sage.

Ivianski, Z. (1980). Provocation at the center: A study in the history of counter-terror. *Terrorism: An International Journal, 4*, 53-88.

Jackson, R. H. & Rosberg, C. G. (1982). Why Africa's weak states persist: The empirical and the juridical in statehood. *World Politics, 35*, 1-24.

Kelman, H. (1973). Violence without moral restraint. *Journal of Social Issues, 29*(4), 26-61.

Koehl, R. L. (1983). *The black corps: The structure and power struggles of the Nazi SS*. Madison, WI: University of Wisconsin Press.

Lasswell, H. D. (1962). The garrison-state hypothesis today. In S. Huntington (Ed.), *Changing patterns of military politics*. New York: Free Press.

Levi, M. (1981). The predatory theory of rule. *Politics and Society, 10*, 431-65.

Lifton, R. (1986). *The Nazi doctor: Medical killing and the psychology of genocide*. New York: Basic Books.

McNeil, W. (1982). *The pursuit of power: Technology, armed force, and society since A.D. 1000*. Chicago: University of Chicago Press.

Nordlinger, E. (1986). Taking the state seriously. In M. Weiner & S. P. Huntington (Eds.), *Understanding political development*. Boston: Little, Brown.

Organski, A. F. K. & Kugler, J. (1980). *The war ledger*. Chicago: University of Chicago Press.

Russett, B. M. (in press). Economic decline, electoral pressure and the initiation of interstate conflict. In C. Gochman & A. N. Sabronsky (Eds.), *Prisoners of war*. Lexington, MA: D. C. Heath.

Sereny, G. (1974). *Into that darkness: An examination of conscience*. New York: McGraw-Hill.

Singer, J. D., Bremer, S. & Stuckey, J. (1972). Capability distribution, uncertainty, and major power war, 1820-1965. In B. M. Russett (Ed.), *Peace, war, and numbers*. Beverly Hills, CA: Sage.

Skocpol, T. (1979). *States and social revolutions: A comparative analysis of France, Russia, and China*. Cambridge: The University Press.

Snider, L. W. (1986). *Identifying the elements of state power: Where do we begin?* Unpublished, Claremont Graduate School.

Stohl, M. (1976). *War and domestic political violence: The American capacity for repression and reaction*. Beverly Hills, CA: Sage.

_____ (1980). The nexus of civil and international conflict. In T. R. Gurr (Ed.), *Handbook of political conflict: theory and research*. New York: Free Press.

Taylor, C. L. & Jodice, D. A. (1983). *World handbook of political and social indicators*, 3d ed., Vol. 1: *Cross-national attributes and rates of change*. New Haven, CT: Yale University Press.

Tilly, C. (Ed.) (1975). *The formation of national states in western Europe*. Princeton, NJ: Princeton University Press.

Trimberger, K. E. (1978). *Revolution from above*. New Brunswick, NJ: Transaction Books.

Walter, E. V. (1969). *Terror and resistance: A study of political violence*. New York: Oxford University Press.

Waltz, K. E. (1979). *Theory of international politics*. Reading, MA: Addison-Wesley.

Zinnes, D. A. (1980). Why war? Evidence on the outbreak of international conflict. In T. R. Gurr (Ed.), *Handbook of political conflict: Theory and research*. New York: Free Press.

Contemporary social science analysis is dominated by utilitarian or functional approaches in which institutional structures are assumed to adapt in an optimal fashion to changing environmental conditions, and the preferences and capabilities of individual actors are ontologically posited. In contrast, an institutional perspective insists that past choices constrain present options; that the preferences and capabilities of individual actors are conditioned by institutional structures; and that historical trajectories are path dependent. Institutional structures persist even if circumstances change. In a world of nuclear weapons and economic interdependence, any adequate analysis of the nature of sovereignty operationalized with regard to transborder controls and extraterritoriality must be informed by an institutional perspective.

4

Sovereignty: An Institutional Perspective

STEPHEN D. KRASNER

Organisms are not putty before a molding environment or billiard balls before the pool cue of natural selection. Their inherited forms and behaviors constrain and push back; they cannot be quickly transformed to new optimality every time the environment alters.
—Stephen Jay Gould, *The Flamingo's Smile*, p. 53

Alternative Perspectives

Over the last five hundred years, the sovereign state has been a powerful instrument of human progress, or, at a minimum, human progress has occurred while sovereign states have been the dominant mode of political organization. The existence of an international system composed of many states facilitated economic development by preventing the consolidation of a single absolutist empire that would have stultified private initiative and by providing an environment sufficiently orderly to permit rational economic

Author's Note: I would like to thank James Caporaso, Raymond Duvall, Barbara Geddes, Mark Granovetter, Nina Halpern, Robert Keohane, John Ruggie, and Alex Wendt for their comments on earlier versions of this paper. This paper was completed while the author was a Fellow at the Center for Advanced Study in the Behavioral Sciences, where financial support was provided by National Science Foundation Grant BNS-8700864.

calculations.[1] This sovereign state system, however, also has some less benign consequences. Because the state system as a whole lacks a sovereign, wars are an immanent possibility. The severity of wars has increased over time, as measured by casualties rather than the frequency of conflict (Goldstein, 1985). With the advent of nuclear weapons, major interstate conflict threatens to destroy human existence. Moreover, even very large states may not be able to cope with economic and other disturbances emanating from the international environment, and the opportunity cost of pursuing autarky is increasing in part because technological changes in communication and transportation have reduced the transactions costs of international commercial activities (Cooper, 1968). It is no longer obvious that the state system is the optimal way to organize political life.

The existence of a suboptimal institutional structure presents an anomaly for most of the theoretical orientations that inform social science research. These perspectives adopt a static viewpoint that is either utilitarian or functional. For both of these orientations, actors are adaptive and outcomes are optimal. History is not particularly important; institutional structures and policies will change if environmental incentives change. A social fact is explained by some other social variable that belongs to the same time period. For contemporary social science this is a "natural" mode of explanation (Harsanyi, 1960:136). In investigating the basic mode of political organization in the contemporary world, the national state, these conventional approaches are not likely to provide either adequate prescriptive guidance or satisfactory explanations. It will be necessary to deploy an institutionalist perspective to construct a suitable explanation for the development and persistence of the sovereign state. An institutionalist perspective regards enduring institutional structures as the building blocks of social and political life. The preferences, capabilities, and basic self-identities of individuals are conditioned by these institutional structures. Historical developments are path dependent; once certain choices are made, they constrain future possibilities. The range of options available to policy makers at any given point in time is a function of institutional capabilities that were put in place at some earlier period, possibly in response to very different environmental pressures.

Conventional Approaches

James March and Johan Olsen have argued that in one form or another utilitarian or functional approaches dominate American social science. These orientations see political activity as an integral part of civil society. Outcomes are the result of individual choice. History is understood as functionalist in the sense that anticipated outcomes result in one single most efficient equilibrium. And finally these perspectives are instrumentalist in that allocation is viewed as the major concern of political activity (March & Olson, 1984:735). The pervasive impact of these orientations, especially utilitarian arguments, is particularly apparent in political science and economics.

In microeconomic theory, market outcomes are a product of the behavior of individual firms and consumers whose preferences and capabilities are taken as given. The realism of the assumption of egoistic individualism is not part of the inquiry of modern economics. (Sen, 1977:322; Moe, 1984:741) The most pristine and imperialistic form of this argument, exemplified in the work of the Chicago School, applies microeconomic analysis to all aspects of human behavior. It assumes that preferences are universal. Gary Becker argues that since "economists generally have had little to contribute, especially in recent times, to the understanding of how preferences are formed, preferences are assumed not to change substantially over time, nor to be very different between wealthy and poor persons, or even between persons in different societies and cultures" (Becker, 1976:5). Customs and traditions, which might from other perspectives be thought of as determinants of values, are seen as devices for dealing with imperfect information. (Stigler & Becker, 1977:82). Stigler and Becker argue that the assumption of unchanging and common preferences makes it possible to avoid the intellectually flaccid position of explaining changes in behavior in terms of unexplained changes in tastes and to abstain from appealing to "whoever studies and explains tastes (psychologists? anthropologists? phrenologists? sociobiologists?)" (Stigler & Becker, 1977:76). (Stigler and Becker, of course, realize how much other social scientists cherish being identified with phrenologists.)

For the Chicago School institutions play very little role either because they accept Coase's theorem, which states that in the absence of transactions costs optimal allocation can be achieved through the market or because they believe that in the not-so-long run, institutions, like any other outcome of behavior, must reflect the preferences and capabilities of individual actors (Moe, 1987:276-277). A shift in incentives or resources will quickly lead to a shift in behavior. In such a fluid environment the concept of institutional structures becomes illusory and meaningless. The utilitarian perspective has also produced arguments that are more sympathetic to the importance of institutions and that potentially complement the perspective elaborated in this chapter. Moe (1987) has referred to this line of argument as the positive theory of political institutions. This mode of analysis treats institutional structures, which cannot be easily changed, as constraining individual actors by eliminating the viability of certain options and influencing resource availability. A stable outcome is one in which none of the individual actors have an incentive to change their behavior (Ferejohn, 1987:2). But even this more institutionally oriented utilitarian perspective must be distinguished from an institutional perspective because it takes preferences and the nature of actors as given. Institutional structures are seen as constraining actors rather than constituting them.

The utilitarian perspective, whether in its more or less institutional version, does not have much to say about failure. It cannot explain why some actors fail while others succeed except to say that those that fail did not act to maximize their utility. Actors may not adjust to environmental opportunities or institutional constraints. Some firms go bankrupt while others thrive. Failures have to be written off as random events (Hogarth & Reder, 1986:S187, S190). Violations of basic assumptions, such as transitivity of preferences, are glossed over by arguing that in the long run there is learning or that, in any event, outcomes are not affected because market forces act as a corrective (Tversky & Kahneman, 1986:S273).

Moreover, even those utilitarian approaches that are sympathetic to institutions, regard them as being always up for grabs. Institutions are not taken for granted. Violating some established pattern of behavior is merely one cost among others. The principal-agent literature is the clearest example of this perspective. Even actors in formal hierarchical relationships are presented as calculators and connivers; weasels always looking for a way to increase their utility if principals fail to monitor them effectively. Hence, utilitarian theory describes a world in which actors are given and unproblematic and in which behavior is fluid and, for the Chicago School, constrained only by resource availability and relative prices.

Examples of this approach abound. In interest-group pluralism, public policy is understood as a product of the pulling and hauling of particular societal groups. These groups are taken as a natural component of the political landscape. Human activity constantly produces changes in power, privilege, and welfare. Political and social structures are never permanent and never the starting point for an analysis. Institutions are, at best, arenas within which group activity takes place. (Binder, 1986:7-10; March & Olson, 1984: 735-736).

In structural or realist theories of international politics, behavior is analyzed as a function of the distribution of power among states and the relative position of a given state. Shifts in the distribution of power will lead to changes in foreign policy and outcomes. The state, understood as a bundle of capabilities within a given territory that are deployed as if they were under the control of a unified rational actor, is taken as a given (Waltz, 1979). Institutional constraints are entirely absent from this analysis. For realists, international politics is a self-help system in which individual states autonomously determine their own actions.

While utilitarian approaches, in various guises, are now the prevailing perspective in American social science, functional arguments still exert some influence, particularly in sociology and, to a lesser extent, in political science. Such theories also posit a world that is fluid and optimizing. Structures, although they may not always be readily visible, develop to fulfill different functions. Change is the result of adaptation to environmental incentives. Prevailing modes of analysis in organizational theory explain organizational structures as rational adaptations to environmental circumstances. They differ more in their descriptions of the environment than they do in their analyses of how the environment affects organizations: Weberians see rational bureaucratic modes of organization as functionally optimal in complex modern societies; Marxists argue that organizations change in response to the needs of capitalist society (DiMaggio & Powell, 1983:156). Although functional theories have been applied to social aggregates and utilitarian theory to individuals, they share a view of human behavior in which the struggle to maximize utility is pursued through adaptation of one form or another to environmental incentives.

Adherents of neoclassical economic theory, interest-group pluralism, structural realism, and structural functionalism have modified their basic arguments in a variety of ways that attempt to take account of factors such as property rights, asymmetrical information, political institutions, and international regimes. But these departures do not violate the Lakatosian hardcore of the actor-oriented approach. Even very sophisticated presentations take actor preferences as given, rather than as an endogenous product of an institutional structure, an assumption that makes it possible to understand actors as searching for an optimal outcome. If preferences are endogenous, this mode of analysis makes little sense. Furthermore, even arguments such as principal-agent analysis in the new economic theory of the firm; or the investigation of equilibrium political institutions (Shepsle, 1986); or the examination of international regimes (Keohane, 1984; Krasner, 1983); tend to be static in that independent and dependent variables are drawn from the same time period.

From an actor-oriented utilitarian or functional perspective, unambiguously dysfunctional behavior presents an anomaly. The most spectacular historical examples of such behavior occur when polities collapse in the face of pressure from some external force that could have been resisted given available material resources, but these resources could not be deployed because of institutional or cognitive constraints. At the end of the eighteenth century, the Polish nobility was unable to overcome a legislative system that gave every member of parliament a veto. Even in the face of extreme external threats, coherent and unified military action was impossible, and the Polish state was dismembered and disappeared from the map of Europe for 120 years.

At the end of the nineteenth century, the Balinese ruling class failed to effectively unite despite pressures from the Dutch. The indigenous system collapsed when one of the major noble houses appealed to the Dutch for support in 1899, a policy which could not be reconciled with the hierarchical cosmology upon which the Balinese theater state was based (Geertz, 1980:39). The indigenous civilizations of the Western hemisphere were unable to comprehend the Spanish. They had only two classifications for human beings, the sedentary civilized and the barbarians. The Spanish were neither one of these, therefore, they had to use the only other category available to them, the sacred. They thought the Spaniards were gods because they had no cognitive alternative, and Aztec civilization was destroyed (Paz, 1987:7). The nation state system has not yet presented quite so extreme an example of dysfunctional behavior, but one is not hard to imagine, and military conflicts and state repression in the twentieth century have taken millions of individual lives even if they have not destroyed the nature of the state system itself.

An Institutional Perspective

This paper is an effort to spell out an alternative approach to understanding how the sovereign state, and social structures more generally, might be understood, an approach that focuses on institutional change and inertia as a major explanatory variable. Institutional arguments have been given greater attention by political scientists in recent years. The basic characteristic of an institutional argument is that prior institutional choices limit available future options. There are two basic reasons why outcomes at some given point in time cannot be understood in terms of the preferences and capabilities of actors existing at that same point in time. First, capabilities and preferences, that is, the very nature of the actors, cannot be understood except as part of some larger institutional framework. Second, the possible options available at any given point in time are constrained by available institutional capabilities and these capabilities are themselves a product of choices made during some earlier period. Thus, an institutional perspective requires first a careful delineation of the nature of particular institutional arrangements because such arrangements are both a dependent variable at time t and an independent variable at time $t + 1$; and second, an explication of how institutional arrangements perpetuate themselves across time even in situations where utilitarian calculations would suggest that they are dysfunctional.

An institutionalist perspective implies that it is necessary to unpack the notion of the sovereign state. What precisely does *sovereignty* mean and how has this meaning changed? How have issues of extraterritoriality and transborder control varied across states and over time? Have state assertions to the exercise of final authority within their own territorial boundaries been challenged by external actors? What kind of transborder movements have states tried to control and how successful have they been? Once unpacked and made problematic, it is necessary to examine how the particular institutional structures of sovereignty regenerate themselves and delimit the range of available policy options and institutional changes.

While social science understands actor-oriented utilitarian and functional perspectives very well, institutional approaches are more illusive.;[2] Cooper and Brady point out that "Institutional analysis has lagged behind behavioral analysis since the advent of the behavioral revolution in the early 1950s. Our ability to handle questions that posit individuals, whether in small numbers or large aggregates, as the units of analysis is far greater than our ability to handle questions that posit institutionalized collectivities in complex environments as the units of analysis" (Cooper & Brady, 1981:994).

There is no commonly agreed definition of what an institution structure is. Oran Young states that "Social institutions are recognized practices consisting of easily identifiable roles, coupled with collections of rules or conventions governing relations among occupants of these roles." (Young, 1986:107). Sidney Verba argues that institutions refer to "generally accepted regular procedures for handling a problem and to normatively sanctioned behavior patterns" (Verba, 1971:300). Alford and Friedland are more expansive stating that the "concept of 'institution' refers to a pattern of supraorganizational relations stable enough to be described—polity, family, economy, religion, culture" (Alford & Friedland, 1985:16). Finally,

Stinchcombe says that an institution can be defined as "a structure in which powerful people are committed to some value or interest." (Stinchcombe, 1968:107).

Despite their differences, these statements do suggest that there are two interrelated characteristics that are central to an institutionalist perspective: the derivative character of individuals and the persistence of something— behavioral patterns, roles, rules, organizational charts, ceremonies—over time. Sociologists have frequently argued that individuals are extremely sensitive to consensual norms. These norms are internalized through socialization. Behavior cannot be understood by examining atomized individuals. At the very least, individuals are confronted with a limited repertoire of social roles and values from which to choose. A particular role or enduring pattern of behavior can only be adequately comprehended as part of a larger social structure. Preferences are developed through involvement in political activity which is structured by institutional arrangements. Routinized procedures for hiring, promotion, and dismissal based on qualifications and performance would, for instance, be standard operating procedure for any formally established corporation in late twentieth century America; such procedures would have been incomprehensible in medieval Europe (Katznelson, 1986:319-320; Granovetter, 1985;483; Alford & Friedland, 1985:7-8). John Meyer and his colleagues have asserted that "A central concern of our analysis is the way in which the institutional structure of society creates and legitimates the social entities that are seen as "actors." That is, institutionalized cultural rules define the meaning and identity of the individuals and patterns of appropriate economic, political, and cultural activity . . . They similarly constitute the purposes and legitimacy of organizations, professions, interests groups, and states . . ." (Meyer, Boli, & Thomas, 1987:12). Alex Wendt, applying structuration theory, which more explicitly focuses on the interaction between macro and micro phenomena, maintains that behavior can only be understood in terms of the interaction between social structures that constitute individual actors and are, in turn, constituted by the actions of these actors (Wendt, 1987).

Second, an institutionalist perspective implies that something persists over time and that change is not instantaneous and costless. If patterns of behavior, roles, collectivities, or formal organizations change rapidly and frequently, then there is little use in invoking an institutionalist argument. Better under such circumstances to focus on individuals without regard to some larger context. Invoking some notion of enduring institutions can only obscure understanding in an environment where patterns of behavior and what are commonly called *institutions* are rapidly changing in response to environmental pressures. While an institutionalist argument does not maintain that such rapid change never occurs, it does imply that such episodes are infrequent and are followed by long periods of either relative stasis or path-dependent change. Changes, from an institutionalist perspective, can never be easy, fluid, or continuous and are more likely to occur at the level of the whole population of organizations, as some types are selected out, than as a result of individual adaptation (Carroll, 1984; Hannan & Freeman, 1977).

Dimensions of Institutionalization

Institutionalization, the tendency of patterns of behavior, norms, or formal structures to persist through time, depends on two dimensions, vertical depth and horizontal linkage. Depth refers to the extent to which the institutional structure defines the individual actors. Breadth refers to the number of links that a particular activity has with other activities, to the number of changes that would have to be made if a particular form of activity were altered.

The definition of actors involves a specification of: (a) endowments in the form of property rights; (b) utilities in the sense of preferences; (c) capabilities in the form of material, symbolic, and institutional resources; and (d) self-identity in that the way in which individuals identify themselves is affected or determined by their place within an institutional structure. Holding environmental pressures and horizontal links constant, the more individuals' basic self-definition is determined by a given institutional structure, the more difficult it will be for that institution to change. Such an institution may collapse because it fails to adapt to changed environmental circumstances, but it will not be undermined by its own members.

With regard to sovereignty, the notion of citizenship is one example of institutional depth. The state bestows citizenship. The very notion of *citizen* in the modern world is intimately linked with the existence of sovereign states. Without such political entities, citizenship as we know it would have no meaning. The depth of citizenship, the extent to which it becomes an important part of an individual's self-definition varies both across and within countries. Nevertheless, it is a powerful source of identity for many people, powerful enough to make many subject themselves to the dangers of violent death, Hobbes's baddest of the bad. States also constitute political communities that define what Michael Walzer (1983) has called *spheres of justice*. The conception individuals have of what is just, a basic component of any preference structure, is determined by membership in a particular political community.

Other examples of institutional structures defining the identity of individuals are even more compelling. Geertz's description of the Balinese aristocracy marching into Dutch machine guns, because this was more consistent with their cosmology than capitulation to foreign rule, is a powerful illustration of the ability of particular self-identities to lead individuals to accept death rather than what would be for them, dishonor (Geertz, 1980). The long list of martyrs shows that violent death is not, for some individuals, the worst possible outcome.

The concept of organizational depth reflects an epistemological stance that is skeptical of assertions of objective reality. It views reality as a social construct. This construction may arise either from the interaction of individuals who attribute meaning to certain events or from a general consensus on the meaning of events that is produced by shared paradigms or shaped by roles. In an uncertain or even unknowable external environment, meaning does not simply present itself in the form of some objective social reality. It is contingent on individual cognitions and possibly, with regard to the depth of institutionalization, on the extent to which these cognitions are determined by the immediate institutional environment within which the individual functions (Meyer et al., 1987:5).

Horizontal linkage refers to the density of links between a particular activity and other activities. If a particular activity can be changed without altering anything else, then there is no linkage. If one modification requires changes in many others, then a particular activity is densely linked. Holding other things constant, the greater the number of links, the higher the level of institutionalization. For instance, the legal requirements for changing the American Constitution are much more stringent than those needed to promulgate a law; that is, many more individuals and legislative bodies must be involved to alter the constitution. These legal demands do correspond to our commonplace understanding of what we mean by stating that a particular practice or norm is institutionalized. We mean that it is hard to change.

The breadth of institutionalization will be influenced by the way in which a particular institution fits into a broader institutional framework. In the case of sovereignty, there are two relevant sets of networks or links. First, national arrangements related to the scope and nature of authoritative control are tied to other arrangements within that same country. States may, for instance, assert control in some areas but not in others because of national legal arrangements, bureaucratic structures, or policing capabilities.

The United States, for instance, has been very reluctant to move toward a system of identity cards to control illegal migration because this would conflict with liberal values, which are deeply enshrined in individual beliefs and embedded in the legal system. The treatment of women's issues in Sweden and Great Britain has reflected more general attitudes toward social welfare (M. Ruggie, 1984).

Second, the authority claims of a particular state are also linked to international regimes and the practices of other states. National actions that are consistent with the principles and norms of existing international regimes, and are reinforced by the behavior and policies of other states, will be more difficult to change than assertions of sovereign authority that are antithetical to existing regimes and contradict or undermine the practices of other states. Some actions inevitably require agreement between two or more states, such as the setting of exchange rates; others are not necessarily contingent on the behavior of other actors but enforcement may be facilitated by general agreement, such as establishing the limits of the territorial sea.

In sum, institutionalization can be conceived of along two dimensions, breadth and depth. *Breadth* refers to the number of links an institution has, the number of other changes that would have to be made if that institution were to be changed. *Depth* refers to the extent to which the self-identities of individuals are determined by their participation in some larger social arrangement. This discussion is illustrated by Figure 4.1.

With regard to both breadth and depth, sovereign states have become increasingly formidable institutions. They influence the self-image of those individuals within their territory through the concept of citizenship as well as by exercising control, to one degree or another, over powerful instruments of socialization. With regard to breadth, states are the most densely linked institutions in the contemporary world. Change the nature of states, and virtually everything else in human society would also have to be changed. Hence, even though environmental incentives have dramatically changed since the establishment of the state system in the seventeenth century, there is little reason to believe that it will be easy to replace sovereign states with some alternative structure for organizing human political life.

Institutions that have high degrees of breadth and depth, that define the nature of actors and have many links with other institutions, are not up for grabs. They are taken for granted. Support does not have to be continually mobilized to sustain them. They are not challenged either because actors accept them as if given by nature (they do not even conceive of alternatives) or because particular behaviors and outcomes seem so fixed that the costs of changing appear to be prohibitive (Jepperson, 1987:4-6). It is exactly

		Breadth: *Density of Links*	
		Low	*High*
Depth: *Extent of Vertical Embeddedness*	*High*	Pennsylvania Dutch	The Modern State
	Low	Medieval Long Distance Luxury Trade	Urban Traffic System

Figure 4.1 Dimensions of Institutionalization

this taken-for-granted quality that distinguishes institutional analysis from even those utilitarian perspectives that recognize the importance of institutions but regard them as being constantly under challenge—constantly subject to the rational maximizing calculations of their members.

An Evolutionary Analogy

Metaphors and analogies cannot be a substitute for analysis; that is, for specifying the relationships between clearly conceptualized variables (Snidal, 1985). But when theoretical conceptualizations are weakly developed, metaphors and analogies can clarify the underlying logic of an argument. One analogy that does help to illuminate the reasoning of an institutionalist perspective is offered by the evolutionary theories of Stephen Jay Gould and Niles Eldredge.

Gould and Eldredge have argued that evolutionary change is characterized by what they term punctuated equilibrium. They contrast their position with the Darwinian synthesis. An evolutionary process characterized by punctuated equilibrium is one in which long period of stasis are broken by short, in geologic time, episodes of rapid speciation. This allotropic speciation occurs in geographically isolated subpopulations usually living at the environmental margin of a particular species. Sharp breaks occur in fossil records because one variant of a species quickly replaces its ancestor as a result of shifts in environmental conditions (Eldredge, 1985: chap. 3 and 148-50; Gould, 1982:383; Gould & Eldredge, 1977:116-117).

In the Darwinian synthesis, change is slow, steady and gradual. Darwin's commitment to gradualism reflected his social environment and his theories parallel those of Smith, Bentham, and other nineteenth century European thinkers who saw history as a pattern of moderate evolution. The Darwinian synthesis, like Adam Smith's political economy, also focused attention on the individual. The mechanism for change was mutation in particular individuals rather than changes in whole species more or less at the same time. Adaptation would be optimal because individual variables provided a very rich repertoire of possible solutions, which could be selected in response to changed environmental incentives. Alterations in the environment would ultimately produce the most functionally efficient biological stock as different responses were played out slowly over a long period of time (Gould, 1982:381; Gould & Eldredge, 1977:145; Eldredge, 1985: 21-22).

Eldredge and Gould have criticized such adaptationist arguments on several grounds. The Darwinian synthesis ignores constraints imposed by previous choices. An optimally adaptive response may not be possible because the gene stock necessary for such a change is simply not present. Earlier adaptations, or even elimination of certain species, channel subsequent developments. The constraints of this channeling must be placed alongside environmental incentives to explain evolutionary change. Gould argues, for instance that "we should not conclude that Darwinian adaptation to local environments has unconstrained power to design theoretically optimum shapes for all situations. Natural selection, as a historical process, can only work with material available . . . . The resulting imperfections and odd solutions, cobbled together from parts on hand, record a process that unfolds in time from unsuited antecedents, not the work of a perfect architect creating *ab nihilo*" (Gould, 1985a:34-35).

Adaptationalist arguments also ignore the possibility that some changes are fortuitous. They may have occurred because two particular structures were genetically bound together, and change in one inevitably induced change in the other. Structures originally developed for one purpose may ultimately come to serve another. One of Gould's most fascinating examples is that wings developed from protuberances whose initial purpose was to facilitate heat regulation for warm-blooded animals. Indeed, it is difficult to imagine, Gould argues, how wings could have developed in any other way, for they are too large to have sprung full-blown, as it were, from the skeletal structures of terrestrial animals (Gould, 1982:383; Gould, 1985b).

Gould and Eldredge developed their theory of punctuated equilibrium in response to these and other problems, as well as in reaction to the fact that the fossil record was more incomplete than the Darwinian synthesis suggested that it should be. If the Darwinian synthesis were correct and change was constant, gradual, and optimally adaptive, then it should be possible to find more or less complete fossil records. But this has not been the case. Missing links are typical rather than the exception. Such gaps in the fossil record are more easily explained by a pattern of development in which change takes place rapidly over a limited period of time and often in a limited geographic area. Evolutionary paleontologists would have to be extremely lucky to construct a complete fossil record.

Gould notes that the gradualist-punctuationalist debate in the largest sense "is but one small aspect of a broader discussion about the nature of change: Is our world (to construct a ridiculously oversimplified dichotomy) primarily one of constant change (with structure as a mere incarnation of the moment), or is structure primary and constraining, with change as a 'difficult' phenomenon, usually accomplished rapidly when a stable structure is stressed beyond its buffering capacity to resist and absorb" (Gould, 1982:383).

Punctuated equilibrium is not a perfect analogy for an institutionalist argument. There is no parallel between the concept of allotropic speciation with its focus on alterations in geographically isolated subpopulations as the driving mechanism for change and an institutionalist perspective. Evolutionary theory does not claim that biological structures can consciously alter their environments in ways that enhance their viability. But other aspects of the Gould and Eldredge's approach are extremely germane. First, an adequate explanation must take into consideration both structures (institutions or biological stocks) and environmental incentives.[3] Second, change is difficult; once a particular institutional structure (biological stock) is established, it tends to maintain itself or, at the very least, to channel future change. Third, optimal adaptation is not always possible because the institutional stock is not available. Features selected during one point in time impose limits on future possibilities. Fourth, historical origin and present utility may require different explanations. A particular structural feature that evolved for one reason (or an institution that was established to cope with certain environmental incentives) may later be put to very different uses. "These evolutionary shifts," Gould argues, "can be quirky and unpredictable as the potentials for complexity are vast" (Gould, 1983:63). Credit cards can be used to open doors. The balancing fins of fish became the limbs for land-based vertebrates. Roman law became one of the pillars upon which notions of private property essential for capitalism were based (Anderson, 1974).

Finally, punctuated equilibrium suggests that explanation rather than prediction ought to be the primary objective of science. In a world of organisms in which present behavior is constrained by structures that evolved in response to past conditions, adaptation will be imperfect and, therefore, unpredictable. Chance and quirkiness heavily influence the organic universe (Gould, 1983:65). This orientation does not imply that all search for regularities should be given up, that history whether evolutionary or human can only be a collection of individual stories. It is possible to delineate general principles and regularities that underlie a variety of unique responses. But a recognition of the importance of *fortuna* does suggest that prediction will inevitably be very difficult. Knowledge of existing institutional stock delimits a range of possible responses to environmental incentives, but does not necessarily determine any particular path. The punctuated-equilibrium approach to evolutionary theory of Gould and Eldredge is a better model for social science than the logical deductive, determinative, and predictive orientation of theoretical physics to which many social scientists aspire, if only rhetorically.

Institutional Persistence

Species reproduce themselves biologically; we know something about how genes work. An institutionalist perspective must delineate mechanisms that account for the perpetuation of institutions over time. Arthur Stinchcombe describes historicist causal imagery in the following way: "Some set of causes *once* (italics in original) determined a social pattern (e.g., the Reformation determined Protestantism in North Europe, Catholicism in South Europe). Then ever since, what existed in one year produced the same thing the next year (e.g., each year each country has the same dominant religion it had the year before)." In such an approach, Stinchcombe goes on to argue, the problem of explanation "breaks down into two causal components. The first is the particular circumstances which caused a tradition to be started. The second is the general process by which social patterns reproduce themselves" (Stinchcombe, 1968:102-103).

Arguments about how particular institutions originate are familiar enough in political science. Certainly the most conventional are actor-oriented utilitarian or functionalist analyses. The explanation for how institutions or enduring patterns begin is no different from explanations for policy change or other more transitory phenomena. Such explanations are not inconsistent with an institutionalist perspective. But an institutionalist perspective suggests that they must be supplemented with an examination of how pre-existing structures delimit the range of possible options. An effort to explain origins would have to take account not only of environmental incentives but also of extant institutional structures, of the genetic stock, not just external conditions.

The second task of an institutionalist perspective involves explaining how institutions persist over time, even though their environments may change. If institutional arrangements change readily when environmental conditions change (or, in the language of the Chicago School, when prices change), then there is little use in invoking an institutionalist perspective; indeed, under such conditions it is not even clear that the very concept of institutions is of any use because the study of what would commonly be called *institutions* would be no different from the analysis of other social phenomena such as policy choices, congressional voting, or profit maximization.

A number of mechanisms can contribute to institutional persistence and inertia. One factor is the ability of an institution to alter its environment. Statist and corporatist explanations have emphasized such possibilities. Legal rules and administrative regulations affect the barriers to entry and exit in different sectors of the economy, and therefore the political capabilities and external legitimacy claims of actors (Hannan and Freeman, 1977:932). Public officials actively cultivate support from private groups and in doing so may alter not only the balance of capabilities but also conceptions of self-interest. Central decision makers can invoke symbols of national unity and thereby influence the attitudes of individual citizens toward specific policy issues. At the very least, there is likely to be a symbiosis between public and private institutions in which preferences and organizational structures are conditioned by long-standing relationships and shared political values (Katzenstein, 1985; Stepan, 1978; Badie and Birnbaum, 1983). Hence, at least at the national level, the depth and breadth of public institutions may increase over time as a result of conscious policies to alter the distribution of power in civil society or to reinforce existing patterns of behavior.

Institutions may also increase their depth through effective recruitment of personnel. In highly professional state agencies with selective recruitment, socialization into the bureaus, ethos can be intense. The more the individuals governing an institution can socialize and select their successors, control the conditions of incumbency, and depict themselves as models for subsequent generations, the easier it is for an institution to be effectively maintained (Poggi, 1978:138; Stinchcombe, 1968:112).

An institution may persist because it can mitigate problems associated with incomplete information. Decisions in complex environments inevitably must be made without full information. Institutions can increase information and distribute it more symmetrically. Robert Keohane has argued that such activities are a central purpose of international regimes, some of which reduce the probability of cheating by establishing monitoring mechanisms and reducing suspicion. This is, as Keohane (1984) notes, a purely functionalist explanation, although one that recognizes that sunk costs can lead to a situation in which all members of an organization might prefer different arrangements but none has the incentive to initiate changes. Oliver Williamson has made similar arguments with regard to the relative merits of hierarchical, as opposed to market, forms of organization. Hierarchical forms of organization, such as the firm, may be more efficient than markets when there is incomplete information, because firms can more easily develop internal mechanisms that diminish or overcome the problems posed by bounded rationality (Williamson, 1975:25).

But such functional analyses do not necessarily imply that organizational structures can be easily adapted if environmental circumstances change. Once commitments are made regarding expertise and standard operating procedures, certain kinds of information processing will be facilitated, but other kinds will be inhibited. In large organizations many different procedures have to be coordinated. Coordination can only be accomplished if the rules are stable, but such stability may lead organizations to persist in behavior that appears to be stupid or counterproductive (Steinbrunner, 1974:78; Nelson & Winter, 1982:37). Locked-in standard operating procedures can potentially yield catastrophic outcomes if environmental conditions rapidly change (Bracken, 1983).

Mark Granovetter (1985) offers a different argument about the way in which organizations contribute to resolving problems of bounded rationality. He argues that the level of shirking, cheating, and dissimulation that occur in economic relationships (although there is no logical or empirical reason to limit his argument to such activities) is heavily influenced by the extent to which transactions are embedded in a network of personal ties. These personal relationships provide information. They also spill over into noninstrumental activities. The relationships become valued as an end in themselves, and they become freighted with concerns that extend beyond short-term utility maximization. Such embedded structures tend to persist because they are functionally useful and become valued in their own right.

Internal resistance to organizational restructuring is another cause of inertia. Such restructuring is designed to benefit the whole organization over the long term. But in the short term it will disadvantage particular subunits by changing their ability to control resources and invoke legitimizing norms. Disadvantaged groups are likely to resist change, and their objections will be particularly telling in environments characterized by high levels of uncertainty because the beneficial consequences of change cannot be persuasively demonstrated (Hannan & Freeman, 1977:931).

Nelson and Winter make an explicit analogy between their theory of the firm and evolutionary theory. They argue that a *routine* is a regular and predictable pattern of behavior. For business firms, routines are applied to all aspects of the activity including production and personnel policies. These routines are the equivalent of genes in evolutionary theory. "They are a persistent feature of the organism and determine its possible behavior (though *actual* behavior is determined also by the environment); they are heritable in the sense that tomorrow's organisms generated from today's (for example, by building a new plant) have many of the same characteristics, and they are selectable in the sense that organisms with certain routines may do better than others, and, if so, their relative importance in the population (industry) is augmented over time" (Nelson & Winter, 1982:14).

Institutions may also persist because they follow path-dependent patterns of development. Path-dependent patterns are characterized by self-reinforcing positive feedback. Initial choices, often small and random, may determine future historical trajectories. Once a particular path is chosen, it precludes other paths even if these alternatives might, in the long run, have proven to be more efficient or adaptive.

Alexis de Tocqueville finds America a fascinating case because the initial conditions, which he sees constraining future patterns of development are so evident. He argues that:

> If we were able to go back to the elements of states to examine the oldest monuments of their history, I doubt not that we should discover in them the primal cause of the prejudices, the habits, the ruling passions, and, in short, all that constitutes what is called the national character. We should there find the explanation of certain customs which now seem at variance with the prevailing manners; of such laws as conflict with established principles; and of such incoherent opinions as are here and there to be met with in society, like those fragments of broken chains which we sometimes see hanging from the vaults of an old edifice, supporting nothing. This might explain the destinies of certain nations which seem borne on by an unknown force to ends of which they themselves are ignorant (de Tocqueville, 1945:28).

Increasing returns of various kinds lead to path-dependent patterns of development in which random initial choices preclude future options, including those that would have been more efficient over the long run. Path dependency can arise for several reasons. There may be increasing returns to adoption: once particular routines are adopted they may become more efficient over time. Because potentially more efficient routines were not chosen in the first place, there is no opportunity to ride them down a learning curve. The system is locked in by small initial choices (Arthur, 1985:5).

Path dependency may also result from network externalities. The more people that choose a particular institutional structure, such as a given telephone system, the more efficient that structure becomes. Other possible routines are frozen out. Over time the changeover gap, the amount that would have to be spent to make some alternative routines equally attractive, increases. Initially decisions may also be locked in by economies of agglomeration. Once a choice is made, other institutions reorient themselves or new services are created; once particular forms of economic activity, for instance, become concentrated in a Silicon Valley or Route 128, it is difficult to relocate them because of the network of financial, legal, and other services that have been created (Arthur, 1984:10; Arthur, 1986:2).

W. Brian Arthur has summarized, in the following table (Figure 4.2), the differences between constant returns, diminishing returns, and increasing returns for different kinds of technological regimes. The same differences could also exist for institutional structures.

With increasing returns, institutions are not necessarily efficient or flexible. Once initial choices are made, it is difficult to explore alternatives because their competitive positions are weakened by the increasing efficiency over time of the initial choice. Final outcomes are not predictable because processes are nonergodic; that is, initial small random shocks do not average out but rather establish long-term trajectories.

Finally, there are circumstances in which classes of institutions, if not particular members of that class, are very likely to persist: namely, situations in which competition is limited, survival is not an issue, and the most important element of the environment is other organizations. Under such circumstances, institutions tend toward isomorphism not because of competition over limited material resources but because of their need to fit into a larger organizational environment. DiMaggio and Powell point to three mechanisms for what they call *institutional isomorphic change:* First, coercion arising from either political pressures from other organizations or from widely shared expectations about legitimate modes of action. Second, mimetic processes in which organizations imitate existing forms, a pattern which is likely to be particularly powerful when goals are unclear. Third, normative pressures that are often embodied in professional associations and selective mechanisms of recruitment (DiMaggio & Powell, 1983: 150-154). In the vocabulary developed earlier in this chapter, *institutional*

	Necessarily Efficient	Necessarily Flexible	Predictable	Ergodic
Constant Returns	Yes	Yes	Yes	Yes
Diminishing Returns	Yes	Yes	Yes	Yes
Increasing Returns	No	No	No	No

Figure 4.2 Consequences of Increasing Returns
SOURCE: W. Brian Arthur, 1984.

isomorphism refers to a situation in which the density of links among organizations is high, implying that structural change will be difficult.

In sum, from a functionalist or utilitarian perspective, organizations persist so long as they contribute to the achievement of some desired goal. An institutionalist perspective need not ignore such considerations. But at a minimum, an institutionalist argument must assert that institutions will not change in lock step with every change in environmental conditions including prices. An institutionalist perspective also points to some more ambitious lines of reasoning. First, institutions may alter their own environment. States (here meaning central decision-making institutions) may, for instance, be able to alter the distribution of power among groups in civil society. Second, institutions may persist because in a world of imperfect information altering established routines will be costly and time consuming, and the consequences of change cannot be fully predicted. Third, certain institutional choices may determine the future trajectory of developments because of path dependencies generated by increasing returns. Institutional structures are locked-in even though there might have been some more efficient alternative. Finally, institutional structures may persist because the material environment is permissive; horizontal links with other organizations then constrain the range of institutional possibilities.

Sovereignty

Sovereignty is a term that makes the eyes of most American political scientists glaze over. It has lost meaning and analytic relevance. Scholars now do talk of the state, by which they usually mean either a central administrative and legal apparatus including especially central decision-making institutions or a polity, the network of institutional ties, behavioral regularities, and values that knit together public and private actors who play some role in formulating the implementing authoritative decisions.[4] Analysts interested in comparative politics in particular have illuminated the relationship between the state apparatus and civil society and the rules that govern interactions between different components of the polity. Students of international relations have been content to take the state, here often defined as a bearer of power capabilities in the international system, as a given. Few international relations scholars have made the nature of the state problematic.[5]

The growing disjuncture, however, between the nature of sovereignty in the contemporary world and functional objectives, both security and economic, suggest that it is time to reflect on the nature of sovereignty; to make problematic for the study of international relations what has previously been taken as an analytic given. Specifically, it is necessary to examine how the authoritative claims of states (taken here to mean the central administrative and legal apparatus) and their ability to implement such claims have changed with regard to international or transnational as opposed to domestic activities. Two issues are involved: First, the assertion of final authority within a given territory; second, efforts to control the transborder movements of people, goods, capital, and culture.

The assertion of final authority within a given territory is the core element in any definition of sovereignty. Strayer avers that "sovereignty requires independence from any outside power and final authority over men who live within certain boundaries" (Strayer, 1970:58; Finer, 1974:79; Dyson, 1980:34). The alternative to sovereignty is either a world in which there are no clear boundaries or a world in which there is no final authority within a given territory. Empires offer an example of the first form of political organization. Empires have borderlands but not boundaries and demand varying kinds of deference from groups within or even beyond these borderlands. The Roman and Chinese empires are two examples of political entities that did not recognize clear territorial boundaries (Kratochwil, 1986:33-36). Feudalism is an example of a polity in which authority varies across issue areas (the church for some questions, the nobility for others) and in which there is not necessarily a transitive ordering of authority within a given issue area. To assert, however, that the core of sovereignty is final authority within a given territory does not exhaust the problem either behaviorally or conceptually. Behaviorally, final authority within a given territory has been challenged in one way or another throughout the history of the state system. This issue was not resolved in the late medieval struggle between secular rulers and religious authorities. In the nineteenth and even the twentieth centuries, the European powers and the United States asserted extraterritorial rights in China, the Ottoman Empire, Egypt, and areas of the Persian Gulf, as well as dictating the customs policies of several Latin American states and Japan. The United States has affirmed the right to issue authoritative directives to the foreign subsidiaries of American corporations, sometimes with success, as with the freezing of Iranian assets on deposit in the overseas branches of American banks, and sometimes without success, as in the attempt to prevent the European subsidiaries of American corporations from providing material for the natural gas pipeline from the Soviet Union.

A second problem with simply treating final authority within a defined territory as unproblematic is that there are territories and spheres of human activity in which only partial sovereignty, that is control over only some issues, is claimed. The exclusive economic zones agreed to in the Law of the Sea Treaty, and accepted even by those states that have rejected the Treaty itself, gives littoral states economic control over an area extending out at least 200 miles, but denies them the right to regulate shipping in this same area. Here is a form of territorial control that is not fully sovereign. The signatories to the Antarctic Treaty have sidestepped the issue of whether states have the right to assert sovereign claims over parts of Antarctica. The European Convention on Human Rights gives individual citizens of the European Community countries the right to appeal directly to the European Court. Conceptually, the core definition of sovereignty is not concerned with explaining the actual claims that states have made with regard to the exercise of final authority. It is one thing to say that states will deny any other entity final authority within their territory, it is another to delineate the actual scope of activities over which states have asserted authority. The public debate over abortion and welfare in the United States illustrates the depth of passion that questions related to the scope of state authority can arouse, because such issues affect not only specific instrumental outcomes but also basic conceptions about the nature of political life.

Questions related to transborder control, as opposed to purely domestic issues, have also exercised states. The claims that states have made with regard to the authoritative control of movements of people, commodities, investments, and information, ideas, or culture across their international boundaries have changed across time and over countries. In some issue areas, all states have accepted the same rules; in others they have followed different norms and practices. One example of variation is the rules governing the entry and exit of people. While there is general agreement that states can regulate entry, there is no agreement on rules of exit, with some states advocating free exit and others denying that individuals are entitled to such a right. The variation can be explained by a utilitarian calculus: national laws reflect either ethnic preferences or economic interests (Weiner, 1985:443-445). Institutionalist arguments hardly seem germane for this issue. But consider a possible counterfactual. What if all states save one had opted for migration rules that provided for the free movement of individuals across borders? It would, then, be difficult for the last state to promulgate regulations that prohibit entry because the costs of enforcement could be high. On the other hand, if all states save one have adopted rules which prohibit exit, it would be less costly for the last state to enforce a rule prohibiting entry. Rules governing the exit and entry of people do involve network externalities: the utility of a particular policy does depend on the choices that have been made by other states.

More generally, if externalities are significant, and choices are irreversible, then small random events at the beginning of a process may be very important in determining the final outcome. For instance, if one or two states opt for a certain pattern of control in a given issue area, and there are substantial network externalities, then all other states may eventually make the same choice even though they would have chosen a different option had they had the opportunity to go first. If there are path-dependent sequences, then initial institutional choices can determine final institutional and behavioral outcomes. Choices that at first blush appear to be fully explicable in terms of a utilitarian calculus, such as policies toward the entry and exit of individuals, may be better understood if the impact of sequences and externalities are investigated.

In other issues, the impact of institutional constraints on available policy options is more readily apparent. The use of mercenaries offers one example. Such forces often dominated European armies during the early modern period. But their importance decreased over time for a variety of reasons, some more utilitarian, such as the fact that they were too dangerous to the rulers that hired them, others more institutional, such as the fact that states were increasingly held responsible for the actions of individuals as the conception of citizen as opposed to subject became widely accepted (Thomson, 1987).

But, does the present situation make sense from a utilitarian perspective? At the very least it poses a problem, because there are countries with material and financial resources whose citizens are reluctant to fight, for instance the United States; mercenaries would seem to be an optimal solution for such states. The United States can support rebellious citizens, the *Contras*, in Nicaragua. American policy makers do not have the option of buying a regiment or two of Gurkhas. The use of mercenaries is constrained by institutional structures that do not produce an optimal result for at least some powerful actors in the contemporary international system. The virtual absence of mercenaries in the present world system is not so easily explained by a utilitarian calculus.

Finally, consider the dominance of the state system itself, the notion that political life must be territorially organized with one final authority within a given territory. Even if this vision is sometimes challenged, no alternative has been effectively articulated and legitimated. Can the dominance of the sovereign state in the late twentieth century be explained from a utilitarian/ functionalist perspective? I began this essay by suggesting that such an approach posed difficulties because nuclear weapons and economic interdependence made it impossible for even the most powerful states to guarantee the lives, and possibly, the well being of their citizens. But the triumph of sovereignty over other possible forms of political organization in the recent past is even more striking. Efforts to convert colonial empires into commonwealths have failed. The Soviet effort to base relations in Eastern Europe on transnational functional agencies rather than state-to-state agreements has eroded over time, despite the continued material domination of the Soviet Union. Most strikingly, decolonization has led to the creation of a large number of states with only the most limited resources and populations. The existence of these states can hardly be explained by their material capabilities. Their survival and being are a function of the larger institutional framework in which they are embodied. Their most potent asset is not their tax base, population, or army, but rather the juridical sovereignty that is accorded by the international community; that is, by the willingness of other states to endorse their existence and the absence of any alternative legitimate form for organizing political life (Jackson & Rosberg, 1982).

The triumph of the sovereign state cannot be understood from a utilitarian/functionalist perspective. The breadth of the state, in terms of its links with other social entities, and the depth of the state, reflected in the very concept of citizenship as a basic source of individual identity, make it very hard to dislodge. Path-dependent patterns of development have been important; once Europe was committed to a form of political organization based on sovereign states, other possibilities were foreclosed. In earlier historical periods this was a result of the imposition of the state system or derivatives thereof, such as colonialism, through conquest. More recently it has reflected the unwillingness to consider other forms of political organization as fully legitimate. The problem of the West Bank, for instance, would be easier to resolve if there were some legitimate option to full sovereignty for the Palestinians or continued Israeli occupation; but no such possibility is acceptable, not simply because of the utilitarian calculus of the actors involved but also because the sovereign state is the only universally recognized way of organizing political life in the contemporary international system. It is now difficult even to conceive of alternatives. The historical legacy of the development of the state system has left a powerful institutional structure, one that will not be easily dislodged regardless of changed circumstances in the material environment.

Notes

1. Such arguments are made by authors from a wide range of political perspectives. The importance of an international system composed of independent states, as opposed to a world empire, is a central component of the world-systems perspective associated with the work of I. Wallerstein (1974). For similar arguments from a neoclassical economic perspective see D. North (1981), and from a sociological perspective putting considerable weight on shared values see M. Mann (1986) and J. A. Hall (1985).

2. There is variation across different social sciences with regard to the frequency with which institutionalist perspectives are invoked. They almost never appear in economics. They are also rarely invoked in political science. They are, however, much more prevalent in sociology where the work of the founding fathers of the discipline, especially Durkheim and Weber, rejected static utilitarian arguments including the notion that the market could be self-regulating. Organizational sociologists have come to take for granted the notions that organizations are not fully flexible and cannot respond instantaneously to changes in environmental conditions and that existing organizational strategies constrain the options open at any given point in time (Carroll, 1984:71-93).

3. For a similar argument by a social scientist concerned with institutions see Moe (1984).

4. For a description of various definitions of the term state see Benjamin and Duval (1985). For analyses that focus on the state as administrative apparatus see Evans, Rueschemeyer, & Skocpol, (1985). My own use of the term state in Krasner (1978) also used this approach. Corporatist arguments focus more on the state as polity. See especially Katzenstein (1985).

5. The major exceptions to this generalization are John G. Ruggie, Friedrich Kratochwil and Richard Ashley. The work of these scholars has greatly influenced my own thinking on these matters making problematic for me questions that I had earlier taken for granted. See, for instance, J. Ruggie (1986), Ashley (1986), and Kratochwil (1986).

References

Alford, R. A. and Friedland, R. (1985). *Powers of theory: Capitalism, the state, and democracy.* Cambridge: Cambridge University Press.

Anderson, P. (1974). *Lineages of the absolutist state.* London: Verso.

Arthur, W. B. (1984). Competing technologies and economic prediction. Options.

_____ (1985). *Competing technologies and lock-in by historical small events: The dynamics of allocation under increasing returns.* (CPER Publication No. 43). Stanford, CA: Stanford University, Center for Economic Policy Research.

_____ (1986). *Industry location patterns and the importance of history.* (Mimeo) Stanford, CA: Stanford University, Food Research Institute.

Ashley, R. (1986). The poverty of neo-realism. In R. O. Keohane (Ed.), *Neorealism and its critics.* New York: Columbia University Press.

Badie, B. & Birnbaum, P. (1983). *The sociology of the state.* Chicago: University of Chicago Press.

Becker, G. S. (1976). *The Economic approach to human behavior.* Chicago: University of Chicago Press.

Benjamin, R. & Duvall, R. (1985). The capitalist state in context. In R. Benjamin (Ed.), *The democratic state.* Lawrence, KS: Kansas State University Press.

Binder, L. (1986). The natural history of development theory. *Comparative Studies in Society and History, 28*(January), 3-33.

Bracken, P. (1983). *The command and control of nuclear weapons.* New Haven, CT: Yale University Press.

Carroll, G. R. (1984). Organizational ecology. *Annual Review of Sociology, 10,* 71-93.

Cooper, J. & Brady, D. W. (1981). Institutional context and leadership style: The house from Cannon to Rayburn. *American Political Science Review, 75*(June), 411-425.

Cooper, R. (1968). *The economics of interdependence.* New York: McGraw-Hill.

DiMaggio, P. J. & Powell, W. W. (1983). The iron cage revisited: Institutional isomorphism and collective rationality in organizational fields. *American Sociological Review,* (April), 147-160.

Dyson, K. H. F. (1980). *The state tradition in Western Europe: A study of an idea and institution.* New York: Oxford University Press.

Eldredge, N. (1985). *Time frames: The rethinking of Darwinian evolution and the theory of punctuated equilibria.* New York: Simon & Schuster.

Evans, P., Rueschemeyer, D., & Skocpol, T. (1985). *Bringing the state back in.* New York: Cambridge University Press.

Ferejohn, J. (1987). *The new institutionalism.* Paper prepared for presentation at the American Political Science Association annual meeting, Chicago (September).

Finer, S. (1974). State-Building, state boundaries and border control: An essay on certain aspects of the first phase of state-building in Western Europe considered in the light of the Rokkan-Hirschman model, *Social Science Information XIII,* 79-126.

Geertz, C. (1980). *Negara: The theatre state in nineteenth century Bali.* Princeton, NJ: Princeton University Press.

Goldstein, J. S. (1985). Kondratieff waves as war cycles. *International Studies Quarterly, 29,* 411-444.

Gould, S. J. (1982). Darwinism and the expansion of evolutionary theory, *Science 216* (April 23rd), 380-387.

_____ (1983). *Hen's teeth and horse's toes.* New York: W. W. Norton.

_____ (1985a). Not necessarily a wing. *Natural History,* (October), 12-25.

_____ (1985b). *The flamingo's smile.* New York: Norton.

Gould, S. J. & Eldredge, N. (1977). Punctuated equilibria: The tempo and mode of evolution reconsidered. *Paleobiology, 3.*

Granovetter, M. (1985). Economic action and social structure: The problem of embeddedness. *American Journal of Sociology, 91* (November), 481-510.

Hall, J. A. (1985). *Powers and liberties*. Oxford: Blackwell.

Hannan, M. T., and Freeman, J. (1977). The population ecology of organizations. *American Journal of Sociology, 82*, 929-964.

Harsanyi, J. C. (1960). Explanation and comparative dynamics in social science. *Behavioral Science, 5*.

Heclo, H. (1974). *Social policy in Great Britain and Sweden*. New Haven, CT: Yale University Press.

Hogarth, R. M. & Reder, M. W. (1986). Editors' comments: Perspectives from economics and psychology. *Journal of Business, 59*, S185-S207.

Jackson, R. H. & Rosberg, C. G. (1982). Why Africa's weak states persist: The empirical and the juridical in statehood. *World Politics, 35* (October), 1-24.

Jepperson, R. L. (1987). *Conceptualizing institutions, institutionalization, and institutional effects*. Paper prepared for the Conference on Institutional Change. Stanford, CA. (May), Center for Advanced Study in the Behavioral Sciences.

Katzenstein, P. J. (1985). *Small states in world markets*. Ithaca, NY: Cornell University Press.

Katznelson, I. (1986). Rethinking the silences of social and economic policy. *Political Science Quarterly, 101*, 307-325.

Keohane, R. O. (1984). *After Hegemony: Cooperation and discord in the world political economy*. Princeton, NJ: Princeton University Press.

Krasner, S. D. (1978). *Defending the national interest: Raw materials investments and U.S. foreign policy*. Princeton, NJ: Princeton University Press.

_____ (1983). Structural causes and regime consequences: Regimes as intervening variables. In Krasner (Ed.), *International regimes*. Ithaca, NY: Cornell University Press.

_____ (1984). Approaches to the state: Alternatives conceptions and historical dynamics. *Comparative Politics, 16* (January), 223-246.

Kratochwil, F. (1986). Of systems, boundaries, and territoriality: An inquiry into the formation of the state system. *World Politics, 39* (October), 27-52.

Mann, M. (1986). The sources of social power. Volume 1: *From the beginning to 1760 A.D.* Cambridge: Cambridge University Press.

March, J. G. & Olson, J. P. (1984). The new institutionalism: Organizational factors in political life. *American Political Science Review, 78* (September), 734-749.

Meyer, J. W., Boli, J., & Thomas, G. M. (1987). Ontological rationalization in the western cultural account. In G. M. Thomas, J. W. Meyer, F. O. Ramirez, & J. Boli, *Institutional structure: Constituting state, society, and the individual*. Newbury Park, CA: Sage.

Moe, T. M. (1984). The new economics of organization. *American Journal of Political Science, 28* (November), 739-777.

_____ (1987). Interests, institutions, and positive theory: The politics of the NLRB. In K. Orren & S. Skowronek (Eds.), *Studies in American Political Development, 2*. New Haven, CT: Yale University Press.

Nelson, J. & Winter, S. (1982). *An evolutionary theory of economic change*. Cambridge, MA: Harvard University Press.

North, D. (1981). *Structure and change in economic history*. New York: Norton.

Paz, O. (1987). The Food of the Gods. *New York Review of Books, 34* (Feb. 26), 3-7.

Poggi, G. (1978). *The Development of the modern state: A sociological introduction*. Stanford, CA: Stanford University Press.

Ruggie, J. G. (1986). Continuity and transformation in the world policy: Toward a neorealist synthesis. In R. O. Keohane (Ed.), *Neorealism and its critics*. New York: Columbia University Press.

Ruggie, M. (1984). *The state and working women: A comparative study of Britain and Sweden.* Princeton, NJ: Princeton University Press.

Sen, A. K. (1977). Rational fools: A critique of the behavioral foundations of economic theory. *Philosophy and Public Affairs, 6*(Summer), 317-344.

Shepsle, K. (1986). Institutional equilibrium and equilibrium institutions. In H. F. Weisberg (Ed.) *Political science: The science of politics.* New York: Agathon.

Snidal, D. (1985). The game *theory* of international politics. *World Politics, 38* (October), 25-57.

Stepan, A. (1978). *The state and society: Peru in comparative perspective.* Princeton, NJ: Princeton University Press.

Steinbrunner, J. (1974). *The cybernetic theory of decision: A new dimension of political analysis.* Princeton, NJ: Princeton University Press.

Stigler, G. J. and Becker, G. S. (1977). De gustibus non est disputandum. *American Economic Review, 67* (March), 76-90.

Stinchcombe, A. (1968). *Constructing social theories.* New York: Harcourt, Brace & World.

Strayer, J. (1970). *On the medieval origins of the modern state.* Princeton, NJ: Princeton University Press.

Thomson, J. E. (1987). *Mercenaries.* Paper presented at the annual meeting of the American Political Science Association. Chicago (September).

Tocqueville, A., de, (1945). *Democracy in America.* New York: Vantage Books.

Tversky, A. and Kahneman, D. (1986). Rational choice and the framing of decisions. *Journal of Business, 59,* S251-S278.

Verba, S. (1971). Sequences and development. In L. Binder, et. al (Eds.) *Crisis and sequences in political development.* Princeton, NJ: Princeton University Press.

Wallerstein, I. (1974). *The modern world system.* New York: Academic.

Waltz, K. (1979). *Theory of international relations.* Reading, MA: Addison-Wesley.

Walzer, M. (1983). *Spheres of justice: A defense of pluralism and equality.* New York: Basic.

Weiner, M. (1985). On migration and international relations. *Population and Development Review, 11* (September), 441-445.

Wendt, A. (1987). The agent-structure problem in international relations theory. *International Organization, 41* (Summer), 335-371.

Williamson, O. (1975). *Markets and hierarchies, analysis and antitrust implications.* New York: Free Press.

Young, O. (1986). International regimes: Toward a new theory of institutions. *World Politics, 39* (October), 104-122.

This article argues that ideas of the state are crucial for understanding contemporary politics in so-called state-societies such as West Germany. It argues that the recent protracted and divisive political battle over state employee personnel policy in the Federal Republic needs to be understood as a conflict involving the power of two nineteenth-century ideas of the German state, on the one hand, and the general modernization of the West German state and transformation of West German elite and mass political culture, on the other.

5

Radicals and the State:
The Political Demands on West German Civil Servants

GREGG O. KVISTAD

This article addresses one case of the complicated relationship between political ideas and public policy. It will suggest that the idea of the state in German politics powerfully informs the political contours of civil service personnel policy in the Federal Republic of Germany. In short, the idea of the German state—or a combination of two particular ideas of the German state—provides the ideological foundation for a politically restrictive personnel policy that has had since 1972 the explicit goal of keeping political undesirables out of the West German civil service. The impact of these ideas of the German state on civil service personnel policy is so powerful as to have overwhelmed other developments in West German politics that would suggest a politically less restrictive policy. Those include a transformative liberalization of both elite and mass political attitudes in the Federal Republic and the appearance of a concept of a liberal German state that denies the legitimacy of a protective bureaucracy occupying a distant

Author's Note: Initially prepared for presentation at the annual meeting of the American Political Science Association, Washington, D.C., August 28-31, 1986. The author would like to thank Reinhard Bendix, James Caporaso, Kenneth Dyson, Jeffrey Herf, Peter Katzenstein, Wolf-Dieter Narr, and David Wilsford for suggestions and comments.

realm above German society. This study attempts to demonstrate that ideas about the state are not just the stuff of metaphysical discourse; such ideas have important value for concrete historical and political analysis.[1]

Civil service personnel policy in the Federal Republic of Germany is not the politically innocuous and largely managerial issue that it tends generally to be in the Anglo-American context.[2] The civil service is very large in West Germany, employing approximately 17% of the working population. It includes three grades of employee—civil servant, white-collar employee, and worker—and within those grades a variety of jobs are included: from Foreign Ministry bureaucrat, to University scientist, to state office janitor.[3] The large number of state employees in itself makes civil service personnel policy politically significant for West German politics. But more important than mere numbers, civil service personnel policy in Germany has been directly political for nearly two hundred years: as will be elaborated, the German civil service has traditionally been regarded as the embodiment of the idea of the state, and its employees have been conceptualized as agents of the state acting to protect and defend German civil society. Who becomes a state employee and what political beliefs state employees hold, then, are directly relevant for thinking about the adequacy of the state's capacity as a political actor vis-à-vis civil society.

This study concurs with the recent call in social science to "bring the state back in" as a concept for the study of modern Western industrial democracies (Skocpol, 1985:3-37; Dyson, 1980:7; von Beyme, 1986: 115-119; Cassesse, 1986:120-130). As students of German politics know, however, the concept of the state has been constantly present in German political discourse and analysis since the beginning of the last century. But the continuous presence of the state concept in these realms has not led to conceptual clarity, especially in West German political discourse in the past two decades. This has been a period of protracted domestic political unrest in the Federal Republic, and a large part of that unrest reveals a fundamental contestation of deeply imbedded German political ideas and practices—for both ordinary political discourse and political analysis. Among the most contested of these phenomena is the concept of the German state and its political significance.

This article will attempt to shed some light on the value of the state concept for the study of contemporary West German politics by bringing it to bear critically on the practice of making positive political demands on all of Germany's public employees. Here we will specifically address the so-called *Radikalenerlass* (radicals decree)—an executive decree that appeared in the Federal Republic in 1972 having the intent of keeping political radicals and extremists out of the West German civil service.[4] It is not surprising that the state concept—never having left German political discourse in the past two centuries—was quite immediately brought in to the debate over the *Radikalenerlass*. This decree had as its object the construction of the material West German state. What was rather surprising, however, was how unclearly this concept was used in political debate and analysis in a society with such a rich ideological tradition of the state. *The* German state was referred to in the debate from the start; exactly *which* German state, however, with which ideological contours, was hardly ever specified. Much of why this decree became one of the most contentious domestic political issues faced by the Federal Republic in the 1970s, it will be suggested here, is attributable to this conceptual unclarity.

In an important book, Kenneth Dyson (1980) has argued that Western Europe can be viewed as the site of two quite different ideological traditions of the state. One, which he calls the *state-society* tradition, is found in societies that ideologically tend to locate public authority in the institution of the state. This state is understood as an authoritative moral and public agent acting to protect and defend civil service. *Stateless societies*, in contrast, tend to understand public authority as located in some immediate emanation from citizens in a society; as a result, such societies do not find a concept of an independent, sovereign state authority familiar or politically relevant. Germany, for Dyson's analysis, is the proto-typical *state-society*. As such, Germany since the end of the eighteenth century has been the site of the appearance of at least eight different concepts of the state: the *Obrigkeitsstaat* (authoritarian state), the *Beamtenstaat* (bureaucratic state), the *Rechtsstaat* (rule of law state), the *Parteienstaat* (party state), the *Fuehrerstaat* (dictator state), the *Bundesstaat* (federal state), the *Sozialstaat* (social state), and the *Wohlfahrtsstaat* (social welfare state).

It could be argued that each of these concepts has a relevance in German politics that is historically specific: the *Beamtenstaat*, for instance, is relevant only for understanding Prussian politics in the *Vormaerz*; the *Fuehrerstaat* idea is relevant for understanding only the National Socialist regime; and the *Bundesstaat* is relevant only for understanding the present-day Federal Republic. In particular cases that argument is surely right (e.g., the *Fuehrerstaat* idea for the NS regime). But generally, such an argument falters in its assumption of an ideological plasticity and tidiness that has concepts neatly appearing and disappearing with the comings and goings of historical regime types. The history of civil service personnel policy in Germany for the past two centuries demonstrates quite clearly how apparently anachronistic concepts of the German state have survived regime changes quite unscathed and continue to serve as ideological foundations for policy formulation and debate.

Most distinctive about all of these concepts of the German state is their incorporation of a more or less implicit dichotomization of the state realm (or leadership realm, in the case of the Fuehrerstaat) on the one hand, and the realm of civil society on the other. This conceptual dichotomization is typically loaded with a positive political significance for the concept of state and a negative or prepolitical significance for the concept of civil society. This broad understanding of the political relevance of state and civil society was formalized by Hegel in 1821 with his *Philosophy of Right*. Subject to critique, interpretation, and misinterpretation from the beginning, Hegel nonetheless left Germany with the legacy of ideologically dichotomizing state and society and of infusing that dichotomization with political meaning.[5]

The *Radikalenerlass* is a policy in West Germany as a *state-society* that has as its object the construction of the material agency of the West German state vis-à-vis West German society. Concepts of the state that would be relevant for understanding such a policy must address the role of the German civil servant in maintaining the German political order. The Beamtenstaat, the Rechtsstaat, and the Parteienstaat ideas all incorporate the ideological dichotomization of state and civil society and suggest a specific political role for civil servants in relation to civil society. The Beamtenstaat and Rechtsstaat ideas developed in nineteenth-century German political thought, while the Parteienstaat idea is a twentieth-century construct.

The Beamtenstaat concept is typically held to be anachronistic for contemporary West German politics because it refers to the political rule by expert, politically reliable, and unelected bureaucrats that characterized the period between the Reform Era in Prussia and the 1848 revolution. The Rechtsstaat idea emerged at about the same time in Prussia and was used as a legitimating concept for the rule of law as applied by a bureaucracy independent of both the Crown and other classes in Prussian society (Chapman, 1959:184; Armstrong, 1973:64-65). The Rechtsstaat idea has been salvaged for the Federal Republic but is now less an active legitimating concept than an ideological foundation—the rule of law—that underlies other more specific concepts like, for instance, the Parteienstaat idea. The Parteienstaat idea was first applied to the politics of the Weimar Republic, but only pejoratively, to denote the illegitimate rule of inexpert political parties. The idea has become, however, one of the central concepts in discussions of current politics in the Federal Republic. Parties in the Federal Republic now not only constitute stable and responsible governments, but they also act as career channels for bureaucratic recruitment.

Though all three of these German concepts of the state dichotomize state and civil society and suggest the importance of the bureaucracy in maintaining the political order, here it will be argued that only the nineteenth-century Beamtenstaat and Rechtsstaat concepts help us to understand the politics of the Radikalenerlass and the contentious debate that followed in its wake in the Federal Republic. The Parteienstaat concept is the only distinctly twentieth-century concept of the three, but it has little value for this policy area apart from suggesting how mainstream political parties determine recruitment at the most senior levels of the bureaucracy. Indeed, it will be argued below that the Parteienstaat concept, relative to the Radikalenerlass, actually suggests a much less politically restrictive response to the question employing political undesirables in the state service.

The purpose of drawing on these historical ideas of the state in German political discourse is not only to gain a clearer understanding of the Radikalenerlass. More generally, it is also to suggest that ideas about political institutions and practices that may rightly be seen as anachronistic for a modern political order generally, may nonetheless be crucial for understanding developments in certain policy areas. Civil service policy in Germany has its own discourse extending back almost two centuries, and the central concept within that discourse is an idea of a protective state that is separated from German civil society. The terms of that imbedded discourse may not appear in, and may even be challenged by, other developments in a changing political order such as West Germany's. But that does not discount entirely the relevance of the old discourse for parts of the modern political order.

Traditional German Statism and the Civil Service

The Nineteenth-Century Beamtenstaat Idea

The first Prussian civil service commission *(Oberexaminationskommission)* was established in 1770. This commission, which controlled promotion and recruitment in the Prussian bureaucracy, began a series of reforms that culminated in the full assertion of bureaucratic independence from the autocratic authority of the Crown in the early years of the nineteenth century (Rosenberg, 1966:178). The Prussian General Code *(Allgemeines Landrecht)* of 1794 established a relatively independent civil service whose members were no longer "royal servants," but rather "servants of the state" (Rosenberg, 1966:191). According to Reinhard Bendix (1964:122-124), this shift signalled the beginnings of the protection of Prussian society by a regularized bureaucracy, which by the end of the century, had come to be closely identified with the maintenance of the legal order.

This shift in identity from royal servant to state servant carried with it a transformation in the training and ascribed status for the Prussian bureaucrat. By the early nineteenth century, the overall competence of Prussian bureaucrats improved as a result of required university training in cameralistics and the use of examinations for promotion (Johnson, 1983:170). Adopting the practice of other German states, Prussia began to require training in law for higher bureaucrats in the 1830s (Schram, 1971:143; Armstrong, 1973:163). The social and political status of the new state servants was secured by the formation of the *Berufsstaende* (professional estates), a fourth *state* estate alongside the nobility, the burghers, and the peasantry (Gillis, 1971:6). The Prussian civil servant estate began, according to John Armstrong (1973:82), to identify itself as a "state above classes." It was at this time in Germany that the tradition began of entrusting the executive responsibility of the state to a body of alleged experts with the proper training and experience (Johnson, 1983:257). By 1815 Frederick William had relinquished almost all of his policy-making authority to his senior officials and had made both the administrative and judicial bureaucracies completely self-governing (Gillis, 1971:27). With no meaningful distinction made at this time between legislation and administration, Prussia, according to Hans Rosenberg (1966:178), was by 1815 a "bureaucratic autocracy."

This body of experts in early nineteenth-century Prussia, however, was not a body of politically neutral administrators. It was, instead, highly politicized, skilled, independent, and critical of the political claims of other estates in Prussian society. Reinhard Bendix (1964:117-122) observes that Germany's "functionalist" response to the question of the political beliefs and actions of civil servants left individual state bureaucrats not neutralized, as in the United States, but rather restrained, in the sense that German civil servants had *particular* rights and duties distinct from those of ordinary citizens. While this was usually not problematic for the overwhelmingly conservative bureaucratic estate, it was also, according to Hans Rosenberg (1966:213), not an empty question in the early nineteenth century:

> "The career open to talent" came to mean career open not to the vocationally most competent, if politically neutral or lukewarm, but to the politically talented with the "right opinion."

A pernicious form of ensuring the political reliability of the new state servants developed in 1815, after Napoleon's defeat. A so-called *Dema-*

gogenverfolgung (persecution of demagogues) against political unreliables in the civil service was begun as a precursor to the more generally applicable and repressive Carlsbad Decrees of 1819.

The main victims of this Demagogenverfolgung were suspected radical university professors allegedly inciting students in the name of Pan-German (not Prussian) nationalism (Conze, 1979:28). Neither bureaucratic reformism, as practiced by Stein and Hardenberg, nor German liberalism, which was just then developing, demonstrated the will or ability to counter this early political repression in the Prussian bureaucracy (Simon, 1955:51-3; Sheehan, 1978:32, 43). And while it was particularly virulent, the Demagogenverfolgung in no sense contradicted the self-understanding of the Prussian bureaucracy's functional politicization. Allowing the bureaucrats of the Prussian Beamtenstaat to be political carried with it the requirement that the politics of the individual civil servant match what was defined as the politics of the state. The policy-making role of Prussian civil servants, their self-identification as embodying the "state above classes," and their conscious rejection of the political claims of others in Prussian society, allowed the Beamtenstaat in the early nineteenth century to utilize the politics of individual civil servants for the purpose of the Prussian state.

The Beamtenstaat of this period was posited as distinct and independent of the pretensions of the nonexpert and *ungebildete* (uneducated) nobility (Sheehan, 1978:26), the "entrepreneurialism" of the commercial middle class (Armstrong, 1973:83), and the political threats of the "mob," which Friedrich Dahlmann (1978:461), a liberal, wrote in 1815, "ignorantly runs after any immediate advantage." The bureaucratic estate had not only freed itself from the fetters of the Crown, but it had also defined itself as the unique embodiment of a state established to protect the public interest of Prussian society (Chapman, 1959:274). This self-definition, to be sure, did not include political neutrality (Mayntz, 1984:175). The public interest was not perceived to be something to be distilled from the interaction of Prussian society's estates; it was, rather, to be defined and acted upon by the state bureaucracy (Edinger, 1986:92). As Reinhard Koselleck (1967:343) notes, it was believed that "The state and its 'spirit' were present only in the civil service, and not in the estate-represented society."

The contours of this early dichotomization of state and society in the Prussian Beamtenstaat changed somewhat after 1848. The strengthening of the bourgeoisie, the formal destruction of the estate system, and the gradual development of ideologies which came to underpin political parties left the bureaucracy still defining itself "above society," but Beamtenstaat ideology now located political incompetence in organized political parties rather than in society generally. In opposition to *Parteien* (parties), the state was ideologically situated as *ueberparteilich* (above parties). Standing above political parties meant rising above narrow partiality, conflict, and self-interest in order, it was alleged, to decipher and act upon the universalistic public interest (Blair, 1978:348). The bureaucracy, embodying the spirit of the state, stood above political parties, but not above politics and policy making.

The Beamtenstaat idea of this period mandated:

(1) the ideological separation of state and society and the identification of the bureaucracy as embodying the spirit of the state;

(2) the attribution of unique political and social status to bureaucrats and the corresponding denigration of other societal actors organized in estates and parties;

(3) the lack of distinction between politics and administration as constituting the bureaucrat's activity;

(4) the definition of a protective role for state bureaucrats who are above conflict and partiality and, thus, uniquely situated to determine the public interest;

(5) the restriction of ordinary rights of citizenship for bureaucrats and the general instrumentalization of their politics for the defined purposes of the state.

The Nineteenth-Century Rechtsstaat Idea

The General Code of 1794 began the process of constructing a *Rechtsstaat* (rule of law state) in Prussia. Replacing the personality of the monarch with the idea of the state as the object of the bureaucrat's actions, the Code marked a significant step toward the legalization of politics in Prussia. The Rechtsstaat idea became anchored in Prussian politics after the state's defeat by Napoleon in 1806; the idea gradually merged with other reform ideas to leave the Rechtsstaat as the principal legitimizing concept of the semi-autonomous bureaucracy estate between 1807 and 1840 (Armstrong, 1973:164-165).

The Rechtsstaat idea had its foundation in Roman law, introduced in Prussia by Napoleon after 1806 (Chapman, 1959:25). Consisting of a finite number of self-sufficient paragraphs, Roman law was regarded as providing all of the norms necessary for providing a technically correct solution to a political dispute (Dyson, 1982a:18). In this view politics is not significantly different from adjudication; indeed, the Prussian civil servant was regarded as holding a position similar to a judge (Chapman, 1959:100). This clearly contributed to the ideological delegitimization of the politics of interest, on the one hand, whether practiced by individuals, groups, or political parties, and the ideological legitimation of the politics of rational deduction, on the other, as practiced by bureaucrats located above society (Schram, 1971:137; Dyson, 1982b:80). The original Rechtsstaat idea thus placed public authority in a unitary and consistent agent, above the conflict and contradiction inherent in society (Johnson, 1983:20).

This Rechtsstaat idea had the progressive effect of politically delegitimizing the arbitrary will of the monarch. The rationality and certainty that the idea introduced into politics left citizens—as well as bureaucrats, who, after 1794, could be dismissed from service only for legally defined infractions— with some recourse against the exercise of political authority. But the Rechtsstaat idea in Prussia developed toward what Nevil Johnson (1983:15) has called a *legal formalism*, because the second part of the nineteenth-century constitutionalist program—establishing responsible party government—failed in Prussia. The Rechtsstaat idea fostered a legal positivism by offering no mechanism for checking the content of legal rules which were deduced and applied in particular cases. On the one hand, the *Rechtsstaat* had a universalistic and moral raison d'être—checking the whim of the monarch. On the other hand, the Rechtsstaat idea alone was inadequate for determining the morality of the laws with which public authority was now to be consistent. The Rechtsstaat notion defined a moral agent, the state as opposed to the personality of the monarch, but it lacked the means to determine whether the activity of that agent was moral. This, as we shall see below, is a problem that the Federal Republic has addressed with its notion of a *streitbare Demokratie* (militant democracy).

The legal formalism of the Rechtsstaat idea in Prussia required civil servants to be trained and conversant in the law. While the simple execution of the law did not itself demand legal expertise, the Rechtsstaat tradition of meshing policy making and administration contributed to making legal training for all senior civil servants obligatory in Prussia by 1846. This original Rechtsstaat idea helped pave the way for the much discussed and frequently criticized *Juristenmonopol* (lawyer monopoly) that has held fast in the senior ranks of the German bureaucracy up to the present day (Blair, 1978:348). The Rechtsstaat idea in effect turned large areas of policy making and administration in Germany into quasijudicial processes (Dyson, 1977:58). Lacking a spirit of compromise, pragmatism, and tentativeness, the original Rechtsstaat idea encouraged public authorities to view social problems as requiring consistent, definitive, and legally mandated solutions provided by trained experts.

The nineteenth-century German Rechtsstaat idea incorporated:

(1) the universalization of political rule by subordinating it to codified law;
(2) the interpretation of law as a consistent and finite set of maxims;

(3) the ideological elevation of the state bureaucracy as a formal unitary moral agent whose job it is to provide political order in a partial, divisive, and conflict-ridden society;

(4) the juridification of social problems by treating them largely as legal questions that have unequivocal, norm-derived solutions.

The Radikalenerlass

What has come to be known as the *Radikalenerlass* (radicals decree) was issued as two separate documents on January 28, 1972, by the federal Chancellor and the Minister Presidents of the West German *Laender* (states) and West Berlin. While the decree appears innocuous—largely a reiteration of standing civil service law (Art. 35 Sec. 1 and Art. 36 BRRG; Art. 52 Sec. 2 and Art. 54 BBG)—and its intent was asserted by Willy Brandt to be the establishment of consistency in West German civil service policy (Duve & Narr, 1978:34), the decree itself produced perhaps more domestic turmoil in the Federal Republic than any other issue in the 1970s. Unlike urban terrorism, which was opposed by virtually all political voices in the Federal Republic (though the means of combatting it were much disputed), the Radikalenerlass generated an utter lack of consensus in West German political debate. Despite continuous stated reassurances of consensus in the *Bundestag* (federal parliament), an institution not known for its divisiveness, the decree left that body stalemated. It generated a particularly politicized and polemical public debate in newspapers and popular journals, a particularly legalistic academic debate in scholarly political science and law journals, and a landmark Constitutional Court decision that confused the issue more than clarified it. It also led to countless demonstrations in the Federal Republic and abroad, over 350 organizations specifically formed to protest the decree, and an international tribunal on alleged human rights abuses in West Germany.

Political elites in the Federal Republic had every reason to settle the Radikalenerlass issue expeditiously. The decree created an unhealthy atmosphere of suspicion and alienation among an entire generation of university graduates at home, and abroad it rekindled considerable doubts about West Germany's political culture (Lepsius, 1982:116). By 1976 Brandt himself came to call the decree and its implementation *grotesque* (Brandt & Schmidt, 1976:48-49). Few were satisfied with the decree and its implementation, but there was no consensus on how to proceed. While the catch-all parties disagreed over particular aspects of the decree, neither a

general shift in mass or elite political consciousness (toward liberal politicization), nor a shift in the state's institutional identity (toward the Parteienstaat)
was powerful enough to assist in overcoming this lack of agreement.

The Radikalenerlass as issued in January, 1972, contains the following
points that are relevant for this discussion:

(1) Only a person able to guarantee the willingness to intervene on behalf of *(ein-
treten)* the free democratic basic order as defined by the Basic Law can be
appointed to the civil service relationship.

(2) This guarantee must be demonstrated at all times—both during work and nonwork hours.

(3) Persons who have engaged in activities that are hostile to the constitution *(verfassungsfeindlich)*[6] may not be appointed to the civil service.

(4) Each individual case must be tested and decided on its own merits.

(5) A person's membership in an organization or political party that pursues goals
hostile to the constitution will typically suffice for the denial of employment.

(6) These principles apply to all levels of public employee in the Federal Republic:
civil servants *(Beamten)*, salaried employees *(Angestellten)*, and wage workers
(Arbeiter) (Denninger, 1977:518-519).

As Philip Blair (1978:350) has observed, political discussion in the Federal
Republic is often formulated as a series of claims about the discrepancy
between constitutional norms and political reality. The controversy over
the Radikalenerlass in the 1970s was infused with this sort of debate. On
the one hand, many activists and legal commentators claimed that the decree
violated a number of the Basic Rights detailed in the first nineteen articles
of the Basic Law (Menger, 1976:105-115; Konow, 1972:47-50; Schmid,
1975:1089-1091; Alt, 1978:593-594; Blanke, 1975:153-169; Wesel,
1975:1-14; Schick, 1975:2169-2175; Seuffert, 1980:612-619). These include freedom from discrimination on the basis of belief or political perspective (Art. 3), the right of free speech (Art. 5), the right to join constitutionally legal organizations (Art. 9), and the freedom to choose one's profession (Art. 12). On the other hand, defenders of the decree tended to point
to a number of so-called *Verfassungsschutzartikeln* (articles for the defense
of the constitution) to justify its constitutionality. These include Art. 18,
which mandates the forfeiture of Basic Rights for anyone who "abuses"
(missbraucht) them "in order to attack the free democratic basic order";
Art. 33, which stipulates that the "law of the civil service shall be regulated
with consideration to the traditional principles *(hergebrachte Grundsaetze)*
of the professional civil service"; and Art. 79, an eternity clause that pro-

hibits any amendment to the constitution that would violate the Bundesstaat principle, inalienable human rights, or the right to resist any attempt to abolish the West German constitutional order. The part of this legalistic debate that is important to consider here, from a slightly different perspective, is the second half: the argument that the Radikalenerlass is constitutional and defensible for the West German political order. We find that the Radikalenerlass was often defended by legal scholars, political commentators, and politicians in the Federal Republic in the 1970s in terms consistent with the nineteenth-century Beamtenstaat and Rechtsstaat ideas discussed above.

The Radikalenerlass and the Traditional German State

The Radikalenerlass and the Rechtsstaat

Since the Federal Republic's founding, the state's political commentators have been fixated on the problematic institutional arrangement of the Weimar Republic (Bracher, 1974:50). Legal scholars comparing the Basic Law of the Federal Republic to the Weimar constitution repeatedly call attention to the latter's indifference and value neutrality (Hoenes, 1972:222; Borgs-Maciejewski, 1973:9; Mandt, 1978:10; Assel, 1972:4; Bulla, 1973:343). It is countered that the "value-ladenness" of the West German constitution, embodied in its *Verfassungsschutzartikeln*, makes the Federal Republic a material Rechtsstaat. It is alleged that this material Rechtsstaat has the means to defend itself, so to speak, unlike the purely formal and legal positivistic Rechtsstaat of the Weimar Republic (Dyson, 1979:391; Johnson, 1983:16; Landfried, 1985:208). The material Rechtsstaat idea not only calls for the rule of law, but it also stipulates what law can and cannot be made. Art. 79 of the West German Basic Law prohibits any amendment that would violate the federal principle, violate human dignity by denying inalienable human rights (Art. 1), or violate the right to resist any attempt to abolish the West German constitutional order (Art. 20). These principles are meant to protect a citizen's human rights and legalize a citizen's resistance to an attempted overthrow of the constitutional order. They might be viewed, in the Anglo-American liberal sense, as rights against state or government authorities.

Art. 79 is joined, however, by Art. 18, another *Verfassungsschutzartikeln*, which empowers public authorities to remove certain Basic Rights from persons who are deemed by the authorities to threaten the free democratic basic order. While this also applies to all citizens in the Federal Republic, it is most relevant for West Germany's public employees—some of whom are the authorities who are to implement this constitutional article. The special applicability of Art. 18—in a sense, the state's right against the citizen—to public employees is justified, according to Klaus Stern (1977: 285), by the "special status" *(Sonderstatus)* of the civil servant relative to other West German citizens. This special status requires the civil servant to be more intensively loyal to and in conformity with the Basic Law than the average citizen (Semler, 1971:107; Lecheler, 1972:232; Matz, 1978:468).

The logic of the Rechtsstaat idea clearly underlies the purported special status of the West German civil servant. The material Rechtsstaat idea grounded in the constitution guarantees the rule of law according to a set of "eternity" principles that no positive law can ever violate. It is argued that this guarantee can be maintained only if a guarantor can be relied upon to provide it. And the guarantor of the rule of law is the German state embodied in its civil service. The role of guaranteeing for eternity the rule of law in the Federal Republic is clearly politically more demanding than merely acting within the law as a citizen. This role sometimes demands invoking or executing the *Verfassungsschutzartikeln* of the material Rechtsstaat, e.g., denying the civil rights of someone threatening the free democratic basic order. Therefore, those who protect German society by activating the material Rechtsstaat cannot themselves, it is argued, threaten the political order that it is their duty to defend. The Radikalenerlass, which limits the political freedom of West German public employees, is thus justified.

The Rechtsstaat idea is also expressed in the Radikalenerlass differentiating neither among the three categories of employee in the West German public service—the civil service, white-collar employees, and workers—nor among functionally different jobs within those three categories. State employees as state employees are considered potential security risks in the Federal Republic. The Rechtsstaat idea of the state as a unitary and consistent political-moral agent is thereby maintained. But the maintenance of this Rechtsstaat idea prohibits a more pragmatic consideration of whether the job a person does as a state employee has any meaningful security implications. More than once in the 1970s the halls of the Bundestag rang with arguments about how such people as state gardeners could conceivably threaten to undermine the free democratic basic order. This less than pragmatic approach to the political beliefs of public employees in the Federal Republic was sanctioned in a 1975 Constitutional Court decision. Concurring with the Court a couple of years later, Ernst-Wolfgang Boeckenfoerde (1978:9) wrote, "the Rechtsstaat is indivisible, [and] that cannot all of a sudden be dispensed with for entrance into the public service."

The Rechtsstaat idea posits that there are many different *jobs* in the state service, but the *agency* of public authority, the Rechtsstaat, is itself singular. As Klaus Stern (1978:384) argues:

> In every civil service relationship there is one and the same state, one and the same basic constitutional value, on behalf of which the civil servant must intervene, whatever he does in whatever function he may be occupied.

While this argument is certainly debatable from the perspective of a public service providing state, it clearly does express the rationality of the Rechtsstaat idea (Johnson, 1983:181). A call for more pragmatism here that would bring the Federal Republic more in line with other Western European states cannot afford to ignore the tremendous power of this Rechtsstaat idea for the West German context (Landfried, 1985:209-210; Chapman, 1959:320). In 1982 the Socialist-Liberal government approved a bill to differentiate among the security risks of different jobs in the civil service. This bill was defeated by the conservative-controlled upper house and never resurfaced when the conservative coalition took power later that year (Braunthal, 1985:8).

The Rechtsstaat concern for consistency appears to have been a major motivation for issuing the Radikalenerlass in the first place. While West German civil service practice is generally homogeneous across the *Laender* and in the federal executive (Johnson, 1983:171), the Radikalenerlass appeared in part as an attempt also to make homogeneous the politics of Laender and federal civil service personnel policy. Such an attempt to remove arbitrariness and inconsistency from official practice is, of course, consistent with a progressive aspect of the Rechtsstaat idea. But the Rechtsstaat idea can also justify an annoying legalism that can lead, according to Klaus von Beyme (1983:15), to the attempt to try "to regulate all possible emergency cases, thus creating a political climate of fear and intimidation."[7]

We might add that to try to enhance consistency and regulate all possible emergency cases and then to fail in that attempt, produces even more fear and intimidation than would be produced if the attempt were successful. Failure to produce consistency, unfortunately, has accompanied the implementation of the Radikalenerlass in the various Laender since 1972. This inconsistency that von Beyme (1983:14) finds most embarrassing about the

Radikalenerlass others—such as victims of the decree—have found intimidating. This ironic challenge to Rechtsstaat consistency that the implementation of the Radikalenerlass constitutes was exacerbated in the summer of 1985 when the Saarland Social Democratic government announced it would no longer officially abide by the decree at all. This unleashed a furor in conservative West German Laender and led one CDU parliamentarian to call Saarland's actions a "scandalous retreat from the Basic Law" that would be pursued in the Constitutional Court (*Sueddeutsche Zeitung*, 1985). The previous appeal to the Court in 1975 did nothing to aid the decree's implementation (Kriele, 1975:210; Damkowski, 1976:1; Loew, 1979:457).

Finally, the Rechtsstaat concept of a state that is unitary and moral and is embodied in the agency of the civil service underlies the demand in the Radikalenerlass that the *entire* public employee—his or her beliefs and actions both during work and nonwork hours—must demonstrate the guarantee to uphold the free democratic basic order. The state of the Rechtsstaat is a single, unified entity; since it has no public and private spheres, its material embodiment, the state employee, has no relevant public and private spheres either. Likewise, moral agency is neither part-time nor revealed only by actions. Thus, the state employee in the Federal Republic has no private or politically irrelevant space in which beliefs and actions need not be accounted for. This line of reasoning is clearly problematic from an Anglo-American liberal political perspective. But the privacy issue has figured only marginally in the West German debate over the Radikalenerlass (Gusy, 1979:206; Staff, 1972:160; Heinemann, 1976:5).

The Radikalenerlass and the Beamtenstaat

Unlike the Rechtsstaat idea, the Beamtenstaat idea is nowhere directly mentioned in the Federal Republic's constitution, nor is it typically to be found in West German political or legal commentary. The Beamtenstaat idea is, however, indirectly referred to in Art. 33, Section 5, of the Basic Law, which states: "Civil service law is to be regulated with consideration to the traditional principles *(hergebrachte Grundsaetze)* of the professional civil service." While drafting the Basic Law the founding fathers of the German civil service allegedly became convinced that the German civil service was "always the most secure support of the state" (Hoenes, 1972:223). Though in terms of legitimacy, democratic parties may have been most advantageously situated of all of Germany's political institutions to assume the political mantle in the Federal Republic after the war (Dyson, 1982b:84), the example of Weimar did not reveal the parties as secure supports of the state. This positive perception of the bureaucracy in 1949 led to the inclusion of Art. 33 Sec. 5, and with it, considerable disagreement over the origins of these traditional principles and how they relate to the rest of the Basic Law. Not a little of this disagreement hinged on whether the traditional principles of the civil service incorporated the nineteenth-century Beamtenstaat idea.

Konrad Kruis (1979:197) argues that the constitution-drafting Parliamentary Council was not trying to link the West German bureaucracy to "reaction and traditionalism" with the citing of these traditional principles, but rather to the "core of the structural principles of the German civil service" that were necessary for the "functioning of the state." Some suggest that these principles extend back at least to Weimar (Stern, 1977:270), while others argue for back as far as the early Prussia absolutist state (Abendroth, 1975:13). On the whole, the principles seem to express at least parts of the early nineteenth-century concept of the Beamtenstaat. The Constitutional Court contributes to that interpretation in its 1975 discussion of these traditional principles. Citing legal commentary published in 1876, 1885, 1928, 1930, 1956, and 1967, the Court writes that the traditional principles of the civil service suggest, "If the civil service is not dependable, then society and the state are 'lost' in critical situations" (*Entscheidungen des Bundesverfassungsgerichts*, 1975:347).

This returns us to the special status of the West German civil service relative to other citizens. The Beamtenstaat idea separates state from civil society and identifies the state bureaucracy as embodying the spirit of the state. It also suggests that the bureaucracy deciphers the public interest and acts to protect and defend the public order. These roles are implicitly contained in the traditional principles which inform the Radikalenerlass.

A number of West German commentators concur with the 1975 Constitutional Court decision on the Radikalenerlass in asserting that Art. 33 Sec. 5 of the Basic Law—the traditional principles of the civil service— takes precedence over everything else in the document for determining the breadth of a state employee's legal political rights (Borgs-Maciejewski, 1973:9; Hoenes, 1972:224; Matz, 1978:468). Klaus Stern (1977:285) argues, "The constitution cannot exclude such restrictions that are necessary for the institutional purpose and maintenance of the functioning capacity [of the civil service]." The institutional purpose and the functioning capacity of the German civil service is partly defined by the Beamtenstaat idea as protecting German civil society from internal and external threat. For this, clearly, the politics of the individual civil servant is relevant: membership in a political party that is deemed as hostile to the constitution, though is not officially banned, it is argued, can produce doubts about the civil servant's understanding of his special protective function vis-à-vis other West German citizens. The legal commentator Martin Kriele (1979:4) vividly suggests that the most important question to ask in the Radikalenerlass debate is, "In which direction will the civil servant shoot?"

Being charged with the special protective duty vis-à-vis the rest of German society places the West German civil servant at least ideologically—though obviously not legally—in something like the separate estate that the original Beamtenstaat idea mandates. State employment is then elevated to something like membership in the state estate. And membership in the state, according to the Beamtenstaat idea, may not be consistent with membership in other associations in civil society. Therefore, civil servant membership in organizations in civil society that pretend to define an alternative political universal—such as an alternative political party—can, from the Beamtenstaat perspective, be very problematic. For this might not only threaten the state's self-defined unique political competence, but also and more immediately, the political order that the state, through its civil servants, is committed to defend.

One precursor to the Radikalenerlass in the Federal Republic, the so-called *Adenauer-Erlass* of 1950, was perhaps more clearly consistent with the original Beamtenstaat idea than the later decree. The Adenauer-Erlass listed thirteen organizations which membership in, or otherwise "taking part in," led to the state employee's immediate dismissal (Brandt, 1976:139; Seifert, 1978:32). The 1972 Radikalenerlass, in contrast, contains no such explicit list of *verfassungsfeindlich* (hostile to the constitution), but not necessarily constitutionally forbidden, parties and organizations. At the same time, however, the decree states clearly that membership in certain organizations and political parties is inconsistent with state employment. While some regard this lack of a list as problematic for the Radikalenerlass (Hoenes, 1972:221), others suggest that an explicit list in 1972 would have been more problematic, for it would undoubtedly have included the newly (re-)founded German Communist Party (DKP). Including the DKP in this list would have almost certainly led to the initiation of banning proceedings against the party, and that, in turn, would have been disastrous for Willy Brandt's recently launched *Ostpolitik*. Brandt, however, has repeatedly denied any such linkage (Brandt & Schmidt, 1976:48).

These nineteenth-century concepts of the German state ideologically underpinning the modern practice checking the politics of West German civil servants also inform, ironically, the one nominal concept of democracy that the Federal Republic has produced. As so-called once-burned children who

have learned their political lesson, West Germans are now said to have constructed a *streitbare*, or *fighting*, democracy that is to protect against any
future internal attack on a German liberal political order (Binder, 1979:30).
Also termed a *wehrhafte* (defensive), *wertgebundene* (value-laden), and
militante (militant) democracy, this construct, while not well-defined, is
the subject of much discussion in the Federal Republic (Lameyer, 1978:173).
The construct is, Peter Graf Kielmansegg (1978:9-10) notes, "a specifically
German affair" because of the experience of the Weimar Republic.

As a construct explicitly of democracy and not of the state, *streitbare
Demokratie* would appear to break new ground in German political thought.
It might connote a broad-based popular mobilization of politically conscious
West German citizens committed to protect the constitutional order. Not
state servants, but ordinary citizens would then be relied upon to protect
the political order from internal subversion. This interpretation of the *streitbare Demokratie* construct, however, is not one typically advanced in West
German political and legal commentary. Instead, *streitbare Demokratie*
seems largely to appear as a concept of the state in West German politics
and not as an authentic concept of democracy. More precisely, the *streitbare Demokratie* concept relies heavily on the Rechtsstaat and Beamtenstaat
traditions for its content; and it in turn relies on the Radikalenerlass as one
of its instruments.

The well-known West German political scientist Kurt Sontheimer
(1972:144) observed that

> Germans tend to go about democracy as an affair of the state, in the style
> of a democratically organized authoritarian state . . . [because it] has not been
> possible to make the citizen understand that democratic order is a mechanism
> by which the people, by delegating representatives, rule themselves.

While this is indeed disputable in part, the ideological link between
democracy and the state in the Federal Republic is intact in a large part
of the Radikalenerlass debate. Ludwig Raiser (1979:116), for instance, suggests that "it is consistent with the principle of a value-laden democracy . . .
that civil service law requires loyalty to the constitution." This pointed assertion of consistency is explicable if the civil servant—regardless of his actual job—is accorded a special status that requires him to maintain the
democratic order. While the Basic Law can only invite West German citizens
to defend the political order, the Basic Law, in concert with civil service
law and the Radikalenerlass, can require West German civil servants to
be willing to defend the political order at all times.

Echoing the Constitutional Court decision of 1975, Juergen Claussen (1980:10) argues:

> The political loyalty oath ensures that in times of crisis and in serious conflict situations, . . . the civil servant will side with the state. The state requires, if it does not want to make itself unreliable...a civil service that . . . defends it in crises.

Similarly defending the Radikalenerlass, Martin Kriele (1978:341) again more dramatically asserts:

> Decisive as if we can trust that on 'day X,' when it goes all-out [*ums Ganze geht*] the civil servant will not have a conflict of loyalty, but that he will support the state and fight its opponents.

This reflects what Karl-Dietrich Bracher (1974:130) has criticized as an "overriding consideration" in West German politics for "the state or some oath to some order of society," and not "an alert constitutional consciousness, a democratic consciousness." It reflects, in other words, the tendency even to reduce a concept of democracy like the *streitbare Demokratie* to a statelike notion. As the sociologist M. Rainer Lepsius (1982:126) suggests, there is a long tradition in Germany of regarding the ethos of *Rechtsstaatlichkeit* (rule of law stateness) as a substitute for democracy.

New West German Politics

The Parteienstaat Idea

The Federal Republic is Germany's only constitutional order that has been praised as a *Parteienstaat* (party state) (Dyson, 1977:6-7). But this concept, it will be suggested here, is largely inconsistent with making the type of political demands on West German civil servants that can be found in the Radikalenerlass. As has been briefly discussed above, nineteenth-century German political and legal theory generally dismissed political parties as having no competence to occupy the positions of state power. The Weimar Republic was called a Parteienstaat, but usually only pejoratively, to indicate that parties during this era were incapable and unwilling to govern Weimar Germany responsibly. This has certainly changed in the Federal Republic. In West Germany's Parteienstaat concept, catch-all political parties are viewed as legitimate contenders for political power—not only for forming governing coalitions, but also for providing from their ranks the personnel for high state offices.

Conceptually, the Parteienstaat idea suggests a transcendence of the dichotomization of state and civil society. The proper functioning of this concept in the Federal Republic, Klaus von Beyme (1983:59-67) argues, has made obsolete and untenable the ideological separation of state and civil society for modern West German politics. Kenneth Dyson (1982b:90; 1979:379-380) notes that this concept of the German state has contributed to greater efforts to accommodate, and not dichotomize, the concepts of state and civil society in West German political and legal commentary. There is even a constitutional foundation for this transcendence or accommodation. Article 21 of the Basic Law defines political parties as formative agents of the political will of the entire West German public. Absent here is the idea that a state body independent of civil society defines the political will of the public. This ideological reconceptualization catapults political parties from narrow, interest-dominated groups to constitutionally mandated institutions with a moral task: the articulation of a universalistic public interest that rises above the representation of partial interests in West German society (Dyson, 1977:10).

This reconceptualization of the role of parties in German politics had much to do with the postwar power vacuum in which every political institution but democratic political parties was tainted by some form of Nazi collaboration (Dyson, 1982b:84). Even if political parties had never previously figured positively in German political thought, their persecution by Hitler and the Allied example of parliamentary democracy secured for them a central role in the reconstruction of the West German polity. The acceptance of this policy-making role and the success that party politicians demonstrated to senior civil servants immediately after the war inspired confidence in the bureaucracy that political parties were legitimate political players (Johnson, 1983:187). In the early years, postwar party membership was sometimes sought by Germans eager to become state employees and needing therefore to demonstrate a democratic value commitment. Party membership provided the seal of approval (Herz, 1957:106). Since then party membership among West German civil servants appears to be less instrumental and more indicating of a genuine democratic value commitment (Dyson, 1982:90; Dyson, 1979:381; Blair, 1978:349; Johnson, 1983:187; Mayntz & Scharpf, 1975:55). Party membership for West German civil servants now is very high—at approximately 65% at the federal level and 85% at the *Land* level it is higher than for any other occupational group in the Federal Republic (Edinger, 1986:144). These developments have led Kenneth Dyson

(1977:11) to conclude that postwar West Germany has witnessed the dissolution of the German state into German civil society.

Changing Political Culture

The political beliefs of West Germans since the war have been of considerable interest to social scientists as well as policy makers. The attitudes of higher civil servants in the Federal Republic have been studied, often, it appears, with the assumptions that if traditional authoritarian, Prussia, or Beamtenstaat political thinking would have a home anywhere in the Federal Republic it would be in the senior civil service. These studies contribute to the Parteienstaat discussion by addressing the political beliefs of those who, at least in the pre-Parteienstaat political context, might be most likely to have authoritarian and antiparty political attitudes. If senior bureaucrats were found to harbor liberal beliefs and positions that reject the state/civil society dichotomization of German politics, then the Parteienstaat construct, it could be argued, which locates political authority in functioning catch-all political parties and not in a distant, professional, unelected bureaucracy, might have a secure place in West German politics.

In a cross-national study of senior bureaucrats, Robert Putnam (1975:89-90) conceptualizes two ideal-types of bureaucrat. The classical bureaucrat has a monistic conception of the public interest, believes in nonpartisan and objective policy making, and feels less than completely congenial towards the political institutions of a pluralist democracy. The classical bureaucrat construct thus appears to embody values very close to what we identified in both the German Beamtenstaat and original Rechtsstaat ideas above. The political bureaucrat, in contrast, has a more pluralistic vision of the public interest, is problem- and not procedure-oriented, and generally accepts as legitimate the political role of parties and pressure groups. This construct, in short, seems relatively consistent with our West German Parteienstaat idea.

Putnam (1975:113) found, apparently to his surprise, that West German higher bureaucrats in 1970 "displayed great sensitivity to and support for the imperatives of politics in a democracy." In other words, higher civil servants in the Federal Republic tended to be more "political"—pluralistic, accepting of conflict, and according a legitimate political role to parties— than "classical" in orientation. This was surprising in part because his classical ideal-type was constructed with the traditional image of the German bureaucrat in mind. Putnam found that the Italian bureaucrat fitted this classical image much better than the German. These data were gathered only a few months after Willy Brandt's Social-Liberal coalition brought into the top layer of the bureaucracy a number of outsiders who were young, politically committed, and fired with egalitarian ideals (Putnam, 1975:98; Aberbach, Putnam, & Rockman, 1981:18, 40, 188). But most of Putnam's sample entered the civil service *before* the SPD-FDP government was formed, and, thus, the political nature of his West German bureaucrats is not an artifact of a recent purge (Putnam, 1975:114-116). This politicization is rather related to age and experience: younger bureaucrats (under fifty years old) who have been in their posts for a relatively short period of time (less than three years) tended to be more "political" than any other section of this sample (Putnam, 1975:115; Aberbach, et al., 1981:40-1). Putnam (1975:116) thus concludes that the transformation of the Federal Republic's modern bureaucracy is the result of a bureaucratic cohort shift and not a shift in the attitudes of individual bureaucrats.

Other studies generally support Putnam's conclusions. Renate Mayntz (1984:192) similarly finds a shift in West German higher civil servant self-identification from a "servant of the state" to an "advocate of the public." Indeed, John Herz's earlier study (1957:99, 113) found senior, but not lower level, West German officials harboring antiauthoritarian and even democratic political views, thus, throwing into doubt the validity of the classical German bureaucratic image for any time in the Federal Republic's history. But tempering this liberal image are the findings of Kaltefleiter and Wildenmann (von Beyme, 1983:152-153), which suggest that West German bureaucrats are particularly intolerant of nonmainstream political activity. Senior civil servants are surpassed only by military elites in their intolerance of so-called deviant political behavior and their readiness to equate that with fundamental opposition to the political order.

These attitudinal studies of West German bureaucratic elites appear generally to demonstrate a liberal democratic politicization of civil service ranks. There seems to be a willingness to try to discern the public good from the interaction of society's interest groups; there is an overwhelming tendency to belong to one of the Federal Republic's catch-all parties; and there is a tendency to tolerate conflict in society—even to see it as politically beneficial—so long as it remains within the parameters of the political status quo. On the whole, the West German bureaucrat of these elite attitudinal studies is very similar to the bureaucrat suggested by the modern Parteienstaat idea of the Federal Republic and quite different from that suggested by the nineteenth-century Beamtenstaat and Rechtsstaat ideas. Only the bureaucrats' readiness to view alternative forms of politics in the Federal Republic as "fundamental opposition" and as threats to the constitutional order complicates this picture. Such intolerance is more consistent with the Beamtenstaat and Rechtsstaat ideas. Generally speaking, however, it appears that the traditional German state/society ideological dichotomization would be of limited relevance to contemporary West German bureaucratic elites. The horizontal pull of the Parteienstaat concept seems to have considerably weakened the vertical pull of the Beamtenstaat tradition, at least for senior bureaucrats (Southern, 1979:154).

Political culture studies of mass attitudes in the Federal Republic suggest a similar conclusion. These studies are concerned generally to measure the extent to which citizens view themselves as rightful and competent political actors. It can be argued that the more participatory a mass public views itself, the more relevant a political concept like the Parteienstaat becomes, which spatially locates meaningful political activity in society and not in the distant realm of a state inhabited by bureaucrats.

Political culture studies of the West German public document a significant transformation of political belief in the last few years. The large number of studies that have appeared reflect the repeated doubts about the reliability of West Germany's mass political culture have been expressed since the Republic's founding (Lepsius, 1982:116). Recent studies, many of them drawing on the 1963 Almond and Verba civic culture study, indicate that West Germany's mass political culture appears quite *reliable*, if by that is meant some level of convergence with the mass political cultures of other Western liberal democracies. David Conradt (1980:212-272) replicated the Almond and Verba study for the Federal Republic and found that by the late 1970s West German citizens had clearly shifted their self-identities from a subject to a civic competence. Political competence is indicated by a growing political interest, a greater respect for West Germany's political institutions, and a growing sense of civil empowerment among West German citizens.

This politicization exists alongside of what Ronald Inglehart in a number of studies (1977; 1985:485-532) has called a burgeoning "postmaterialist" value orientation in modern industrial societies. This post-materialist orientation is constructed from so-called quality-of-life values that deemphasize traditional economistic demands like high wages and low rates of unemployment and inflation. In these studies Inglehart (1977:262-290; 1985:495, 514, 524) found no significant differences between the West German populace and other advanced industrial societies in terms of the breadth and intensity of postmaterialism. In a conclusive and exhaustive discussion of this shift, Baker, Dalton, & Hildebrandt, (1981:136-159) devoted a whole volume to this attitudinal transformation in the Federal Republic, similarly finding the development of a New Politics that values participation and other quality-of-life issues over the Old Politics of economism and limited popular participation.

The Radikalenerlass and New German Politics

These two survey literatures detailing the transformation in both elite and mass political attitudes in the Federal Republic together support, at a different level of analysis, the theoretical understanding of West Germany's Parteienstaat as liberal-politicizing and transcending the ideological barriers between state and civil society. These attitudinal studies demonstrate that West German elite and masses are thinking less traditionally about the nature of politics, the state, and their own political participation. Combined, this new concept of the Parteienstaat in the Federal Republic and these attitudinal findings suggest a conclusion that is clearly inconsistent with the nineteenth-century Beamtenstaat and Rechtsstaat concepts argued above as underlying the Radikalenerlass.

While the Parteienstaat concept and these studies suggest an unprecedented modernization and liberalization in both political thought and German political attitudes, it has been argued here that nineteenth-century ideas of the state and civil society are still alive and well in the Federal Republic, servicing both the formulation of the Radikalenerlass policy and the contentious political debate that followed in the decree's wake. The Radikalenerlas conceptualizes a state distinct from civil society, a state that protects civil society from internal subversion, and a state that must therefore be concerned with the politics of the persons who embody its authority. This is neither the state of the West German Parteienstaat nor of recent West German elite and mass political culture studies. The protracted political battle over the decree from the day it was issued in January, 1972, revealed the tension between liberal, and to some extent postliberal, political development in the Federal Republic, and the continuing relevance—at least for this policy area—of traditional nineteenth-century concepts of the German state. The uncertainty and unclarity that attended the Radikalenerlass debate indicated a political order that was ideologically unsettled, or *verunsichert*, as one leading West German political scientist formulated it (Sontheimer, 1979).

Are we to conclude from this discussion, then, that West Germany at this historical juncture is the home of some wide but tidy ideological gulf between nineteenth-century statist political thought on the one side and liberal and postmaterialist attitudes and concepts on the other? The answer is obviously no; the picture is much murkier than that. For one, civil service personnel policy is only one, relatively narrow, policy area. Furthermore, it could even be argued that old political concepts like the Beamtenstaat and the Rechtsstaat ideas, as pre-Hitlerite concepts, actually helped to legitimize the new West German political settlement in its early years. It mattered less that these concepts were born in authoritarian or semi-authoritarian nineteenth-century contexts and more that they were German (but not National Socialistic) ideas that emphasized the legality of politics. As such, they could be called on for the post-Hitler reconstruction of a political order in desperate need of legitimating political concepts.[8]

The West German Parteienstaat idea is also arguably not a purely liberal concept that transcends the old nineteenth-century German dichotomization of state and civil society. The Parteienstaat concept, we must remember, remains a concept of *Staat* and not of *Demokratie* or *Republik*. Kenneth Dyson (1977:6-10) argues that the Parteienstaat concept in the Federal Republic today implies less that the West German state has become like the political party conceptualized by nineteenth-century political thought than that political parties in the Federal Republic have become "heirs to state norms." This means that parties in the Federal Republic have adopted not only the organizational rigidities of bureaucracies—which is obviously not unique to the Federal Republic—but also the moral function of speaking "for the whole people" in the political arena (Smith, 1982:69). In replacing traditional concepts of the state like the Rechtsstaat and the Beamtenstaat in West German political discourse, the Parteienstaat concept does not wholly discard the values of that old discourse. Speaking for the whole, which was the German state's function in the nineteenth century, is now the role of catch-all political parties.

Conclusion

A solution to the question of political undesirables in the West German civil service that would be more consistent and pragmatic than the Radikalenerlass and its implementation failed to appear in the Federal Republic in the 1970s, it has been argued here, in part because of the power of two surviving nineteenth-century concepts of the state in West German political discourse. The logic of the Beamtenstaat and Rechtsstaat ideas helped to prevent a satisfactory—from the perspective of any West German political actor—solution to this question which became in the 1970s one of the most contentious issues in West German domestic politics. Pulling in the opposite direction from these ideas of the state and the Radikalenerlass were the Parteienstaat concept and convincing evidence of an increasingly politicized and participatory elite and mass public in West Germany. But this ideological construct and changing political culture were together not powerful enough to displace the strength of the Beamtenstaat and Rechtsstaat ideas for this policy area.

These nineteenth-century concepts of the state and the nonparticipatory politics that they endorse have been even more sharply attacked in the 1980s in the Federal Republic. Green political ideology, which politicized the diffuse antiauthoritarianism of West Germany in the late 1960s and early 1970s into a slightly more focused antistatism in the early 1980s, clearly rejects any political concept that elevates the state bureaucracy to a position of expertise and decision making vis-à-vis the rest of society. In fact, there is a strong current in Green ideology that rejects even the liberal Parteienstaat concept as little more than another statist notion that legitimizes removing meaningful political participation from ordinary West German citizens (Kvistad, 1987:211-228).

This article points to the danger of adopting any one *Schluesselbegriff* or key concept as defining of a modern changing political order like that of West Germany. It has been argued that two concepts of the German state, which are viewed as generally anachronistic for understanding West German politics today, are in fact crucial for understanding the contentious issue of civil service personnel policy in the Federal Republic since 1972. While the relevance of these nineteenth-century concepts of the state is bound to fade in the Federal Republic, this study suggests that such a process is protracted and uneven. Modern political orders are not all of one piece. It is only by calling on two-century-old ideas of the German state that we are able to begin to understand the breadth and depth of contemporary political conflict and transformation in the Federal Republic.

Notes

1. The classical account of the relevance of the idea of the state for modern social science is Nettl (1968:559-592).

2. Obviously, the McCarthy era in the United States is the clear exception to this generalization. But it was also the clear exception to the American experience, indebted more to the peculiar conjuncture of foreign policy, domestic anticommunism, and the demogogy of one man, than to a broader historical and conceptual tradition defining the political role of state employees.

3. Unless otherwise noted, *civil service, public service,* and *state service* will ᵥᵥ ᵤₛₑᵤ ᵢₙ-
terchangeably here. That is also the case with *civil servant, public servant,* and *state employee.*
It should be kept in mind that Germany has historically distinguished among three levels of
state employment and *civil service* is typically used to denote only the highest level, the *Beamten.*

4. The state as a concept figures centrally, if not always critically, in West German literature
on this topic. Anglo-American literature, however, set in a different ideological tradition, often
views the Radikalenerlass as a civil liberties issue (Conradt, 1986:65). This is a mistake, I
believe, if only because it suggests an Anglo-American liberal concept of *negative* freedom
from the state—a concept utterly foreign to the German political tradition. As James Sheehan
(1978:43) has shown, German liberalism has consistently understood liberty as something a
strong state provides and protects, not something that a strong state threatens. While the
liberalism of the small Free Democratic Party in the Federal Republic mistrusts the state along
Anglo-American lines, this is a weak position in German politics built on a weak tradition.
The Radikalenerlass may in an abstract sense be a civil liberties issue, but it is not primarily
that in West German politics. Adopting a civil liberties approach to the Radikalenerlass, furthermore, forecloses anything but a mildly critical liberal condemnation of the decree. It does
not service an explanation of either the decree or the political turmoil that the decree produced.

5. I have attempted to deal with Hegel's relevance for the problem of politics and the German civil servant in my unpublished Ph.D. dissertation (Kvistad, 1984:32-65).

6. *Hostile* does not nearly connote the intensity of the German word *feindlich,* which literally
translated is something like *enemylike.*

7. On the legalism of the Federal Republic's political culture, see Johnson (1983:262-266);
Landfried (1985:209); Blair (1978:348); Southern (1979:154); and Conradt (1986:62).

8. I am indebted to Kenneth Dyson for this suggestion.

References

Abendroth, W. (1975). Das Problem des Berufsverbots fuer Marxisten, Sozialisten und radikalen
Demokraten und die Entscheidung des Bundesverfassungsgerichts. *Marxistische Blaetter,
5,* 125-129.

Aberbach, J., Putnam, R., & Rockman, B. (1981). *Bureaucrats and politicians in western
democracies.* Cambridge, MA: Harvard University Press.

Alt, F. (1978). Vertrauen ist besser: Kritik am Radikalenerlass. *Evangelische Kommentare,
10,* 593-594.

Armstrong, J. (1973). *The European administrative elite.* Princeton, NJ: Princeton University Press.

Assel, H. G. (1972). "Die Grundrechte: Ewiges Fundament oder wandelbare Satzung?" *Aus
Politik und Zeitgeschichte, 1-2,* 3-15.

Baker, K., Dalton, R., & Hildebrandt, K. (1981). *Germany transformed: Political culture
and the new politics.* Cambridge, MA: Harvard University Press.

Bendix, R. (1964). *Nation-building and citizenship.* New York: John Wiley and Sons.

Binder, G. (1979). Der Aufsatz: 100 Jahre Sozialistengesetz—ein Lehrstueck: Stellungnahme
zu dem Beitrag von Karl-Ludwig Guensche und Klaus Lantermann." *Aus Politik und
Zeitgeschichte, 12,* 25-33.

Blair, P. (1978). Law and politics in Germany. *Political Studies, 26*(3), 348-362.

Blanke, B. (1975). 'Staatsraeson' und demokratischen Rechtsstaat: Einschraenkung der Berufsfreiheit als Sonderrecht fuer den Staatsapparat und Ausbuergerungsrecht gegen die Linke." *Leviathan, 2,* 153-169.

Boeckenfoerde, E.-W. (1978). Verhaltensgewaehr oder Gesinnungs-treue? *Frankfurter Allgemeine Zeitung, 273,* 9.

Borgs-Maciejewski, H. (1973). Radikale im oeffentlichen Dienst. *Aus Politik und Zeitgeschichte, 27,* 3-22.

Bracher, K.-D. (1974) *The German dilemma: The throes of political emancipation.* London: Weidenfeld and Nicholson.

Brandt, E. [Ed.] (1976). *Die politische Treuepflicht: Rechtsquellen zur Geschichte des deutschen Berufsbeamtentums.* Karlsruhe: C. F. Mueller Juristischer Verlag.

Brandt, W. & Schmidt, H. (1976). *Deutschland 1976: Zwei Sozialdemokraten im Gespraech.* Hamburg: Rowohlt.

Braunthal, G. (1985). The West German decree against radicals: A major civil rights controversy. (Mimeo, 1-11).

Bulla, E. (1973). Die Lehre von der streitbaren Demokratie: Versuch einer kritischen Analyse unter besonderer Beruecksichtigung der Rechtssprechung des Bundesverfassungsgerichts. *Archiv des oeffentlichen Rechts, 98,* 340-360.

Cassesse, S. (1986). The rise and decline of the notion of the state. *International Political Science Review, 7*(2), 120-130.

Chapman, B. (1959). *The profession of government: The public service in Europe.* Princeton, NJ: Princeton University Press.

Claussen, J. (1980). Zur politische Treuepflicht der Beamten. *Zeitschrift fuer Beamtenrecht, 1,* 8-19.

Conradt, D. (1980). Changing German Political Culture. pp. 212-72. In G. Almond and S. Verba (Eds.). *The civic culture revisited.* Boston: Little, Brown & Company.

_____ (1986). *The German polity,* 3rd ed. New York: Longman.

Conze, W. (1979). *The shaping of the German nation.* New York: St. Martin's Press.

Dahlmann, F. (1978). Ein Wort ueber Verfassung. In E. K. Bramsted & K. J. Melhuish (Eds.). *Western liberalism.* London: Longman.

Damkowski, W. (1976). Radikale im oeffentlichen Dienst: Funktionen und Folgen einer Entscheidung des Bundesverfassungsgerichts. *Recht im Amt, 1,* 1-12.

Denninger, E. (Ed.), (1977). *Freiheitliche demokratische Grundordnung,* Band II. Frankfurt am Main: Suhrkamp Verlag.

Duve, F. & Narr, W.-D. (Eds.), (1978). *Russell-tribunal—pro und contra: Dokumente zu einer gefaehrlichen Kontroversen.* Hamburg: Rowohlt.

Dyson, K. (1977). *Party, state and bureaucracy in Western Germany.* Beverly Hills, CA: Sage.

_____ (1979). The ambiguous politics of western Germany: politicization in a 'state' society. *European Journal of Political Research, 7,* 375-396.

_____ (1980). *The state tradition in western Europe: The study of an idea and an institution.* New York: Oxford University Press.

_____ (1982a). West Germany: The search for a rationalist consensus, pp. 17-46. In J. Richardson (Ed.) *Policy styles in western Europe.* London: Allen & Unwin.

_____ (1982b). Party government and party state, pp. 77-100. In H. Doering & G. Smith (Eds.), *Party government and political culture in Western Germany.* New York: St. Martin's Press.

Edinger, L. (1986). *West German politics.* New York: Columbia University Press.

Entscheidungen des Bundesverfassungsgerichts (1975), *39,* 16. Tuebingen: J. C. B. Mohr.

Gillis, J. (1971). *The Prussia bureaucracy in crisis: 1840-1860*. Stanford, CA: Stanford University Press.

Gusy, C. (1979). Die 'Eignung zu einem oeffentlichen Amt' gem. Art. 33 II GG. *Recht im Amt, 11*, 201-227.

Heinemann, G. (1976). Freimuetige Kritik und demokratischer Rechtsstaat. *Aus Politik und Zeitgeschichte, 20-21*, 3-5.

Herz, J. (1957). Political views of the West German civil service, pp. 96-135. In H. Speier & W. P. Davison (Eds.), *West German leadership and foreign policy*. Evanston, IL: Row, Peterson, & Company.

Hoenes, E. R. (1972). Beamte als Verfassungsfeinde. *Der oeffentliche Dienst, 12*, 221-228.

Inglehart, R. (1977). *The silent revolution: Changing styles among western publics*. Princeton, NJ: Princeton University Press.

_____ (1985). New perspectives on political change. *Comparative Political Studies, 17*(4), 485-532.

Johnson, N. (1983). *State and government in the Federal Republic of Germany*, 2nd. ed. London: Pergamon.

Kielmansegg, P. (1978). Ist streitbare Demokratie moeglich? *Frankfurter Allgemeine Zeitung, 127*, 9-10.

Konow, K. O. (1972). Grenzen der schriftstellerischen Betaetigung der Beamten. *Zeitschrift fuer Beamtenrecht, 1*, 47-50.

Koselleck, R. (1967). *Preussen zwischen Reform und Revolution*. Stuttgart: Ernst Klett Verlag.

Kriele, M. (1975). Feststellung der Verfassungsfeindlichkeit von Parteien ohne Verbot. *Zeitschrift fuer Rechtspolitik, 9*, 201-204.

Kriele, M. (1978). Verfassungsfeinde im oeffentlichen Dienst—ein unloesbares Problem?, pp. 335-347. In M. Funke (Ed.) *Extremismus im demokratischen Rechtsstaat*. Duesseldorf: Droste Verlag.

_____ (1979). Der rechtliche spielraum einer Liberalisierung der Einstellungspraxis im oeffentlichen Dienst. *Neue Juristische Wochenschrift, 1/2*, 1-8.

Kruis, K. (1979). Berufsbeamtentum—Aergernis oder Forderung der freiheitlichen rechts- und sozialistaatlichen Demokratie? *Politischen Studien, 244*, 189-201.

Kvistad, G. (1984). *Radicals and the German state: Hegel, Marx, and the political demands on German civil servants*. Ph.D. dissertation. Berkeley, CA: University of California.

_____ (1987). Between state and society: Green political ideology in the mid-1980s. *West European Politics, 10*(2), 211-228.

Lameyer, J. (1978). *Streitbare Demokratie: eine verfassungshermeneutische Untersuchung*. Berlin: Dunker and Humblot.

Landfried, C. (1985). Legal policy and internal security, pp. 198-221. In K. von Beyme & M. Schmidt (Eds.) *Policy and politics in the Federal Republic of Germany*. New York: St. Martin's Press.

Lecheler, H. (1972). Die Treuepflicht des Beamten—Leerformel oder Zentrum der Beamtenpflichten? *Zeitschrift fuer Beamtenrecht, 8*, 228-237.

Lepsius, M. R. (1982). Institutional structures and political culture, pp. 116-129. In H. Doering & G. Smith (Eds.), *Party government and political culture in western Germany*. New York: St. Martin's Press.

Loew, K. (1979). Bundesverfassungsgericht gaenzlich missverstanden. Nochmals: Mitgliedschaft in verfassungsfeindlicher Partei und oeffentlicher Dienst. *Deutsche Verwaltungsblatt, 12*, 456-458.

Mandt, H. (1978). Grenzen politischer Toleranz in der offenen Gesellschaft: Zum Verfassungsgrundsatz der streitbaren Demokratie. *Aus Politik und Zeitgeschichte, 3*, 3-16.

Matz, U. (1978). Extremisten im oeffentlichen Dienst. *Die oeffentliche Verwaltung, 13/14*, 464-468.

Mayntz, R. (1984). German federal bureaucrats: A functional elite between politics and administration, pp. 174-205. In E. Suleiman (Ed.) *Bureaucrats and policymaking: A comparative overview*. New York: Holmes & Meier.

Mayntz, R. & F. Scharpf (1975). *Policy-making in the German federal bureaucracy*. New York: Elsevier.

Menger, C.-F. (1976). Parteienprinzip und Zugang Radikaler zum oeffentlichen Dienst. *Verwaltungsarchiv, 1*, 105-15.

Nettl, J. P. (1968). The state as a conceptual variable. *World Politics, 20*(4), 559-592.

Putnam, R. (1975). The political attitudes of senior civil servants in Britain, Germany, and Italy, pp. 87-127. In M. Dogan (ed.) *The mandarins of western Europe*. New York: John Wiley and Sons.

Raiser, L. (1979). Der 'Radikalen-Erlass': Pruefstein eines demokratischen Rechtsstaates? *Zeitschrift fuer Evangelische Ethik, 2*, 106-117.

Rosenberg, H. (1966). *Bureaucracy, aristocracy and autocracy: The Prussia experience 1660-1815*. Boston: Beacon Press.

Schick, W. (1975). Der 'Radikalenbeschluss' des Bundesverfassungsgerichts—Inhalt und Konsequenzen. *Neue juristische Wochenschrift, 48*, 2169-2175.

Schmid, R. (1975). Pflichttreue, nicht Treuepflicht. *Merkur, 11*, 1089-1091.

Schram, G. (1971). Ideology and politics: The rechtsstaat idea in German politics. *Journal of Politics, 33*(1), 133-157.

Seifert, J. (1978). Ueber die Geschichte der Berufsverbote in Deutschland. *Vorgaenge, 3*, 4-9.

Semler, J. (1971). Duerfen Beamte verfassungsfeindlichen Parteien angehoeren? *Zeitschrift fuer Beamtenrecht, 4*, 107-111.

Seuffert, W. (1980). Der oeffentliche Dienst in der freiheitlichen Grundordnung. *Die neue Gesellschaft, 7*, 612-619.

Sheehan, J. (1978). *German liberalism in the nineteenth century*. Chicago: University of Chicago Press.

Simon, W. (1955). *The failure of the Prussian reform movement*. Ithaca, NY: Cornell University Press.

Skocpol, T. (1985). Bringing the state back in: Strategies of analysis in current research, pp. 3-37. In P. Evans, D. Rueschemeyer, & T. Skocpol (Eds.), *Bringing the state back in*. New York: Cambridge University Press.

Smith, G. (1982). The German Volkspartei and the career of the catch-all concept, pp. 59-76. In H. Doering & G. Smith (Eds.), *Party government and political culture in western Germany*. New York: St. Martin's Press.

Sontheimer, K. (1972). *The government and politics of West Germany*. London: Hutchinson University Library.

————— (1979). *Die verunsicherte Republik*. Muenchen: R. Piper & Co.

Southern, D. (1979). Germany, pp. 107-155. In F. Ridley (Ed.) *Government and administration in western Europe*. New York: St. Martin's Press.

Staff, I. (1972). Stellungnahme von Juristen zu der Ministerpraesidentenkonferenz vom 28.1.72. *Blaetter fuer deutsche und internationale Politik, 2*, 160-162.

Stern, K. (1977). *Das Staatsrecht der Bundesrepublik Deutschland*, Band 1. Muenchen: C. H. Beck'sche Verlagsbuchhandlung.

_____ (1978). Die Verfassungstreue des Beamtenbewerbers: Eine Verfassungsforderung. *Zeitschrift fuer Beamtenrecht, 12*, 381-384.

Sueddeutsche Zeitung (1985). Saarland hebt Extremistenbeschluss auf. (June 26).

Von Beyme, K. (1983). *The political system of the Federal Republic of Germany.* New York: St. Martin's Press.

_____ (1986). The contemporary relevance of the concept of the state. *International Political Science Review, 7*(2), 115-19.

Wesel, U. (1975). Das Gericht und die Krise: Warum Sybille Plogstedt nicht an der Freien Universitaet arbeiten darf. *Leviathan, 1*, 1-14.

nt examines two contrasting views of state authority in France and reopens the
'strong" versus "weak" states. To do so, it explores the traditional Rousseauian
strong state and contrasts it to an opposing view that emphasizes administrative
heterogeneity even in so-called strong states. The argument applies these views to the French
state and develops a reconciliation of them. I argue that it is useful to conceive of state authority
and structures in terms of "tactical advantages" that states may or may not have at their disposal
in relations with civil society. State traditions structure over time the tactical advantages states
may have. Strong state structures and the tactical advantages these give to the state enable
it to shape politics by employing more effectively policy instruments to induce and constrain
political behavior and policy outcomes. The state's tactical advantages influence what interest
groups do politically and their effectiveness. Thus, the French state possesses tactical advantages that enable it to structure the role interest groups play. The "weaker" American state,
by contrast, does not possess tactical advantages that give it a comparable capacity to dictate
inducements and enforce constraints on politics. But there are also important limits to the French
state's strength. One of the most important of these is the French state's vulnerability to direct
action, or exit from normal politics.

6

Tactical Advantages Versus Administrative Heterogeneity: The Strengths and the Limits of the French State

DAVID WILSFORD

The traditional strong state view, dating in France at least from Colbert
and made intellectually congenial by Rousseau, takes the state as the sole
embodiment of the public interest with commensurate powers against
political and social manifestations of private interests. An opposing view
emphasizes that, whatever the theory of the state, the state bureaucracy is

Author's Note: I wish to thank James A. Caporaso, Henry W. Ehrmann, Arend Lijphart,
and Frank L. Wilson for their critical advice during the preparation of this chapter, as well
as the French government for the privilege of serving as a Chateaubriand Fellow in 1985-1986.
The research reported here was undertaken during that period.

in fact so heterogeneous, embodying so many conflictual interests, that strong state power is a fiction. I will juxtapose these two views of state power and authority and then, addressing the French case, turn to a way of reconciling them that accords sufficient importance to the fact that *strong* states such as the French can indeed do things that *weak* states cannot, but that, equally, there are important limits to strong state power. We will see that one of the most important of these limits is the French state's vulnerability to direct action and other extreme forms of protest, that is, exit from normal politics.

Rousseau and the Strong State

"If the general will is to be able to express itself, it is essential that there should be no partial society within the State and that each citizen should think only his own thoughts" (Rousseau, cited in Ehrmann, 1983:183). For Rousseau, man's principal problem is his inevitable disunity resulting from society. All intermediate associations between individuals and the state—the "partial societies"—are condemned as perverters of the general will. The state then becomes the only means, however imperfect, of overriding the divisive forces of particular wills and instituting a unifying general will. But to be unoppressive, the state must rely on the rule of law, failing the appearance of the Legislator, whose role resembles that of Plato's philosopher-king. The rule of law in turn depends on civic virtue, hence the importance attached by the Jacobins to state education. The state at once embodies and also induces the general will.

The idea of the strong state has proved compelling in French history and politics and dates from well before Rousseau. The rise of modern French administration begins in the Middle Ages and continues through the Renaissance with the crown's struggles to subdue and control from the core a periphery that was often rebellious and always remote. Birnbaum (1982) argues that the presence of a state depends on resistance from the periphery during the emergence from feudalism. The stronger and more widespread the resistance, the stronger the central authority had to become to consolidate the realm (see also Wilsford, 1985). The *intendants* were early agents of this administration. They were sent out from the center to the periphery to rule in the name of the crown. These intendants were early precursors to today's prefects.

Indeed, one might distinguish between the rhetoric of absolutism and the reality of provincialism, resistance, and the constant problem of revolts

(Dyson, 1980:153). Mousnier (1970) emphasizes the continuing vertical lines of loyalty under the *ancien régime* and considers them holdovers from feudal organization of authority relationships. Similarly, Goubert (1969) sees absolutism as a process of dialogue between (often) opposing social forces. There seems little doubt that ideal absolutist rule was severely mitigated in practice by conflicts and subversion. Further, as Bendix has argued (1978), in one important way absolutist rule of the *ancien régime* was not absolutist, nor centralized, at all: To consolidate the realm and control localities, the crown was dependent on a far-flung network of intendants. But to be effective intendants had to be granted a large measure of independence, for it was they who ruled, administered, negotiated and adjudicated on the spot. The contradiction of decentralizing to rule from the center parallels prefect-community relations in France today (see Grémion, 1976; Worms, 1966, 1968; Pitts, 1963).

The French crown's activities gave rise early on to the growth of bureaucracy and centralization—in the armies, in finance, and in an array of interventionist techniques such as grants of monopoly, credits, and subsidies that were used to push nascent industries in the directions the crown saw fit. As Tocqueville argued (1967:98-128), the Revolution and Napoleon's subsequent rule did by no means raze the administrative edifice. Rather, the centralization of the administration was furthered. Napoleon, moreover, established the first *grande école*—polytechnique—to provide him with the technical corps necessary to his vast projects. Napoleon also took the rationality of the Enlightenment, which has always informed the outlook of French administration, to new heights through the Code Napoléon, the metric system, and numerous administrative innovations.

In both the German and French conceptions of the state, a leading role has always been assigned to the public bureaucracy (Dyson, 1980:157-158). Rousseau's notion of the general will as a social bond gave sovereignty to the nation through the state. Further, the Declaration of Rights, following Rousseau, stated, "The Law is the expression of the General Will." But operationalizing such slippery concepts poses problems. The lawmaking instrument, for example, whether an executive or a parliament, or whether a parliament that follows the will of the people or one that exercises independent judgment, has been a contentious question in French political history. Robespierre identified the general will as identical to the will of the Assembly. Its members, much like Burke's trustees, represented not individual interests, but the nation. The strong Assembly gave way to Bonapartist rule, which eliminated participation in favor of a chief of state whose power rested on the direct will of the people, excluding intermediaries. With Napoleon, the state becomes again identified with a single ruler, as it was identified under the *ancien régime* with the crown. And of course to rule over a large territory, the single ruler requires large teams of administrators and bureaucrats. The importance of the public bureaucracy as the chief agent of the state, in turn the embodiment of the public interest, becomes clearer. The state exemplifies that highest rationality.[1]

The French strong state tradition, as the German, views the public bureaucracy as the guardian of the public interest.[2] The administrative corps is to be devoted to public service and the needs of the nation, made up of nonpartisan actors in a politicized society, actors concerned solely with serving an enduring and definable public interest (Schonfeld, 1984:235). Much more than its American counterpart, the French bureaucratic corps sees itself as—and society sees it as—the enlightened interpreter of the *volonté générale*.

This bureaucratic mission means that French high functionaries feel that they act with the authority to perform a special duty. This duty involves the constant definition and defense of the general interest in the face of all who would assert particular or partisan interests contrary to the interests of the whole, or of France. This sense of mission is not unlike the preaching, teaching, and proselytizing of a religious order. The order in French bureaucratic politics is the *grand corps*. Its training grounds are the *grandes écoles*. The mission gives high functionaries in France the perception that the state has an interest that is both definable and defendable. It also shapes their understanding of where interests lie, which of these are compatible with the state's interest, and what types of conduct by decision makers and outside groups are appropriate to this administrative-political universe:

> The ideology which justifies [the monopoly of the state] is that of the general interest. The [French] administration has in effect succeeded in taking over the general interest for itself. No one can incarnate the general interest in the place of the administration except perhaps the political power at the very top. Legitimacy is always on the side of the administration. Individuals, groups, collectivities and political representatives—with the exception of those who are part of the government, and even then . . . —are always suspected of partiality. Thanks to this ideology, the administration can impose its vocabulary, its own mode of reasoning and its competence on the rest of society (Crozier, 1974:24).

The emphasis on *texts* is a common feature illustrative of this French administrative process. In France, high civil servants often deal with groups' opposition by pointing to the text. This conveniently removes direct responsibility from the civil servant, for he or she merely *administers*, (*gérer* in French) a text that has previously been duly negotiated and approved. *On gère les textes* in the French administrative vocabulary. This approach neatly cuts off other avenues of possible recourse to the groups, In this system, the *hauts fonctionnaires* foster an image of themselves as remaining apart from politics and applying the law impartially. This view of the high civil service in France is also supported by a strong juridical administrative law tradition (see Schonfeld, 1984; Favre, 1981). It is not important how much the view corresponds to descriptive reality. It is important that the view is widely shared as desirable.

Rousseau's thought captures the profound contradictions that many see in the French, for it argues simultaneously for both the state—an overriding central organization—and the individual—"each citizen should think only his own thoughts." The fabulous contradictory formula of anticorporatism, glorification of the State, and individualism had its origins in part in the oppressive guild practices of the *ancien régime* (Ehrmann, 1983:182ff). The Chapelier law of the Revolution outlawed all associations. It was rescinded in 1901, but French associations—all interest groups—are still required to register with the Ministry of the Interior, though legal status is automatic once registered. Since 1936 the ministry may also dissolve certain associations that it deems a threat to the state. This power was freely used after the events of May and June 1968. What is important to note about the French associative law, compared to the American context, is that it exists in the first place. Freedom of association is guaranteed, but surveillance of groups by the state, through registration, is also considered essential. The law is at once enabling and limiting. By contrast, the control of private associations in the United States is confined to regulation of lobbying and political campaign financing—and of course to the occasional and not inconsequential red-baiting by movements such as McCarthyism.

The view of the state as the sole entity capable of embodying the collective interest is also manifested in French language. *Etat* in French is the only word for state that normally begins with a capital letter (Nettl, 1968: 567) in contrast to other political vocabulary. Further, the expression *interest group (groupe d'intérêt)* is seldom used or even understood by the average educated French person. While the academic worlds of French political science and sociology know and use *interest group* terminology, its use there was adopted from American academic vocabulary. Far more common are *pressure group (groupe de pression)* and *lobby*, both pejorative expressions denoting a persistent action or influence that constrains or subverts. This pejorative view of interest groups changes the vocabulary used in describing what interest groups do, as well. In French, groups do not articulate their interests, they *défendent leurs droits*, or defend their rights. Indeed, understanding politics in France necessitates understanding the importance of *droits*, or rights. The system of *droits acquis* means that interests are not interests but rights. Otherwise they would signify particular wills, partial societies, and a host of concepts tied to a state of nature, free-market view of man and politics. *Droits*, on the other hand, are acquired *by decision of the state* in its incarnation as the expression of the general will, or public interest. That is, they are given. As such, they may be taken away. Hence *défendre*. Interest groups in France must constantly justify their pursuit of interests. In the strong state tradition, justification is accomplished in part by this vocabulary.

Administrative Heterogeneity

Perhaps the most influential recent critique of the received view of the French state is Suleiman (1970). The ideal-typical Rousseauian view of the strong state stresses the state's proper independence and autonomy in defining and defending the general will. This view is supported by the dominance of a highly sophisticated juridical tradition in French administrative science. This tradition places great emphasis on the study of formal rules and procedures. Suleiman argued, however, that this view of the French state was misleading and that the scholarly emphasis on the study of formal rules and procedures was misplaced. For Suleiman, the "sacrosanct state" constituted neither a good description of French administration nor a good prescription. In later work (1974), Suleiman showed that the French administration was not homogeneous nor nonpartisan, but made up of cross-cutting, conflicting interests. *Hauts fonctionnaires* are not impartial servants of infallible, uniform legal structure. Their views and goals conflict across ministries and *directions*, between *directions* and ministerial *cabinets*, and between *grands corps*. One locus of constant combat, for example, lies between the finance and other ministries (Ehrmann, 1961a).

Crozier (1963) had begun chipping away at the traditional, sacrosanct view of the French state with his argument that formal rules do not fully account for administrative behavior. While organizations such as bureaucracies have extensive, detailed rules to prescribe appropriate action for all situations, these rules inevitably fail because of unanticipated events for which the rules do not provide. The administrative machine breaks down, prompting a modification of the rules or the addition of new ones to take care of problems. But in a vicious cycle, unforeseen events continue to occur, leading to new crises. Routine, where formal rules are valid descriptions of administrative behavior, alternates with crisis, where innovation and adaptability—departure from formal rules—reign.

Crozier's model of French administrative behavior stresses the heterogeneity of the administrators and their interests, depending upon their positions within the administration. While detailed and precise rules are persistently promulgated to govern behavior, and while decision making is in principle centralized, in fact various strata of the administrative hierarchy are highly isolated from each other. Within each stratum, a premium is placed upon egalitarianism that leads to the refusal, or avoidance, of cooperation and participation in hierarchical decision making. Thus, the bureaucratic system cannot cope with change and postpones change as long as possible. Only eruption of crisis forces change, which is imposed from the top, ensuring its inadaptability to individual requirements.

Dupuy and Thoenig (1983) criticized Crozier for neglecting the administrative organization's capacity to adapt. They argued that French administration has mechanisms that adjust decision and rulemaking mistakes to make them tolerable to outside actors who must interact with the administration. As Schonfeld (1984)[3] notes, their argument is less a critique of Crozier than an extension of his work, for theirs is a model of administrative interaction with the outside world, while Crozier confined himself to internal dynamics. Indeed, Dupuy and Thoenig follow Crozier and Suleiman in portraying a bureaucracy frequently at odds with itself and open to influences from outside.

The State and Its Tactical Advantages

The traditional and opposing views capture two faces of the French state. An exploration of the state's "tactical advantages" can reconcile the two views so that sufficient importance is accorded to the fact that strong states can do things that weak states cannot, but that equally there are important limits to strong state power. The French state, insofar as its authority is concentrated in bureaucrats and bureaucratic departments, supported by a strong state ideology, enjoys an upper hand in politics. *Impermeable*, often used to describe a strong state, is not adequate, for it denotes the impossibility of penetrating the state's structures.[4] But the strong state's tactical advantages over politicians and interest groups shape politics in important ways. By contrast, the weak American state—with its dispersed authority structure, (see Neustadt, 1960; Heclo, 1977, 1978; King, 1978; Rockman, 1981)—enjoys fewer tactical advantages. The state tradition and the mechanisms inherent in the state's organization of authority provide constraints and opportunities that structure *but do not determine* interest group behavior and policy outcomes.[5]

Tactical advantages are methods and procedures and the capacity to employ them that the state may use for short range objectives. They may or may not be combined over time in the planning or maneuvering to achieve long range objectives, or strategy. When sufficiently numerous, they suggest the state's superior position in arranging relationships between the state and groups in civil society. The idea implies that states with tactical advantages may more easily arrange their relationships with interest groups and that strong states are strong in part because they have more tactical advantages at their disposal. Thus, they may more often gain the ends *they* seek because of methods and procedures at their disposal that weak states do not enjoy, at least to the same extent.[6] The notion of tactical advantages avoids determinism wherein the various parts of the state are taken as a unit always acting in concert and wherein politicians and interest groups only win if the state wants them to, which is what *impermeable* implies. Tactical advantages possessed by strong states mean that compared to weaker states, politicians and interest groups have to work harder or differently in pressing their case. This does not mean they will not win. Tactical advantages may also help to explain how certain groups in France are favored and others shut out, a state power of some consequence. In the United States it is more difficult to favor or shut out interest groups, for there are always the alternative legislative or judicial arenas that may be resorted to. Indeed, changing arenas is often an explicit strategy in American interest group politics (see Wilsford, 1984). There is something different about the French state, which is partially and imperfectly captured by the word *strong* and sometimes by the word *impermeable*. This needs to be understood better because it is still difficult to grasp practically what a strong or a weak state is. Tactical advantages is an heuristic device for beginning to do this.

Katzenstein (1978; n.d.) tried to capture the ways states interact with interests, at least in part, with "policy networks" and "parapublic institutions," but this underplays the possibility of state capacity to act independently of interest groups, that is, to structure the context in which interest groups act politically—especially in France. For Katzenstein, policy networks and parapublic institutions are necessary for the successful implementation of policy and exist to aggregate sectoral interests for the state to act upon. This tends to reduce the state to a predominantly reactive posture once the initial arranging of interests is accomplished. It may also imply that the state does no more in arranging interests than respond to social imperatives. But in France, the state plays a more important initiating and structuring role and interest groups by contrast are reduced to a reactive posture. When true, this carries important consequences for policy outcomes that cannot be accounted for by Katzenstein's model.[7] Katzenstein's concepts may be more appropriate in depicting state-interest group cooperation in the West German, Austrian or Swiss cases (see Katzenstein, 1984, 1985), where, as Dyson notes (1980:155-185), the state tradition is distinct from the French. The German state tradition places great importance on the state's responsibilities for seeing to it that essential social partnerships are healthy. The partners' legitimacy is not questioned. Further, the social partners *cooperate*. This is a crucial support that is regularly withheld by some French groups, such as the labor unions. In France, the Rousseauian view of the general will and the public interest pits the state against all entities, like interest groups, which represent "particular wills," or private interests.[8]

What Are the French State's Tactical Advantages?

[The state] represents not only a particular manner of arranging political and administrative affairs and regulating relationships of authority but also a cultural phenomenon which binds people together in terms of a common mode of interpreting the world (Dyson, 1980:19).

In his seminal work on Western European states, Dyson distinguishes between *state* and *stateless* societies. By these he means no more than the difference between societies that have an historical and intellectual tradition of the state as the institution that embodies the public power and societies that lack this tradition. Dyson's distinction is analogous to that of *strong* and *weak* state used here.[9] *The strong state is not omnipotent, nor is the weak one powerless*. Rather, the distinction signifies varying conceptions and realities of general state authority vis-à-vis interest groups. The collective conception of a strong state, and the formal institutional arrangements that back it up, assign the strong state more tactical advantages than its weak counterpart. This does not mean that the strong state will always win its political battles against interest groups, nor does it mean that the strong state can even always or usually decide *itself* upon a unified position to take with an interest group or set of groups on an issue. Nor does it mean that the state does not help interest groups or vice versa. Relations of mutual support abound in both France and the United States. But it does mean that the strong state has advantages in its dealings with interest groups that the weak state lacks.

The importance of the state is not in acting homogeneously or monolithically in promoting or arranging at its will a universe of interest group activities and thus, perhaps, policy outcomes. This is the chief problem with theories of neo- or liberal corporatism. They too often take the state as a unit whose constituent parts act in concert. Even in the strong state, agencies and departments are often motivated by conflicting interests and pursue conflicting goals. And in the absence of conflict, they may simply be inefficient. Rather, the state is important as a collective concept which informs the way interest group *and* bureaucratic actors view proper relations between the state and groups. Thus, as Dyson argues,

> the values, beliefs and expectations characteristic of [a] state tradition of authority . . . affect *groups' perceptions of their interests* . . . The idea of the state forms part of the considerations which groups have in mind when determining *where their interests lie* and *what types of conduct* will appeal to decision-makers and the public (1980:3; my emphasis).

One way of fixing empirically what the strong state in France is and what its consequences are for interest group politics is by examining what I have termed tactical advantages. The French state is—empirically—a specific formal organization of authority. This organization of authority is complemented by a specific—empirical—set of behavior patterns, of those who fill the roles of the state and of those, like interest groups, who interact with the state's officials in the hope of certain decisions. Behavior patterns plus formal organization of authority interact in complex ways. Behavior and attitudes inform authority's organization; similarly, the organization of authority informs behavior and attitudes.

How does state organization of authority influence interest groups' behavior in France? It does so with inducements and constraints which structure political action. Its authority position gives the French state tactical advantages which enable it to induce and constrain types of political behavior. Claiming neither an exhaustive list nor that they work in the same way on every issue, some of the important tactical advantages of the French state are: (1) the government's proposal and decree powers; (2) an arena legislature; (3) a strong executive independent of the legislature; (4) the tradition of powerful ministerial *cabinets*; (5) an extensive bureaucratic elite homogeneously trained; and (6) a judiciary of limited powers. We will also see subsequently that the French state is abetted in its use of these tactical advantages by both ideological and non-ideological fragmentation of most interest sectors.

Some of these advantages derive from the constitution of the Fifth Republic. While a behavioral approach might tend to ignore formal legal arrangements, law and constitutions provide the larger settings for legal, institutional and political relationships. As the Colliers observed, "the adoption of laws is a major step in the decision process through which state intervention . . . crystallizes." Law and constitutions are highly visible policy statements "around which political battles are fought, won and lost, and around which political support is attracted, granted and withheld" (1979: 971). This does not mean that concentrating on laws and legal relationships renders a full picture. Written rules do not obviate the necessity of adapting or applying universals to specific cases, nor do they avoid unintended consequences.

The Government's Proposal and Decree Powers

The first tactical advantage of the French state is the preeminent position in lawmaking assigned to the executive by the 1958 constitution. For example, all finance laws and constitutional laws are reserved to government initiative, as are almost all organic laws. Parliament is prohibited from initiating increases in government expenditures or reductions in government revenues. By contrast, the American constitution reserves this prerogative to the House of Representatives. Initiative on constitutional laws is reserved to the president, on the advice of the prime minister, and to members of parliament. Despite the latter provision, no constitutional law has been proposed by members of parliament. Similarly organic laws are most often proposed by the government, though members of parliament occasionally propose organic laws without great hopes they will pass. Of 30 organic law bills by Assembly members from 1973 to 1977, only 1 became law. For the same period, of 7 Senate bills, 2 became law (Massot, 1979: 116-132).

For the Fifth Republic, only an average of 15% of laws passed each year are of parliamentary origin. Success rates are another indication of the executive's supremacy in lawmaking. From 1973 to 1977, 90% of bills introduced by the government became law; only 5% of parliamentary bills became law (Massot, 1979:129-130). Thus, Avril argued that parliamentary initiative has become devoid of significance. Even under the Fourth

Republic, 70.4% of the 2655 laws promulgated corresponded to Government proposals (Avril, 1972:24, 101). In a similar estimate, Goguel (1954:681) noted that only 27% of the laws passed between 1946 and 1951 were initiated by members of parliament.

Apart from constitutional provisions and their application since 1958, an even more important advantage to the government is derived from its powers of intervention in parliament's consideration and adoption of legislation. First, the government fixes all agenda items and the order of their consideration. This permits the government to monopolize sessions of the Assembly and the Senate for the discussion of its own bills. Further, parliamentary committees, which study government proposals, cannot block their final consideration by refusing to report them, as can American congressional committees. When committees refuse to cooperate, the government may proceed directly to parliamentary consideration and the text considered is the original text submitted by the government.

The government holds an additional advantage in the limited amending powers of parliament. If a committee amends a text before reporting it, the government may oblige consideration of its original bill. But the government itself may amend any text being considered. Further, the constitution provides for parliamentary votes on all or part of a text, retaining only amendments proposed by or accepted by the government.

Decrees are an important area of lawmaking reserved entirely to the executive. Decrees permit the government to modify laws and are juridically binding. A law modified by decree is often decades old. Decrees in France are a combination of American implementation regulations and independent lawmaking. The 1958 constitution permits vast domains of policy making to be regulated by executive decree.

These constitutional provisions give the government great advantages over the consideration and adoption of proposals in all domains of lawmaking. Nevertheless, they do not militate against government attention to coalitions and compromise. Alliances are still necessary because countervailing forces must be taken into account. But the tactical advantage of proposal and decree powers means that coalition and compromise assume less widespread importance in French politics than in American.

An Arena Legislature

Polsby (1975) has argued that a useful way of comparing legislatures is to place them along a continuum from transformative to arena institutions, expressing variations in the legislature's independence from outside influences (1975:277). The transformative legislature puts its own imprint on legislation—by originating it, modifying it or killing it. That is, the content of legislation and the outcome of the legislative process is in significant ways *transformed* by the legislative body. For Polsby, the American Congress is the epitome of the transformative legislature. By contrast, the arena legislature cannot place its own substantive institutional imprint on legislative outcomes because it lacks the powers—formal or informal—to do so. Rather, it serves as an arena for conflict between other power centers. In the arena legislature, political forces come together to hash out issues over time. The British House of Commons exemplifies this end of the continuum. The House of Commons may enjoy formal legislative powers, but in a responsible party system, it is in fact an arena for social and political debate. The party, not the legislature, controls legislative outcomes.

In these terms, the 1958 constitution transformed the French parliament from a transformative to an arena legislature. This has in turn transformed the policy-making process. In the Fourth Republic, interest groups pressured parliament, in particular individual deputies, as party discipline was weak. Some parties were in fact little more than electorally organized interest groups. Interest groups and political parties also collaborated for electoral purposes. Interest group pressure on bureaucrats was relatively inconsequential, for the administration was pressured by deputies in the place of— and on behalf of—interest groups.

The arena legislature of the Fifth Republic reversed these relationships. Since 1958, interest groups—who migrate to where power is exercised— concentrate on ministers and bureaucrats. The individual deputy is relatively less pressured than before, although under majority two-round voting he must establish a secure geographic constituency. Likewise, there is less collaboration between interest groups and candidates or political parties for electoral purposes (see Meynaud, 1962a; Wilson, 1983).[10]

But even with the Fourth Republic's transformative legislature, functionaries became more important to interest groups as the state extended and its work became more technical. In economics and finance, for example, "complexity has reduced the role of Parliament [during the *Fourth Republic*] to the benefit of the executive" (Meynaud, 1957:574-575). The phenomenon is the more exaggerated considering the instability of governments under the Fourth Republic. Governments rose and fell according to constantly shifting parliamentary coalitions. The high civil service were by contrast stable. "[Under the Fourth Republic] reasons for political disorder had not been removed and no disciplined majority emerged in parliament [so] constitutional provisions were flouted. Using only slightly different techniques than before the war, parliament found ways to surrender its sovereign powers as the lawmaking authority to the executive. Yet as if to compensate for such weakness, it continuously shortened the life span of succeeding governments" (Ehrmann, 1983:304). In the Fifth Republic, parliament is restricted to meeting a maximum of six months of the year so that "the government has the time to reflect and to act" (Debré, 1966:46). Not only have interest groups adapted to changes in institutional paths of access from the Fourth to the Fifth Republics, moving from legislature to administration, it is debatable how transformative the legislature of the Fourth Republic was. In both regimes, evidence suggests that the state administration held a preeminent position in policymaking.

A Strong Executive Independent of Parliament

Executive power is not just stronger due to the first tactical advantage (the government's proposal and decree powers) and not just by default of the second (a weak legislature). It is strong in its own right. The president in the Fifth Republic enjoys a power base independent of the legislature, for he is directly elected (Ehrmann, 1963) for a seven year term. Deputies' terms may last no more than five years. (Senators serve nine-year terms, but are elected indirectly; in lawmaking, the Senate is less important than the National Assembly.) The president may also dissolve the Assembly. In the Fourth Republic, parliament directed the state politically. By contrast, the Fifth Republic locates political control in an elected executive. This control is centered in the president. Despite the prime minister's strategic position and the wide range of his duties, throughout the Fifth Republic the president has controlled the cabinet in both its makeup and its action (see Massot, 1977).

Of course, in an important variation on the traditional Fifth Republic pattern, the March 16, 1986 legislative elections gave a parliamentary majority to an RPR-UDF coalition opposing the president. Moreover, the 1958 constitution permits parliament to deny confidence to the government—that is, the prime minister and the cabinet—chosen by the president. To resolve an eventual impasse, the president—short of resigning—would presumably appoint a prime minister and cabinet acceptable to the opposing parliamentary majority. After the March 1986 election, in a theretofore untried arrangement of *cohabitation*, Mitterrand appointed the RPR's Chirac prime minister and accepted his proposed government (with the exception of two portfolios, Foreign Affairs and Defense). Of course, *cohabitation* damaged the president's strategic position, although Mitterrand managed to con-

serve a great deal of influence in foreign policy decision making. Insofar
as the prime minister under cohabitation is more clearly responsible for
the successes or failures of government policies, Mitterrand was able to
skillfully place himself above the fray, avoiding identification with the
failures of Chirac's government as 1987 wore on. The parliamentary role
in votes of confidence is important only as and if a governing coalition which
opposes the president begins to fall apart.

In spite of the uncertainties of *cohabitation*, however, the executive
centered strong state is perforce easier to direct politically than the true
parliamentary regime because authority is not dispersed throughout a collective legislative body. The strengthening of the executive and the weakening of parliament by the 1958 constitution make the actions and decision
making of the strong state more coherent and efficient. For the time being,
cohabitation merely transferred strong executive powers from the president to the prime minister.

The Tradition of Powerful Ministerial Cabinets

The tradition of powerful ministerial *cabinets* focuses the political direction of French administration more than the American. The French *cabinet*
should not be confused with the English "cabinet," that is, the group of
all secretaries or ministers chosen by the executive to head bureaucratic
departments. The second institution, in French, is the *Conseil des Ministres*,
or Council of Ministers. There is no strict American equivalent to the French
ministerial *cabinet* as a cohesive decision-making and policing unit serving
the minister and apart from functional units in the ministry. In American
departments, the secretary's top associates are generally institutionalized
in the deputy, under- and assistant secretaries, at once political appointees
of the president (who sometimes but not always follows the recommenda-
tion of the secretary they will serve) and heads of functional units. The
French minister has more freedom to compose his *cabinet* as he wishes
and its members work for him on constantly changing tasks. They also check
on heads of functional departments, or *directions*, trying to ensure that directors act in the minister's interest, political or other. Further, fewer American
civil servants serve in the high echelons surrounding the secretary than
French civil servants serve in the ministerial *cabinets*.

The Fifth Republic cabinet, or *Conseil des Ministres*, like its British
counterpart and unlike its American counterpart, constitutes a generally effective decision-making team under the direction of the president (or prime
minister, if the two are cohabitating) and adheres to a doctrine of cabinet

responsibility. Aberbach, Putnam, and Rockman (1981) argue that both British and French cabinet members tend to better resist the bureaucratic interests of their departments compared to their American counterparts. The ministerial cabinet, a mix of political and technical brains chosen by the minister, serves to focus the minister's directives in a more effective way than any American counterpart. It also serves as the center for inter-ministerial bargaining.

During the Third and Fourth Republics, with frequent changes of government in a parliamentary dominated system of weak parties and constantly shifting coalitions, the ministerial cabinet was viewed as lending stability to the political administration of the bureaucracy (Ehrmann, 1983:282). Suleiman (1974:187ff) argued, however, that administrative instability during the Fourth Republic was more apparent than real. While coalitions and governments changed frequently, many ministers retained their portfolios across several changes of government. Nevertheless, under any republic the ministerial cabinet has been "at once the brain of the minister and, with regard to the administration, the eyes of the master. A study group on the one hand, a means of supervising on the other" (Massigli, 1958:25; cited in Suleiman, 1974:187). The problems of bureaucratic politics and responsiveness to political directives exist most everywhere. But by contrast with the American state, where unclear boundaries of authority and fragmented power centers (Rockman, 1981:914) accentuate the difficulties of political direction of bureaucratic policy making and implementation (see also Heclo, 1977), the ministerial cabinet gives the French minister an instrument of focused control over bureaucrats.[11]

An Extensive Bureaucratic Elite Homogeneously Trained

The structure of the bureaucratic corps in France gives the state an additional tactical advantage over groups in the society and the economy. *Le droit administratif* in France, the *hauts fonctionnaires* and their *grandes écoles* clearly constitute a powerful ensemble of discipline, science, doctrine and profession. Future high ranking civil servants go through a rigorous and highly developed training and socialization process in a limited number of advanced state schools. The *grandes écoles* feed into the *grands corps* and form an administrative technocracy that is much more cohesive in its values and norms than its American counterpart. Two *grandes écoles* dominate the education of future high functionaries—and not incidentally that of future high executives and scientists in French industry—and they feed into a limited number of top corps. The *Ecole Nationale d'Administra-*

tion trains those who enter the *Inspection des Finances*, the *Conseil d'Etat* and the *Cour des Comptes*. *Polytechnique* trains those who will join the *Corps des Mines* or *Ponts et Chaussés*. Entrance is strictly limited and rigidly controlled through competitive examination. Both schools emphasize a curriculum of rational science, the one administrative science, the other natural and engineering science, which orients problem solving toward activist interventionism and a belief in the value of systematic analysis and the powers of reason and intelligence in confronting problems of all kinds (cf. Bodiguel & Quermonne, 1983:passim). In administrative sciences, the number of classic texts is great, their codification advanced, their sophistication remarkable, and their authors illustrious. This corps phenomenon in France is characterized by an insular separation from the outside world (especially from civil society, and even, sometimes, from duly elected politicians), a maintenance of prestige through a strict limiting of numbers, a cultivation of an attitude of special privilege and duty, and a profound internalization of an ideology of public service in the general interest (cf. Birnbaum, 1978:70-73).

The importance of this bureaucratic corps and its common training in the *grandes écoles* is that administrators—bureaucratic, political, and the combination found in the ministerial *cabinets*—share a common view of the *role* of the state, its mission and its options, even if there are different interests and conflicts over them from one ministry to another, from one *direction* to another or between a *direction* and a *cabinet*. The values, beliefs and expectations characteristic of a state tradition of authority and its training grounds (the *grandes écoles*) affect bureaucrats' perceptions of their interests and of the state's interests. Indeed, it gives them a perception of the State having an interest that is definable and defendable. The idea of the state shared by bureaucrats who staff its positions shapes their judgment of where interests lie, which of these are compatible with the state's interest and what types of conduct by decision makers and the public are appropriate to the administrative-political universe.

A Judiciary of Limited Powers

In conflicts with groups, the French state, like the British, enjoys an advantage that its American counterpart has lacked since *Marbury v. Madison:* a judiciary of limited powers with little tradition of judicial review. This subordinate and often downright weak judicial power dates from the French absolutist state (see Anderson, 1974). The Revolution strengthened the asymmetry between judiciary and executive or parliament even though it put forth certain citizen rights in the Declaration of the Rights of Man. Freedom of thought and expression, freedom to own property, freedom from arbitrary detention, and the presumption of innocence until proven guilty were all mentioned. Article 2 carried citizen rights furthest by proclaiming that the fundamental purpose of political organization was to preserve the individual's natural rights, including the right to resist oppression. But absent were any provisions for judicial appeal when these rights were violated. In general, the executive or the legislature as the sovereign incarnation of Rousseau's general will both determined the general interest *and* protected individual rights. But protecting individual rights was secondary. This led to many contradictions for the sovereign power often proclaimed that the general will, or public interest, superceded individual rights. This problem is compounded by the Rousseauian view of rights, inalienable in the American vocabulary, as fosterers of disunity.

Not until the Third Republic were individual liberties extended in more specified ways with guarantees of right of assembly and press freedom in 1881, of formation of trade unions in 1884, of association without prior government approval in 1901,[12] and of religious freedom in 1905. The Constitution of the Fourth Republic in 1946 added equal rights for women, the right to employment, to collective bargaining and to strike (Hayward, 1973:199).[13]

No institutional enforcement of these rights was provided as they were enacted. There is no independent, sovereign agency that protects them for the citizen *from* the State. Rousseau's heritage inhibits division of state sovereignty, along the American pattern. The strong state is antithetical to Montesquieu's thought. Separation of powers and checks and balances to safeguard citizens' rights are incompatible with a view that assigns the state the principal and positive role for determining the citizen's interest *through* the collectivity. For Rousseau and the strong state tradition, to divide the state (whether embodied concretely by parliament or executive) is perforce to weaken it and open it to the attacks of particular wills. But in American thinking, the particular wills must be *protected*.

The institutional asymmetry of French regimes and the philosophy underlying this asymmetry lead to limitations of civil liberties in France that would be less tolerated in Britain or the United States. As Hayward (1973:121) notes, the French believe that civil liberties have eroded *since* World War II, but they also tend to believe that censorship and telephone taps are the normal order of things and, in some vague ways, do serve a national interest—at least sometimes and under the condition that oneself is not the subject of censorship or tapping. French law provides for no *habeas corpus*, police tap telephone lines and open mail, and the government pressures in various ways newspapers and magazines that it considers threats to the public interest. Such threats may be no more than publicizing a scandal involving a government official. In such a case, the government has occasionally intervened with (nationalized) banks to cut credits to the offending organization. Despite constitutional guarantees against arbitrary detainment, the celebrated *garde à vue* permits police to hold suspects up to 48 hours without charges.[14]

The 1958 Constitution continues the tradition of limited judicial review. A constitutional council was established to pass on the constitutionality of parliamentary laws. But the executive is not subject to review by the Council and originally only the president, the prime minister, and the presidents of the Senate and the National Assembly could refer questions of constitutionality to it. In 1974, a provision was added permitting 60 deputies or 60 senators to submit cases.[15]

Executive behavior is the preserve of the Council of State, a multifunctional institution. The government consults the Council on bills it wishes to submit to parliament and on more important decrees and regulations as they are prepared. The Council also advises on the interpretation of the constitution. While the Council's advice is not binding, Ehrmann notes (1983:334) that "its prestige is so high that its recommendations are seldom ignored." The Council also rules on claims of the citizen or groups against the administration. The Council may find official acts illegal—whether those of a minister or a mayor—and annul them and grant damages to plaintiffs. While this function has led the Council to be described as "the great protector of the rights of property and of the rights of the individual against the State, the great redresser of wrongs committed by the State" (Barthélemy, 1924:199; cited in Ehrmann, 1983:334), it is nevertheless limited. Enforcement of its decisions depends on the very administration that may be the object of the ruling. The government often validates questionable administrative acts by legislation during or after the Council of State's consideration of them. Hayward (1973:127) also noted that administrations, particularly the finance ministry, are skilled at circumventing decisions. He estimated that a third of Council decisions remain unenforced. Further, delay is significant. The Council's case backlog is estimated at three years. Currently 17,000 cases await judgment. Yet government reforms aimed at expanding the Council's juridical capacity have met opposition from the Council's own members, who jealously guard their elite status (*Le Monde*, March 15, 1985).

Citizen rights are especially problematic in France because of the state's strong police powers and the close institutional links between the police, prosecutors, and judges. The French judicial system is characterized by executive control at all levels (see Ehrmann, 1983:178-179; Hayward, 1973:128-132). While entry is by examination, promotion is frequently political, as the executive seeks to consolidate its influence on judicial decision making by promoting those that agree with it politically and moving those that disagree to less desirable posts. The Ministry of Justice also directly controls public prosecutors.[16] Lack of judicial independence was institutionalized in the 1958 constitution. Article 64 makes the president the sole guarantor of judicial independence. For de Gaulle, judicial power was part of the "indivisible authority of the state" and was entrusted "in its entirety to the President of the Republic by the people who have elected him" (cited in Ehrmann, 1983:178). Limited judicial access and limited judicial powers give the state greater autonomy in its relations with civil society, both individuals and groups.

Ideological Fragmentation of Interests

Ideological fragmentation of interest sectors in France abets the state's use of its tactical advantages. From labor unions to medical associations, the lines of demarcation which distinguish interest groups from each other within an interest sector tend to fall not according to functional categories, although these exist as well, but along ideological cleavages. For example, while less than 20% of the French industrial workforce is unionized, at least three major unions, the *Confédération Générale du Travail* (CGT), the *Confédération Française Démocratique du Travail* (CFDT), and the *Force Ouvrière* (FO), compete for members in each plant. Ideological fragmentation constitutes an opportunity, a consistent one, presented to the state and used in conjunction with its tactical advantages to structure politics.

Many other interest sectors in France, such as agriculture or medicine, are also ideologically fragmented, presenting consistent opportunities to the French state for domination. Physicians fragment ideologically over *political* issues. In the small but influential subsector of medical professors, three associations compete to represent the subsector's interest. They are distinguished by ideological politics. Indeed, there are no medical *associations* in France, only medical *unions (syndicats)*. The difference in terminology points to a more political defense of sectoral professional interests in France compared to the ostensibly apolitical nature of many American associations that base their claims of representativeness in part on neutral technical issues.

Ideological fragmentation of most interest sectors contributes to the lack of legitimacy of interest groups in state dominated French society. It is difficult to convincingly claim representativeness for an interest when your group is not the only one making the claim and when all claims are colored ideologically. French directors (agency heads) commonly distinguish between the legitimate and illegitimate interests they must deal with (Suleiman, 1974:337-340). For the state administrator, lobbies and *groupes de pression* represent a private interest within an interest sector. These groups are not *sérieux*, an important concept to the French (see Wylie, 1957). Administrators prefer "professional organizations" and contacts with them are considered valuable because these groups are *sérieux*, meaning reasonable, sincere and able to be counted upon, in short, *responsible*.[17] One director in Suleiman's study explained the distinction (1974:338): "An interest group—that is, a lobby—is one that defends its specific interest. A professional organization is one that defends not a private interest but a group [sectoral] interest." Another director noted: "An interest group or a pressure group has very limited interests, whereas professional organizations represent the interests of a whole profession." In the health care sector, for example, for negotiations over the 1985 *convention* (fee agreements) Georgina Dufoix, minister of Social Affairs and National Solidarity, *designated* two medical confederations as representative of the profession (the *Confédération des Syndicats Médicaux Français* and the *Fédération des Médecins de France*) and *conferred upon them* the right to negotiate with the *caisses d'assurance maladie* (*Le Médecin de France*, November 29, 1984:18). Groups that are *sérieux* seek the public interest, not the private. The state determines who is *sérieux* and, therefore, a legitimate partner in the search for the public interest. For the state, groups that are not *sérieux* are by its own definition seeking a private interest that obviates the collective good.

The Symbolism of Consultation

Ideological fragmentation of interests enables the bureaucracy to consult different interests as policy is formulated, giving the appearance of substantive input into decision making. But this consultation takes on a superficial significance, for it enables the state to simultaneously find support for its own view while ignoring or diffusing opposition. Consultation often amounts to no more than a symbolic benefit to interest groups (see Edelman, 1964).

Contacts may be frequent, especially with "legitimate" groups, but there is no pattern of necessarily substantive consultation such as that between the American administration and interest groups (see Chubb, 1983). Suleiman's respondents (1974:333ff) argued that consultation served an informative and persuasive function—from the administration to interest groups: "My job is to explain and to inform . . . . Contacts [with interest groups] are necessary. But I think I can say that we always manage to have our view prevail," argued one director. Another reported: "We always consult. It doesn't mean that we listen, but we consult. We don't always reveal our intentions. We reveal only as much as we think it is necessary to reveal." Thus, Suleiman argued that one important function of consultation was the opportunity it gives the administration to present interest groups with *faits accomplis*, that is, decisions it has made before consultation.

Consultation tends therefore to occur late in the administrative decision-making process, in contrast to the frequent American practice of early consultation as proposals are formulated (Chubb, 1983). Suleiman (1974: 335-336) described a typical policy process: The preparation of texts, whether laws, decrees or reforms, begins in secrecy within a small administrative group. Gradually, the initial group seeks the agreement and cooperation of other groups within the ministry and then from other ministries. Once a final text is agreed upon by the administration, interest groups are approached and informed of the proposed policy. A closed approach is essential, one director reported to Suleiman, "because otherwise there will be opposition over every provision and the text will never get drawn up" (1974:335-336). Another director commented, "We ask for [interest groups'] advice only *after* we have a completely prepared text. And we do this just to make sure that we haven't made some colossal error" (1974:336).

Yet consultation is frequent, much of it institutionalized in advisory commissions which meet regularly. Mignot and d'Orsay (1968:92) estimated the number of commissions at over 15,000. Ehrmann (1983:204) estimated 500 councils, 1200 committees and 3000 commissions, which bring together members of organized interest groups and the bureaucracy at the national level. Ehrmann notes that the Ministry of Finance alone consults more than 130 committees. If consultation means as little as some directors and interest group leaders claim, with different reasons, why does the state engage in it?

First, consultation in France differs from the American in important ways. In general, the state initiates more contacts in France and creates or facilitates the creation of more groups suggesting that consultation is often part of a formal strategy by the state to control interest sectors. Second, consultation often serves as a symbolic benefit, which administrators use to forestall interest group opposition, particularly of protest and direct action common to France. Even such supposedly pacific groups as physicians or hospital interns are quite willing to exit traditional political channels and engage in demonstrations and strikes. Since 1981, French physicians have mounted five large demonstrations aimed against proposed government reforms and hospital interns have struck twice. Threatened or actual social disturbances are a powerful influence on the administration to preserve at least the formalities of consultation.

Groups of course are not fooled by the formalities of consultation. They realize that in normal politics the administration has an upper hand in policy making and that their influence in the consultative process is often minimal. In reforms of health care, private education and a host of other policies, conservative interest groups were regularly consulted by the Socialist administration. But in a curious paradox, both sides knew that conservative group views would almost not at all be taken into account by the Socialists. Why the minuet? Because the Socialists, like all administrators, were influenced by persistent false hopes of forestalling opposition to reforms; likewise, conservative interest group leaders were influenced by persistent false hopes that their opinions might make a difference. In the end, consultation served no substantive purpose. The administration promulgated reforms; conservative groups organized demonstrations and boycotts. Abuse of consultation has reduced even its symbolic benefits.

Faced with protest, administrative symbolism persists. The government may publicize symbolic concessions to protesting groups ''only to retract or deform them after the demonstrators have demobilized'' (Wilson, 1983:906). With striking hospital interns, the government first satisfied interns' demand for restitution of prestige titles. Only after the strike continued and it was clear that symbolism would not suffice to diffuse protest in a strategic policy area did the government satisfy interns' second demand for pay increases. Another reason for substantive government concessions was its new sensitivity to fighting too many public battles at once. For the government, the truckers' strike of February 1984 was easier, for it responded more easily to symbolic concessions. It is difficult for independent truckers (owner-operators) to remain organized over time. The government conceded several demands, but then waited for the situation to diffuse. The state's tactical advantages often enable it to retract or not implement concessions that are not symbolic.

The Triumph of Consensus Over Conflict in French Administration

The executive and bureaucratic powers and advantages of the French state make it stronger than many of its Western democratic counterparts. But these tactical advantages do not mean that either the executive or the bureaucracy always acts homogeneously. Even within the more purely bureaucratic parts of French administration, strategic positions and resources differ. For example, *directions* and ministerial *cabinets* are one important locus of administrative conflict.

Bureaucrats of the French state, in political and administrative incarnations, may be thought of in terms of Rockman's (1981) analysis of American *regulars* and *irregulars*. *Regulars* in France, like their American counterparts, are viewed as advocates of parochial interests. They want rational policies. They tend to think small, incrementally, and do not see the world in manipulable terms. They are cautious and balanced in their approach. *Irregulars*, like their American counterparts, are viewed as generalists working in the presidential or ministerial interests. They want action: that is, presidential or ministerial decisions rationally managed. They tend to prize innovation, aggressiveness and enthusiasm for presidential or ministerial directives. They are more ambitious and purposive.

French irregulars may be divided between (1) floating *hauts fonctionnaires* and (2) politicians brought in by ministers. Both serve in the ministerial *cabinet*. Floating *hauts fonctionnaires* share similar elite training (usually *Polytechnique* or *ENA*, both *grandes écoles*) and have come to dominate the *cabinets*, by about 90%. Their similar background and training give them similar views of their appropriate roles and of the role of the state. That they man the ministerial *cabinets* enables them to provide the essential institutionalized link between generalized administrative expertise and the political needs of the moment, for the cabinets are powerful operating bases. Further, many of the more political appointments to the cabinets are "politicians" who started as *polytechniciens* or *énarques*. Their early government service was spent in the normal bureaucracy. Increasingly in the Fifth Republic, civil servants launch political careers in order to work their way to the top. Giscard, Chirac, Fabius, Rocard, Chevènement, Jospin and Joxe are notable examples. Thus, there tends to be a homogeneity (which nevertheless should not be exaggerated) to the political aspects of French state administration that is lacking in the United States.

There is also more floating of high civil servants in France than in the United States. Evidence suggests that regular and irregular characteristics are more attached to role position and, because of greater floating, an individual French political or administrative bureaucrat changes his own behavior from job to job (Suleiman, 1974:222ff). Members of ministerial *cabinets* become directors, and vice versa. In general, the most important difference between regulars and irregulars in France compared to Rockman's observations in the United States is that irregulars across ministries are tied more closely together and more closely with the president's and prime minister's personal offices. One reason is the more tightly organized character of the French cabinet, or Council of Ministers. Compared to its American counterpart, the cabinet is a cohesive decision-making body, much more responsive to the president's wishes and/or those of the prime minister.[18]

The operational tool for the effectiveness of cabinet decision making is the ministerial *cabinet*. The complex, interlocking nature of the *hauts fonctionnaires* and their floating among *cabinets*, in and out of high politics, and back and forth between administrative units *(directions)* and *cabinets*, combine with their increasingly specialized administrative training (the *Ecole Nationale d'Administration*, or *ENA*)[19] to make the separation of politics and bureaucrats less problematic than in the United States. There is more overlap between high civil servants and politicians. This, in turn, gives the state greater capacity for coherent decision making, even if it is mistaken, and ensures greater bureaucratic implementation of political decisions, other things being equal.

But while the extensive bureaucratic corps generally shares a homogeneous elite training and many of its highest members combine administrative and political perspectives, this does not mean that bureaucrats and politicians don't fight, between and among themselves, between *cabinets* and *directions*, between vertical and horizontal administrations, or between the finance ministry and everyone else. But the French state's heterogeneity is qualified by the strong state tradition. We have seen that bureaucrats—and politicians—hold a common view of the *role* of the state, its mission and its optics, even if these are manifested in different interests and conflicts over them from one ministry to another, from one *direction* to another or between a *direction* and a *cabinet*. Perhaps the most important tactical advantage available to the French state is the tradition of state power, which gives it a preeminent role in state-civil society relations. With the establishment of the *Ecole Nationale d'Administration*, Debré wrote:

> The training—one need not hide this—also has a moral objective. It is not one of the missions of the school to play politics or to impose a particular doctrine. But the School must also teach its future civil servants '*le sens de*

l'Etat,' it must make them understand the responsibilities of the Administration, make them taste the grandeur and accept the servitudes of the *métier* (Debré, 1946; cited in Suleiman, 1978).

The values, beliefs and expectations characteristic of a state tradition of authority and its training grounds (the *grandes écoles*) affect bureaucrats' perceptions of their interests and of the state's interests. They believe that the State has an interest that is definable and defendable. A common idea of the state shapes administrators' judgment of where interests lie, which of these are compatible with the state's interest and what types of conduct by decision makers and the public are appropriate in this administrative-political universe. French administration is obviously heterogeneous, thus, permeable to interest group pressures and susceptible to internal conflict. But one consequence of the state tradition informing French administration is that permeability and conflict are of secondary importance to overarching consensus.[20]

Inducements and Constraints on French Interest Group Politics

The French state uses its tactical advantages to administer inducements and constraints on interest group politics. The state structures the game interest groups play. Fewer alternative arenas within the state (i.e., an independent judiciary) places its executive and bureaucratic institutions in a preeminent strategic position to structure interest representation.

First, the French state officially recognizes groups, thus sanctioning them; but it may also withdraw recognition (in extreme cases, groups may be outlawed by the state). Second, the state subsidizes many groups. These funds often provide crucial resources for offices, personnel, equipment and research, all indispensable to organizing and articulating interests. In this way, the state serves much the same function as private foundations in the American group system (see Walker, 1983). But the state can and does withdraw subsidies, making organization and articulation of interests more difficult, as happened to some conservative groups when the Socialists assumed power.

Opening and Closing Policy Arenas

One important way the state uses its tactical advantages to structure, that is to induce and constrain, interest group activity and policy outcomes is by opening or closing policy-making arenas. As Schattschneider (1960) argued, the scope of conflict—in his terms *private* or *social*—is important in determining what decisions are made, that is, the winners and the losers. An open arena has many participants; a closed arena has few. The character of the French political system and the tactical advantages of the state mean that it can open or close policy-making arenas more easily than its weaker counterpart. That is, it induces wider participation by involving more interest groups, as in agricultural policy making in France after 1981 (see Keeler, 1983). Or it constrains participation in policy making by closing out interest groups, as in agricultural policy making in the 1960-81 period (see Keeler, 1981a, 1981b).

One way the state opens and closes policy-making arenas is by the discretion ministers and bureaucrats enjoy in deciding whom to consult and whom to listen to among the consulted. Wilson reports one interest group leader complaining that too often formal consultation is just that: formal but not substantive. His respondent recounted discussing a proposed measure in a ministerial committee meeting, then seeing the final text of the measure printed the next day in the *Journal Officiel* (1983:900). Similarly, with the reorganization of medical education and hospital administration, one medical association leader reported: "Of course, we and other medical associations were invited to the ministry. But in the end, and even during discussions, the outcome was clear. The government had made up its mind and therefore 'listened' only to those medical groups which shared the government position." We have seen that consultation is frequent, but that there is no substantive pattern to it. Access does not necessarily equal influence, even if it is structured and regular. Consultation does not necessarily equal negotiation.

We have also seen the limits of recourse to the judiciary. Changing arenas, when possible, is an important resource the interest group may use to open a policy-making arena (Wilsford, 1984). But the legal avenue is heavily circumscribed by the constitution in France, and a different ethic of the law and judicial review permeates French thinking. As a labor leader said, "We have no illusions about the effectiveness of legal action. We believe the strength of the social forces is more influential and that it even influences the judges as they render their decisions" (Wilson, 1983:904).[21]

Similarly, legislative support is generally useful only in the long term. We have noted that the 1958 constitution grants most substantive lawmaking powers to the executive. Many areas of policy making are regulated by decree and many decrees cannot be changed or may be modified only slightly by the legislature. In 1984, some conservative groups expended great efforts lobbying members of the Senate, held by the conservative opposition. Their aim was a series of votes opposing various Socialist reforms. Yet under the Fifth Republic constitution, Senate votes are not very significant, as the government may return a bill to the National Assembly for final determination. Why lobby the Senate? One conservative group leader answered, "As a last resort. There was nothing else to do. And it is important to keep the opposition involved for when they return to power." Legislative support is often confined to preparing the ground for future changes of government. The Senate voted its opposition to the proposed reforms; the government proceeded to implement them anyway.

The French State Is Vulnerable to Direct Action, or Exit from Normal Politics

The French state is a very strong state. It is autonomous and skilled at avoiding capture in many policy areas. But, paradoxically, in its strength lies also its weakness. For the French state, by dealing highhandedly with its opponents, cuts them off from normal avenues of political negotiation. In doing so, it forces its opponents to exit normal politics. They go to the streets in demonstrations, strikes, boycotts, and sometimes riots. Opponents of state decisions—such as students opposing university reform, such as interns opposing reforms of medical education, such as physicians opposing departmentalization of hospitals, such as shopkeepers opposing the spread of supermarkets, or such as farmers opposing changes in agricultural policy—have no alternative.

Direct action occurs with great prevalence in French politics. For example, in the first half of the 1984 alone, extreme protest characterized a multitude of interest sectors: Milk producers blocked roads (*New York Times*, May 10, 1984; May 13, 1984). Farmers and winegrowers blocked roads, demonstrated, tore up street surfaces, and harassed occupants of public buildings (*New York Times*, March 27, 1984). Pork and poultry farmers blocked railway lines, hijacked trucks carrying imports, and battled riot police in small towns (*New York Times*, January 25, 1984). Public workers struck (*San Diego Union*, March 9, 1984). So did steel and shipyard workers (*New York Times*, March 31, 1984). Steelworkers sacked courthouses and tax offices (*New York Times*, March 30, 1984) and cut railway lines (*New York Times*, April 3, 1984). They also burned buildings, smashed bank windows, and battled police with acid and steel bolts (*New York Times*, April 5, 1984; April 6, 1984). Tens of thousands marched in Paris (*New York Times*, April 14, 1984). Throughout Spring 1984, both Catholic and non-

Catholic groups, including both conservatives and socialists, protested the
socialist government's proposed reforms of private education. This protested culminated in one of the largest demonstrations in postwar France
on June 22, 1984, when well over 500,000 gathered to march in Versailles.
The movement forced the government to withdraw its program entirely,
and it provoked the resignation of prime minister Pierre Mauroy.

Protest of this kind is not just characteristic of socialist rule. In November-
December 1986, massive student protests—attended by some violence—
also forced the conservative Chirac government to completely withdraw
its proposed university reforms. His higher education minister, Alain Devaquet, resigned. In December 1986-January 1987, the French national
railroads (the SNCF) were reduced to 25% service during the peak
Christmas-New Year's holiday period by a series of wildcat strikes, which
various union leaders struggled to control. By most any index, direct action occurs more often in France than in the United States. This feature
of French politics is general and recurring. The student demonstrations of
1986-87 are a particularly revealing example of this pattern of extreme protest in France.

The central issue in this replay of the 1968 student strikes and riots was
how to make the necessary tradeoff between high quality universities and
egalitarian access to university education in a system crying for innovation, reform and material resources. Long before the March 16, 1986 election, Chirac pledged to reform French universities by giving them more
autonomy to run their affairs, by allowing them to issue degrees under their
own names, by encouraging them to hustle private financing for crucially
needed new programs, and by permitting them to be selective in choosing
which students to admit. Three weeks of violence—involving hundreds of
thousands of students and including demonstrations, strikes and riots—forced
Chirac to withdraw his program of reforms.

Traditionally, of course, French universities have always been closely
controlled from Paris by the Ministry of Education: In the Jacobin state
tradition, all degrees are issued in the name of the French Republic, financing comes solely from the state with numerous restrictions and limitations,
and all students who have passed the high school *baccalauréat* must be admitted if they apply. Chirac thought that such an educational system stifled
innovation and lowered quality overall. In one sense, he was correct. French
universities have long suffered abominable budget shortfalls, lack of basic
equipment and personnel, seriously deteriorating physical plants, severe
space shortages, and low technical and professional salaries. Essentially

open enrollment policies means that many students, especially in the first undergraduate years, have no business pursuing a higher degree but are in the university because of lack of employment opportunities elsewhere. Unemployment in France has hovered above 10% for many years; proportionally it is concentrated in the younger age groupings. Further, talent is drained off by the prestigious *grandes écoles* where entrance is by competitive examination and postgraduate job opportunities are numerous and lucrative.

Chirac aimed his neoliberal reforms in higher education at these problems. By most measures the proposed reforms were relatively weak. Permitting universities to establish and administer their own degree programs and encouraging the competitive hiring of teachers and enrolling of students were ideas not incompatible with Chevènement's socialist "elite republicanism," a euphemism for improving quality by stressing competition and high standards. And these reforms certainly would not have made the French university system over into the image of the American.

But a vast student movement sprang up against the reform proposals, which had been subjected to rather lackadaisical debate in the National Assembly and the Senate. The movement mobilized hundreds of thousands in a week's time and sustained a program of strikes and demonstrations over three weeks. The movement was so strong and sometimes so violent—riot police injured dozens, one died, and highly valued property was destroyed—that Chirac was forced to withdraw his program, not in part but completely.[22]

Four factors characterized the development of these student demonstrations and the government's eventual capitulation to student demands. These factors are common to the extreme protest that often takes on forms of direct action in many sectors of the French state's policy making.

First, the movement exhibited a spontaneous character. The demonstrations and strikes began at the grassroots, well outside the normal channels of the national student organizations. Second, consequently, traditional student leadership was taken by surprise by these events and struggled throughout the three weeks to catch up. In fact, the grassroots directed the events from the beginning and, in this case, never permitted the traditional leadership to coopt the movement. Third, the state was not only taken by surprise by the movement—as it is so often by the spontaneous character of much direct action—but it found itself without an interlocutor with which to negotiate a settlement, this given the grassroots character of the movement. Traditional leaders were shunted aside. The grassroots never permitted a new leadership to form and replace the old. With whom can the state negotiate when no one has the authority or legitimacy to speak for the movement?

Last, Chirac committed the same error in the name of ideological principles as had the socialists upon assuming power in 1981: He interpreted his election victory of March 16, 1986 as a mandate by the French for a sweeping series of neoliberal reforms. Throughout the spring, summer, and early fall 1986, French administration worked overtime to enact measures that privatized many industries and banks, set in motion the privatization of the largest state owned television network, liberalized currency and trading regulations, eliminating some of them entirely, reformed sections of the tax code, especially reducing taxes for higher income brackets, enacted a variety of policies designed to encourage more private investment—in general a French turn toward neoliberalism and Reagan style rhetoric. Yet the French no more voted for these policies than they had for the extreme Socialist platform of 1981. Rather, they voted in protest against an incumbent government. There was, thus, no widespread support in public opinion *in favor* of reform.

We have seen that the French state's authority is concentrated in bureaucrats and bureaucratic departments. They embody the Rousseauian view of the general will which pits the state against all entities, like pressure groups and labor unions, which embody or epitomize "particular wills," or private interests. They also share Colbert's view of how to use state instruments to seek policy goals. They exercise broad control over many aspects of French life, like the country's educational system or its health care system, which in the United States are more or less autonomous. We have seen the numerous advantages that the French state's structure gives these civil servants and their political leaders in day to day decision making. We have seen that the state's use of these advantages severely handicaps outside groups, such as students, teachers, physicians, shopkeepers, farmers, or many others who are concerned.

In this system, the French state is clearly vulnerable to direct action and violent protest. One reason is the way laws and decrees are formulated. Outside input into administrative decision making tends to occur late in the French political process—if it occurs at all. Warning signals of possible or probable opposition and violence are often ignored. The closed policymaking process characteristic of French administration avoids the problems of opposition and delay, but it is also dangerously vulnerable to this explosive protest.

When conditions are ripe, direct action can be extremely effective. Naturally, the student uprisings of 1968 are an example. They wrought sweeping reforms in the same university system that Chirac wished to reform in 1986. And in 1984, massive, nonviolent demonstrations by Catholics and non-Catholics, conservatives, and socialists forced Mitterrand's socialist government to withdraw proposed reforms of private schools. Direct action often stalls the state's plans.

Crozier identified alternating periods of routine and crisis in the French bureaucracy. The rigidities of the strong state and its use of tactical advantages make change hard to come by. As Hayward noted (1973:11), "a regime organized to minimize the impact of change postpones and accumulates a backlog of overdue business." Nevertheless, change cannot be forever postponed, no matter how strong the state is. Exit and direct action are recurring themes in French politics and they sometimes succeed in bringing about crises that force the state to change its planned course of action. The vulnerability of the French state lies in its encouragement of the buildup of overdue business. This makes massive resistance paradoxically more likely than in other regimes that are better at accommodating dissent through strategic change or cooptation. In May 1968, spontaneous alliances arose between students and workers, neither particularly well organized beforehand, and strikes and demonstrations spread extensively across France, prompting a series of sweeping reforms. We have seen that the November-December 1986 student protests also arose spontaneously from the grassroots, persistently threatening to entirely bypass traditional student leaders. The December 1986-January 1987 train strike also began as a series of wildcat actions. Paradoxically, the strong French state is sometimes weak indeed.[23]

Conclusion

In a range of policy-making areas, the French state engages in broad discretionary decision making. Zysman (1978), for example, argues that the French state was the main force in postindustrial modernization and the restructuring of industrial sectors, that it was able to protect its farmers by negotiating effective subsidies from German industry in European Community pricing, and that it supports certain French industries by playing trader of package deals with other countries in the international marketplace. Hall (1986) argues that nothing short of an economic miracle in the postwar transformation of France was attributable to extensive state intervention in the society and the economy.

The character of the French state's intervention in the economy and the society is also evident historically. Consider that in the seventeenth century, shops for making saltpetre (essential to the manufacture of gunpowder) were set up all across France, but only with the help of capital supplied directly by the crown. The French kings subsidized and otherwise encouraged large, capital intensive ventures in many new industries. They participated in the formation of enterprises by grants of special privileges and grants of land, buildings and advances of cash. They also enforced enactments that determined the overall shape of new industrial sectors, such as how concentrated they would become (Nef, 1957:58-88).

French administrators have long used state power to shape the economy and protect France's interests as they perceive them. Colbert executed a policy of mercantilism to protect domestic industries. He also used central power to break down internal tariffs, improve roads and canals and reform commercial codes. Napoleon mounted an extensive continental blockade using centralized state power. During the 1896 depression, Méline, the minister of agriculture, pushed through a series of tariffs blocking agricultural imports in an effort to use the state to protect French farmers. More recently, Edouard Balladur, minister of the economy and finance in the 1986 Chirac government, intervened in the bidding for the privatization of the Compagnie Générale de Constructions Téléphoniques, a major switching manufacturer, and awarded the purchase to a consortium led by the Swedish firm L. M. Ericsson over a superior offer—both technologically and financially—which had been put together by AT&T. Balladur and others who were part of the French state felt that Europeans should be careful not to allow too prominent an American presence in a technological industry crucial to advanced communications (*New York Times*, April 30, 1987).

There is of course no guarantee that a strong state, operating with maximum autonomy, will make the right decisions. The strength of a state is measured by how effectively it may implement its chosen policies and how effectively it may cope with domestic or international opposition. But the inherent correctness or viability of policy is another matter entirely. The French state, for example, has traditionally played a great role in structuring the character of its high technology sectors. In computers, it quite easily blocked the sale of Machines Bull to General Electric in 1964. The state did so because it considered the sale counter to the general interest and because it possessed the tactical advantages necessary to execute this decision. Bull continued to lose money and a year later the state concluded that the sale would have to take place after all. Yet because of steadily deteriorating performance, the terms arranged with GE were significantly less advantageous to the French state. For example, it had to cede GE complete instead of partial control of Bull. Later the state launched a new computer firm, *Compagnie Internationale pour l'Informatique* (CII), which quickly turned into a financial abyss, swallowing state subsidies as fast as they could be granted (cf. Zysman, 1978:285-287).

But in nuclear energy, in contrast to these apparent failures, the French state not only developed a comprehensive and cohesive plan for development of reactors, it executed this plan with a speed and thoroughness that contrasts directly with the American state's role in developing nuclear energy and with the subsequent character of the American nuclear power industry. Of any western industrialized state, the French set the most ambitious development targets for nuclear power. The Messmer government in 1974 planned that by 1985, nuclear power would provide 25% of France's energy needs and 70% of its electricity (Cohen & Gourevitch, 1982:34). The goal was met. France is currently the leading nation in per capita nuclear power and second in total capacity. The French state executed a program based on a uniform reactor design (the conventional light water reactor) and speedy approvals for construction. Consequently, in contrast to the United States, where delays result not only from differences and experimentation in design but also from environmental groups' challenges to construction permits, the French can build many more reactors more quickly and more cheaply per unit. In addition, the French state has incorporated the whole nuclear cycle in its development plan. It has the world's only major reprocessing plant and went forth with a breeder reactor when all other countries were cancelling theirs (Cohen & Gourevitch, 1982:34-40).

But of course the full consequences of this extraordinarily effective decision making are not always clear. The French state wished to develop its nuclear energy sector to reduce its severe dependence on oil and gas imports. It did so effectively. On the other hand, France's gigantic investment in nuclear development makes it the hostage of downward oil prices. The potential danger of nuclear power could also conceivably demonstrate that the French state was wrong to proceed so fully.[24] Likewise, the state chose to commit enormous resources to the Concorde supersonic transport plane and to the construction of a third international airport at Roissy. Both were successfully completed, but the Concorde was clearly a financial albatross. Many argue that the Charles de Gaulle facility was also not only not needed but excessively expensive in economic and social costs.[25] *The effectiveness of state decision making is in no way logically related to the correctness or desirability of subsequent policy outcomes.* Sometimes it is and sometimes it is not.

In an important and elegant study, Feigenbaum (1985) argues that in fact the practice of *pantouflage*—or the ongoing exchange of high functionary and high management personnel between the public and private sector—mitigates the effectiveness of the French state's decision making. Based upon his investigation of oil politics and the French state, Feigenbaum concludes that the interests favored by state policy making after the oil shocks of the 1970s were those of high state and corporate administrators—essentially one and the same socioeconomic elite. However, not only is Feigenbaum's argument about oil policy making not generalizable to many other policy areas, he does not recognize the distinction between *effectiveness* on the one hand and *correctness or desirability* of various policy outcomes on the other. The French state's decision making in response to oil shocks was extremely effective. By Feigenbaum's own evidence, it was at once rapid, coherent, and comprehensive. That the resulting policies imposed severe and lamentable economic and social costs on certain groups cannot be challenged, as Feigenbaum argues with great sensitivity. But this in no way constitutes evidence that the French state is either weak or ineffective. Describing elite decision making that favors itself and judging normatively who should pay social and economic costs of a policy are not inhabitants of the same logical plane.

The strong state tradition in France serves as an overriding factor of consensus in an otherwise extremely plural society. The French state's ideology protects the state's interests. These are sometimes perceived as those of functionaries or as those of privileged groups in the economy or the society. But just as often, or perhaps more often, the state's interests are perceived as the amalgam or distillation of the interests of all, the community, the whole that is France. This state ideology protects the role of the functionary, and it protects the centralization of the system. But it does not protect political institutions such as those that make up the regime type. To the contrary, the regime type is highly vulnerable in France to passing crises and humors. A succession of political regime changes ranging across all types litters the landscape of France's political history.

There is such high politicization over issues and between political parties in France, charged by an all encompassing and violent polemic, that it is difficult for the institutions of a political regime type to become anchored solidly in French political culture. There has never been a *political* consensus in France, which like Americanism in the United States (see Hartz, 1955) could serve to bind elements together in agreement over the modalities and institutions of governance and change. In France, the strong state bound the fractious society together. The strong state itself was all that warring elements could agree upon, each hoping it would serve its own purposes.

The overall relations between society and the state in France are characterized by what may be called *state-dominated pluralism*. In a system of extreme pluralism of groups, the focal point of both policy making and interest group activity is found in the bureaucratic departments. This gives the French state, through its bureaucratic institutions, more capability for control over interest group activity than is found in the "neutral" state of traditional pluralist theory, wherein policy outcomes are sometimes characterized as the "sum of vectors" pushing in upon the state from society.

Of course, in state-dominated pluralism, the state and its structures are by no means homogeneous. The strong state is by no means all powerful. Centers of power compete within the vast French bureaucracy. Perhaps some groups can play opposing centers of power off one another, thus enhancing their own maneuverability in the bureaucratic universe. However, the strong French state is strong in part because it eliminates much access to alternative arenas of policymaking and influence, such as a powerful legislature or judiciary. When groups cannot play conflictual interests within the bureaucracy against each other, they have little other recourse but to exit the political system altogether. This feature points to the French state's high vulnerability to direct action—walkouts, boycotts, demonstrations, strikes—and other forms of sometimes violent protest. The state in state-dominated pluralism is more effective at policy making than its American pluralist counterpart, but it may not necessarily be more successful and it is clearly ineffective at absorbing protest.

Notes

1. The French view of the state is also informed by the Roman model. Peyrefitte (1976), for example, indicted the French for an excessive love of centralized power, which he attributed to both Catholicism and the Latin heritage of "Caesarism without Caesar." For a critique of Peyrefitte's view of *le mal français*, see Dumont (1979).

2. This of course assumes that there can be a single public interest and not an inevitable plurality of public interests, a major difference between continental and Anglo-Saxon traditions which affects politics.

3. See Schonfeld's excellent review of French administrative studies (1984).

4. The permeability of French administration is another way of looking at unified versus heterogeneous state structures. The best discussions are Meynaud (e.g., 1957, 1961a, 1961b,

1962a, 1962b) and Ehrmann (e.g., 1957, 1958, 1961a, 1961b). They argued that technocrats split between horizontal and vertical administrations and between the finance ministry and all others. Concerns were twofold: First, does the technocrat deal from a superior position with underfinanced and poorly (technically) trained interest groups? Does this harm the representative capacities of the administration? Second, do interest group pressures and *pantouflage* cloud the technocrats' vision of the general will, or public interest?

Ehrmann (1961a) argued that vertical administrations (organized according to a single sector, such as agriculture) were more permeable to organized interest group pressure than horizontal administrations, like finance, whose responsibilities cut across interest sectors. On the other hand, the concentration of authority in bureaucratic departments can lead to intense interest group pressure on bureaucrats and *pantouflage*, or the switching between bureaucratic and business or other private sector posts; thus, interest groups often exert more influence on bureaucracies than is good for the public interest, particularly in a postwar setting requiring radical policy changes to promote sorely needed economic growth. In *Organized Business in France* (1957), Ehrmann argued that the state directs far less than it protects. In an interest sector lacking a countervailing force (such as unified labor), business succeeded in demanding protection from competition. Ehrmann accounted for problems of economic development in postwar France in more general interest group-society terms: "In France, social and political values, aspirations and ideologies have been divisive for so long that there has rarely existed substantial agreement on the 'rules of the game' determining the administration of the *res publica*. A political vacuum has resulted into which the interest groups have extended their activities and their intransigence, while the machinery of the state has veered uneasily between collaboration with and submission to the groups (Ehrmann 1957:475).

Meynaud (1961a) saw that administrative permeability to interest groups is complex and that some bureaucrats want only the maximum for their clientele groups regardless of the public interest. But he argued that many bureaucrats bring a larger view to administrative questions. Further, group cooperation is often indispensible to implementing public policy. Both sides profit. In the end, both views are correct; it depends, as both noted, on which part of the bureaucracy we talk about. There is always a difference between ministries and between issue areas, and these not only crosscut but are also unstable. That is, they change over time.

5. Naturally there are often important differences between issue areas, or policy-making arenas. The dynamics of a state's relations with organized groups in agriculture, energy, health care, foreign affairs or many other sectors respond to varying imperatives (see Krasner, 1977, 1978; Katzenstein, 1976).

6. The idea is not the same as corporatism, meaning a particular way of arranging state-industry-labor relationships (see Schmitter, 1974). That is strategy, or the long term, ongoing organization of relationships.

7. As with much work on corporatism, Katzenstein concentrates on state-industry-labor relations. Most often, the concepts developed are not applied to other interest sectors, with the exception of agriculture (see Keeler, 1981a, 1981b).

8. In fact, as Kvistad (1986) argues compellingly, at least three important concepts of the state can be found in the German tradition. Two of these emerge from nineteenth century German political thought: the *Beamtenstaat* and the *Rechtsstaat*. The *Beamtenstaat*, or bureaucratic state, identified the bureaucracy as embodying the "spirit" of the state. Bureaucrats held a preeminent and arbitrating position over other politically interested actors, such as parties, corporations and organized groups. The *Rechtsstaat* emphasized the rule of law, subordinating political rule to legal codes which embodied consistent and finite sets of maxims. The state bureaucracy in this system served as a formal unitary moral agent whose respon-

sibility it was to impose political order onto a partial, divided, conflict ridden society. Both maintained a strict separation of state from society. Both are similar in many respects to the French tradition wherein public power is entrusted to a high civil servant that is viewed as superior to always suspicious private or societal interests.

In twentieth century Germany, the rise of the *Parteienstaat* mitigates the traditionally crucial state-society distinction because catch-all parties are seen not as political organizations of society set against the universality of the state but rather as legitimately assuming the duties of the state and providing the personnel for its offices. The party serves as the bridge between the state and society. Naturally, in France, political parties compete for power through both presidential and legislative elections, and, especially with *cohabitation*, the importance of the majority parliamentary parties is signified. But philosophically and empirically, French parties still do not serve as a replacement for the high civil service, its training grounds in the *grandes écoles* and the importance of the state as a unitary entity which overrides and overarches private interests. Rather, if anything, we will see, the *hauts fonctionnaires* and the *grand corps* members populate the parties, instead of the other way around, as in West Germany.

9. Nettl (1968) captures some of this distinction by explicitly approaching the state as a conceptual *variable*: ". . . more or less stateness is a useful variable for comparing Western societies and . . . the absence or presence of a well-developed concept of state relates to and identifies important empirical differences in these societies" (1968:591-592).

10. The electoral incentives for deputies changed with the 1985 reform law instituting proportional one-round voting in departments for National Assembly seats. The most likely long-term effects of this change would have been a weakening of the importance of the geographical constituency base and a strengthening of the party's role in drawing up the electoral lists. On the other hand, parties may have been weaker inside parliament, for it would have been more difficult to establish a majority and coalition politics could have assumed more importance. But the 1986 Chirac government fulfilled its campaign promise to reinstitute (by ordinance) the previous system, two-round majority voting in individual geographic constituencies.

11. For a history of the *cabinet*'s development, which may be traced to Louis XIV, and a detailed account of its functioning, see Searls (1978).

12. In 1971 the Constitutional Council ruled unconstitutional a law—passed in the wake of May 1968 and mounting social unrest on the left—permitting the government through the prefect to refuse registration to groups *suspected* of objectionable activity. Hayward's account (1973:123) is instructive, not only for the state's view—and the view of the political class—of its proper authority, but also for the state's advantages in lawmaking: "[With the law t]he government would thus be in a position to decide in advance whether an association should be presumed to be illicit and even in the event of a contrary decision by the courts, delay the association [from] acquiring legal personality meanwhile. [With case backlog, the government would benefit from delay in the association's appeal.] Having initially intended to proceed by decree, the minister of the interior accepted the council of state's advice that a Bill would be necessary and secured parliamentary permission to discuss his Bill as a matter of urgency. It was rushed through the assembly between 2 A.M. and 4:30 A.M. on 24 June 1971, at a period when the parliamentary timetable was particularly congested." The essential point is that very recently—even though in the end it lost—the state attempted to curb individual rights, guaranteed by the constitution, in the name of the public interest. It almost succeeded. At least one could argue for the deterrent effects of the state's boldness and tenacity. How much were other groups thereby intimidated? (See Ehrmann, 1983:330-331; Hayward, 1973:122-124.)

13. But French labor unions are as ambivalent about collective bargaining and negotiations

as management. The anarcho-syndicalist tradition means that, despite the political differences that divide the major labor confederations ideologically, unions are united by reluctance to abide by contractual obligations to not strike before the expiration of a negotiated agreement (see McCormick, 1981).

14. The *garde à vue* provision was originally established to allow rural police time to contact the *préfecture*, a purpose now obsolete. It is now often used to interrogate suspects in the hope they will confess (see the film *Garde à Vue*, 1981).

15. Especially useful summaries may be found in Ehrmann (1983:328-333) and Hayward (1973:121-124). There is important evidence to suggest that the Constitutional Council may be coming to play a more important arbitrating (or moderating?) role between left and right since 1981 (see Keeler, 1985; Keeler and Stone, 1987). Nevertheless, the Constitutional Council in no way approaches the importance of the Supreme Court in the American political system. Keeler may overstate his case, for despite the fact that especially after 1981 the Constitutional Council became much more significant as a check on government power, it remains that its jurisdiction is far narrower than the American Supreme Court, far fewer people or groups may bring cases to it, and the whole area of decrees is outside its purview. Further, the indisputably increased activity of the Constitutional Council since 1981 may be partially epiphenomenal: Not since the initial government of the Fifth Republic had a government gotten so many substantive, far-reaching reforms through parliament as did the socialists from 1981 to 1983. Conservatives direly needed an avenue of recourse; they used the available one to the fullest.

16. However, the recent sentence of life imprisonment to Georges Ibrahim Abdallah, the Lebanese terrorist leader, surprised many French and foreign legal observers. The prosecutor, following government instructions, asked for "moderation" in the form of a maximum sentence of ten years. It was widely known that the Chirac government feared renewed terrorist attacks on French territory and in Paris especially, such as those that wounded more than 150 and killed 10 in bomb explosions during September 1986. But such judicial independence from the government is still very rare; the Abdallah case does not in itself constitute a new pattern (see *New York Times*, February 23, 1987; February 24, 1987; March 1, 1987).

17. Of course, definitions of *sérieux* and *responsible* depend upon one's view. For administrators, groups seen as *sérieux* tend to be those that are helpful and therefore liked. The important point is that the French ideology of the state supports such rationalizing evaluations. American bureaucrats, lacking such a supporting ideology, must at least pretend that all groups have equal access and are subject to evenhanded decision making. Traditions of the state inform not only what are acceptable group demands and activities; they inform how the bureaucrats interact with the groups.

18. Or to the wishes of the prime minister alone in an arrangement of *cohabitation*. But of course in any of these variations, the cabinet, or Council of Ministers, also serves as a locus of bargaining within the governing party or coalition.

19. This training is ironically generalist rather than specialist, for the graduate of ENA is expected to be a fast learner and to perform many different tasks in widely differing sectors in the course of his career (see Suleiman, 1978).

20. Some will argue that important cracks are appearing in the once overarching French reliance on centralization and state intervention—which has characterized the French administration at least since the fourteenth century (cf. Nef, 1957). Two recent examples provide compelling but far from sufficient evidence for this proposition. The first is the measures decentralizing certain areas of local governance from Paris and the prefects to individual localities undertaken by the socialist governments from 1981 to 1984. There is no doubt that some im-

portant decisions formerly reserved to the central authorities may now be made by municipal and regional councils, as well as some—but limited—raising of revenues is also limited and perhaps most important, it is still too early to assess the long term effects of these changes.

Second, the whole philosophy of privatization and deregulation that the 1986 Chirac government borrowed from Thatcher and Reagan seriously questions the traditional French reliance on state intervention and overarching control of the economy and society. Again, it is far too early to assess the long term effects of the privatization of such large firms as Saint-Gobain, the banks or the television network TF1, or the deregulation of currency exchange, the stock market and investment. In particular, insofar as these changes may redound to the detriment of the French economy in future cyclical downturns, support for them may dwindle rapidly. In any case, Chirac's interpretation of his March 16, 1986 election victory as a mandate for change in these areas was a grave misinterpretation of what the electorate knew very well it was doing, that is, voting against socialists rather than for conservatives. In any case, Mitterrand's socialist governments from 1983 to 1986 had already turned from an all-encompassing reliance on state intervention and state control for the solution to vexing economic and social problems to a liberalization and withdrawing of the state from many domains, ranging from currency regulation to enterprise management to social welfare programs.

Reliance on the state in the face of vexing problems was often embodied in the mechanism of public ownership of enterprises and important industrial sectors, such as mining, steel or shipbuilding. That the French have been "taking the state back out" is indisputable. This movement probably comes about as a result of a ten year *conjoncture de crise économique* in which the French economy performed poorly and state intervention was seldom successful in turning industries or firms around, much less making them more internationally competitive. In fact, the French state has realized that its traditional interventionist techniques do not always work, and it has moved *just as actively* toward withdrawing from areas that it previously controlled closely, or permitting, under supervision, more liberty than before.

21. Despite limits, the Council of State's authority to rule on citizen or group claims against the state sometimes proves useful. Groups subject to government decrees may oppose them wholly or in part at the Council. Groups representing professors protested the government's decree establishing elections to organize *conseils supérieurs* which control the nomination and promotion of university faculty. The Council ruled illegal the decree's provisions for representation on these *conseils* (April 19, 1985).

22. The first strike movement began among a very small number of students at the Paris XIII campus, well outside of Paris and not particularly known for its radical or activist students. *Le Monde* (November 21, 1986) headlined a short article in its back pages, "Students Against the Devaquet Law: First You Have to Know How to Start a Strike," referring with some derision to the dismal and isolated results of the first day. By November 28, the movement had spread to most of the Paris campuses and to some of the larger provincial universities. On November 29, 200,000 students marched in Paris, 400,000 marched at various demonstrations in the provinces. The majority in the National Assembly, and indeed the government itself, had already divided on how best to handle the crisis. On December 1, the government withdrew several of what it considered the most objectionable features of the reforms. By December 5, most teachers in France had come to favor the students' demands. On December 8, the student was killed by the riot police and Alain Devaquet, the Higher Education minister, resigned from the government. Finally, on December 9, the government withdrew the reform bill entirely (see especially *Le Monde*, November 22, 1986; November 28, 1986; November 29, 1986; December 2, 1986; December 3, 1986; December 5, 1986; December 7-8, 1986; December 9, 1986).

23. Clearly, direct action, particularly concentrated and coordinated action from a relatively strategic group like physicians or train workers, sometimes reduces the effectiveness of the state. But several conditions may be required: First, the group or groups must be relatively strategically placed in society or the economy. Second, unified, concerted action must characterize the movement. Physicians, interns, the events of May 1968, the student protests of late 1986 all exhibit this element. By contrast, the December 1986-January 1987 train strikes were plagued by differences between the principle unions—the CGT, the CFDT and the FO—which permitted the state to play a waiting game and finally settle for a symbolic two percent pay raise. Further, the *école libre* demonstrations in 1984 are instructive: Massive numbers of citizens were involved; they crosscut many social and political categories. Much of the Socialist electorate was involved. But third, demonstrations may not suffice. Particularly from smaller but strategically placed groups, a concerted strike or boycott may be more effective. Economic action not demonstrations worked for hospital interns.

24. In 1987, two accidents occurred at the Tricastin enrichment plant and at the Superphénix breeder reactor. In the first, uranium hexachloride gas escaped from a faulty valve. The gas is only moderately radioactive but highly toxic. In the second, about 25 tons of sodium coolant were discovered to have leaked from the breeder reactor. The sodium is not radioactive but ignites on contact with water (*New York Times*, April 15, 1987).

25. Feldman (1985) is one to argue this point. In a study comparing planning in Britain and France, he wishes to revise the view of French central planning as superior to British "pluralist decision making." He examines two cases, the Concorde project and the construction of third international airports outside London and Paris. In the case of the Concorde, both French central planners and British administrators subject to pluralist pressures stuck to the money losing project to the bitter end. The French did so because their technocracy is autonomously capable of doing so if it wishes despite any societal pressures. The British did so because labor unions objected to the loss of jobs which would attend the project's cancellation. (French labor unions objected also, but according to Feldman's logic, the opposition was irrelevant to the planners' strategic calculations.) With the third international airport, French planners proceeded in the face of societal opposition and imposed great economic and environmental costs to achieve completion of the Charles de Gaulle facility at Roissy. But completion they did achieve. The British administrators, on the other hand, never managed to overcome opposition, and chose instead to expand Heathrow, the existing facility. In retrospect, this alternative was far less costly and more than sufficient to resolve the problem at hand.

References

Aberbach, J. D., Putnam, R. D., and Rockman, B. A. (1981). *Bureaucrats and politicians in western democracies*. Cambridge, MA: Harvard University Press.

Anderson, P. (1974). *Lineages of the absolutist state*. London: New Left Books.

Ashford, D. (1985). The British and French social security systems: Welfare state by intent and by default. In D. Ashford & E. W. Kelley (Eds.) *Nationalizing social security*. Greenwich, CT: JAI Press.

_____ (forthcoming) *Political development of the welfare state*.

Avril, P. (1972). *Les Français et leur parlement*. Paris: Casterman.

Barthelemy, J. (1924). *Le gouvernement de la France*. Paris: Payot.

Bauer, R. A., De Sola Pool, I., & L. A. Dexter (1963). *American business and public policy.* New York: Atherton.

Bendix, R. (1978). *Kings or people.* Berkeley, CA: University of California Press.

Berger, S. (1974). *The French political system.* New York: Random House.

Birnbaum, P. (1982). The state versus corporatism. *Politics and Society, 11*(4), 477-501.

———— (1978). *La classe dirigeante française.* Paris: Presses Universitaires de France.

Bodiguel, J.-L., & Quermonne, J.-L. (1983). *La haute fonction publique sous la ve république.* Paris: Presses Universitaires de France.

Cater, D. (1964). *Power in Washington.* New York: Random House.

Chubb, J. E. (1983). *Interest groups and the bureaucracy: The politics of energy.* Stanford, CA: Stanford University Press.

Cohen, S. S. and Gourevitch, P. (Eds.), (1982). *France in a troubled world economy.* London: Butterworths.

Collier, R. B. & Collier, D. (1979). Inducements versus constraints: Disaggregating corporatism. *American Political Science Review, 73* (December), 4, 967-986.

Crozier, M. (1963). *Le phénomène bureaucratique.* Paris: Seuil.

———— (1974). La centralisation. In M. Crozier (Ed.) *Où va l'Administration française?* Editions d'Organisations, Paris.

Debre, M. (1966). Speech before the Council of State. In W. G. Andrews (Ed.) *European political institutions.* Princeton, NJ: Van Nostrand.

———— (1946). *Réforme de la fonction publique.* Paris: Imprimerie Nationale.

Dumont, J. (1979). *Erreurs sur le mal français ou le trompe-l'oeil de M. Peyrefitte.* Paris: Vernoy.

Dupuy, F. and Thoenig, J.-C. (1983). *Sociologie de l'Administration française.* Paris: Armand Colin.

Dyson, K. (1980). *The state tradition in western Europe.* London: Oxford University Press.

Edelman, M. (1964). *The symbolic uses of politics.* Urbana, IL: University of Illinois Press.

Ehrmann, H. W. (1983). *Politics in France,* 4th ed. Boston, MA: Little, Brown.

———— (1963). Direct democracy in France. *American Political Science Review, 57,* (December) 4, 883-901.

———— (1961a). French bureaucracy and organized interests. *Administrative Science Quarterly, 5* (March) 4, 534-555.

———— (1961b). Les groups d'intérêt et la bureaucratie dans les démocraties occidentales. *Revue Française de Science Politique, 5* (séptembre) 3, 541-568.

———— (1958). Pressure groups in France. *Annals of the American Academy of Political and Social Science, 319* (September), 141-148.

———— (1957). *Organized business in France.* Princeton, NJ: Princeton University Press.

Favre, P. (1981). La science politique en France depuis 1945. *International Political Science Review, 2* (1), 95-120.

Feigenbaum, H. B. (1985). *The Politics of public enterprise: Oil and the French state.* Princeton, NJ: Princeton University Press.

Feldman, E. J. (1985). *Concorde and dissent: Explaining high technology project failures in Britain and France.* New York: Cambridge University Press.

Fiorina, M. P. (1977). *Congress: Keystone of the Washington establishment.* New Haven, CT: Yale University Press.

Freeman, J. L. (1955). *The political process.* New York: Random House.

Goguel, F. (1954). Les méthodes du travail parlementaire. *Revue Française de Science Politique, 4* (octobre-décembre) 4, 674-708.

Goubert, P. (1969). *L'ancien régime*. Paris: Colin.

Gourevitch, P. (1980). *Paris and the province: The politics of local government reform in France*. Berkeley, CA: University of California Press.

_____ (1977). The Reform of Local Government. *Comparative Politics, 10* (October) 1, 69-88.

Gremion, P. (1976). *Le Pouvoir périphérique: Bureaucrates et notables dans le système politique français*. Paris: Seuil.

Hall, P. (1986). *Governing the economy: The politics of state intervention in Britain and France*. New York: Oxford University Press.

Hartz, L. (1955). *The liberal tradition in America*. New York: Harcourt Brace Jovanovich.

Hayward, J. (1973). *The one and indivisible French republic*. New York: Norton.

Heclo, H. (1978). Issue Networks and the Executive Establishment, pp. 87-124. In Anthony King (Ed.), *The new American political system*. Washington, D.C.: American Enterprise Institute.

_____ (1977). *A government of strangers*. Washington, D.C.: Brookings Institution.

Jones, C. O. (1982). *The United States congress: People, place and policy*. Homewood, IL: Dorsey Press.

Katzenstein, P. (1984). *Corporatism and change: Austria, Switzerland and the politics of industry*. Ithaca, NY: Cornell University Press.

_____ (1985). *Small states in world markets: Industrial policy in Europe*. Ithaca, NY: Cornell University Press.

_____ (1976). International relations and domestic structures: Foreign economic policies of advanced industrial states. *International Organization, 30* (Winter) 1, 1-45.

_____ (ed.), (1978). *Between power and plenty: Foreign economic policies of advanced industrial states*. Madison, WI: University of Wisconsin Press.

_____ (n.d.) *Policy and politics in west Germany: A semisovereign state*. Ithaca, NY: Cornell University.

Keeler, J. T. S. (1985). Confrontations juridico-politiques: le Conseil constitutionnel face au Gouvernement socialiste comparé à la Cour suprême face au New Deal. *Pouvoirs, 35*, 133-148.

_____ (1983). Reform, revolt and retrenchment in socialist France: The new politics of agricultural policymaking, 1981-83. In J. S. Ambler (Ed.) *France under socialist leadership*. Philadelphia, PA: Institute for the Study of Human Issues.

_____ (1981a). Corporatism and official union Hegemony: The case of French agricultural syndicalism. In S. Berger (Ed.) *Organizing interests in western Europe: Pluralism, corporatism and the transformation of politics*. Cambridge: Cambridge University Press.

_____ (1981b). The corporatist dynamic of agricultural modernization in the fifth republic. In W. G. Andrews & S. Hoffman (Eds.), *The fifth republic at twenty*. Albany, NY: State University of New York Press.

_____ & Stone, A. (1987). Judicial-political confrontation in Mitterrand's France: The emergence of the constitutional council as a major actor in the policymaking process. In S. Hoffman & G. Ross (Eds.), *Continuity and change in Mitterrand's France*. New York: Oxford University Press.

King, A. (1978). The American polity in the late 1970s: Building coalitions in the sand, pp. 371-396. In A. King (Ed.), *The new American political system*. Washington, D.C.: American Enterprise Institute.

Krasner, S. D. (1977). Domestic constraints on international economic leverage, pp. 160-181.

In K. Knorr & F. N. Trager (Eds.) *Economic issues and national security*. Lawrence, KS: Regents Press of Kansas.

_____ (1978). *Defending the national interest: Raw materials investments and U.S. foreign policy*. Princeton, NJ: Princeton University Press.

Kvistad, G. O. (1986). *Radicals and the state: The political demands on West German civil servants*. Paper presented to the American Political Science Association, Washington, D.C. (August).

Massigli, R. (1958). *Sur quelques maladies de l'Etat*. Paris: Plon.

Massot, J. (1979). *Le chef du gouvernement en France*. Paris: Documentation Française.

_____ (1977). *La présidence de la République en France*. Paris: Documentation Française.

McConnell, G. (1966). *Private power and American democracy*. New York: Knopf.

McCormick, J. (1981). Gaullism and collective bargaining: The effect of the fifth republic on French industrial relations. In W. G. Andrews & S. Hoffman (Eds.), *The impact of the fifth republic on France*. Albany, NY: State University of New York Press.

Meynaud, J. (1962a). Les Groupes de pression sous la Ve République. *Revue Française de Science Politique, 12* (3), 672-97.

_____ (1962b). *Nouvelles etudes sur les groupes de pression en France*. Paris: Colin.

_____ (1961a). A propos de la Technocratie. *Revue Française de Science Politique, 11* (séptembre) 3, 671-683.

_____ (1961b). Les organisations professionnelles et le pouvoir. *Annuaire de l'Association Suisse de science politique, 1* (1), 11-26.

_____ (1957). Les groupes d'intérêt et l'administration en France. *Revue Française de Science Politique, 7* (3), 588.

Mignot, G. & d'Orsay, P. (1968). *La machine administrative*. Paris: Seuil.

Mousnier, R. (1970). *La plume, la faucille, et le marteau*. Paris: Presses Universitaires de France.

Nef, J. (1957). *Industry and government in France and England 1540-1640*. Ithaca, NY: Great Seal Books.

Nettl, J. P. (1968). The state as a conceptual variable. *World Politics, 20* (July) 4, 559-92.

Neustadt, R. (1960). *Presidential power*. New York: John Wiley.

Peyrefitte, A. (1976). *Le mal français*. Paris: Plon.

Pitts, J. R. (1963). Continuity and change in bourgeois France. In S. Hoffman, et al., *In search of France*. Cambridge, MA: Harvard University Press.

Polsby, N. (1975). Legislatures. In N. Polsby & F. I. Greenstein (Eds.), *Handbook of political science*, vol. 5. Reading, MA: Addison-Wesley.

Rockman, B. A. (1981). America's *departments* of state: Irregular and regular syndromes of policy making. *American Political Science Review, 75* (December) 4, 911-927.

Schattschneider, E. E. (1960). *The semisovereign people*. New York: Holt, Rinehart, Winston.

Schmitter, P. C. (1974). Still the Century of Corporatism? *Review of Politics, 36* (January) 1, 85-131.

Schonfeld, W. R. (1984). Sociologie de l'administration française. *Tocqueville Review, 6* (Spring-Summer) 1, 233-239.

Searls, E. (1978). The fragmented French executive: Ministerial *cabinets* in the fifth republic. *West European Politics, 1* (May) 2, 161-176.

Suleiman, E. N. (1978). Higher education in France: A two-track system. *West European Politics, 1* (October) 3, 97-114.

_____ (1974). *Politics, power and bureaucracy in France: The administrative elite.*

Princeton, NJ: Princeton University Press.

_____ (1970). The French bureaucracy and its students: Toward the desanctification of the state. *World Politics, 23* (October) 1, 120-170.

Tocqueville, A., de (1967). *L'Ancien régime et la révolution.* Paris: Gallimard.

Walker, J. L. (1983). The origins and maintenance of interest groups in America. *American Political Science Review, 77* (June) 2, 390-406.

Wilsford, D. (1984). Exit and voice: Strategies for change in bureaucratic-legislative policymaking. *Policy Studies Journal, 12* (March) 3, 431-444.

_____ (1985). The *conjoncture* of ideas and interests: A note on explanations of the French revolution. *Comparative Political Studies, 18* (October) 3, 357-372.

Wilson, F. L. (1983). French interest group politics: Pluralist or neocorporatist? *American Political Science Review, 77* (December) 4, 895-910.

Worms, J.-P. (1968). *Une préfecture comme organisation.* Paris: Centre de Sociologie des Organisations.

_____ (1966). Le préfet et servants notables. *Sociologie du Travail, 8* (juillet-septembre) 3, 249-275.

Wylie, L. (1957). *Village in the Vaucluse.* Cambridge, MA: Harvard University Press.

Zysman, J. (1978). The French state in the international economy. In P. J. Katzenstein (Ed.) *Between power and plenty.* Madison, WI: University of Wisconsin Press.

In political theory the state has been enjoying a conceptual rebirth even while some activities have been receding. The state, however, remains conceptually ambiguous and is, thus, molded into many different conceptual forms. Three of those forms are discussed in this paper—the decision-making state, the production state, and the intermediary state. The first relates to the organization and architecture of decisional authority; the second to the public and distributive goods supplied by the state; and the third to the interconnections between state organization and the organizations of civil society.

Although the state lacks unique definition as a concept, its value lies in bringing together the most important macrolevel connections of the polity, the society, and the economy, which cannot otherwise be adequately analyzed in isolation from one another. In particular, the state provides a focus for the study of statecraft within a given constellation of institutional and interest formations and public cultures. And yet, statecraft itself cannot be detached from an analytic focus on the role of incentives, which must be effectively manipulated in order to preserve the fundamental functions of the state.

7

Minding the State—Or a State of Mind?
Issues in the Comparative Conceptualization
of the State

BERT A. ROCKMAN

The Resurgent (Yet Possibly Receding) State

It is ironic that just as liberal neoclassical economics has experienced a tremendous resurgence in the 1980s, the concept of the state, also, has ex-

Author's Note: This is a revised paper originally prepared for the Conference on Rolling Back the Frontiers of the State, Research Committee on the Structure and Organization of Government, International Political Science Association, under the auspices of the Institut de Recherches Juridiques Comparatives, Paris, France, October 1-3, 1987. It has benefitted from insights offered by James M. Malloy, Alberta Sbragia, Douglas Ashford, and from the cogent comments of James A. Caporaso. I am grateful, as well, to the University Center for International Studies at the University of Pittsburgh for its support.

perienced a spectacular renewal in its centrality to political theory. While state activities are being trimmed or at least reordered, the state itself has burgeoned as an organizing concept in the analysis of society. "Bringing the state back in" and "state-centered theory" have been the marching themes of scholars seeking to understand the intricate and causally ambiguous connections between public authority and private interest—or, in language more apt to be employed by the aficionados of the concept, the relations between the state and civil society.

In certain of its more concrete aspects, of course, the state never had to be brought back in because, clearly, it never left. Particularly, in the countries of Anglo-American culture and institutional tradition (the so-called stateless societies), the state has been absorbed into other categories of analysis—government, administration, and political (usually party) organization. For a number of reasons, however, in the Anglo societies any broader, abstract, or more encompassing conceptions of the state (putting aside the brief moment of neo-Hegelian thinking that flourished at the end of the nineteenth and the beginning of the twentieth century) have played until recently only a modest role in the development of Anglo-based political theory.

From an intellectual standpoint, the foundations of Anglo political thought have been built on empirical traditions and, later, positivist modes of inquiry that are skeptical of nonoperational abstractions. As well, contractarian assumptions traditionally have dominated Anglo political thinking in regard to the relationship between public and private spheres, and between state authority and society. Even the theorist of Leviathan, Thomas Hobbes, got there by way of contractarian premises. Vesting authority in the Leviathan, to borrow from present language, represented an efficient means by which rational individuals pursuing their self-interest could arrive at a stable equilibrium.

There are, of course, a great many other interesting reasons that the state, as a concept, has played a lesser role in the Anglo political cultures—legal traditions and philosophy, the manner in which authority became consolidated and institutionalized, and so forth. Nonetheless, the theme of bringing the state back in particularly has blossomed in the United States where the prior level of theory (rather limited) was consistent with the profile of the state itself (relatively small).

In general, the themes and methodologies of Anglo-American political analysis have emphasized the demand side of politics and government. For example, during the 1960s when studies of childhood socialization to politics were especially fashionable, theoretical focus was placed on the values of diffuse support and a participative citizenry. Focusing on the balance between support for the system and demands made upon it reduced the state to the famous "black box," which vaguely transformed demands so as to produce a reservoir (or deficit) of political legitimacy (Easton & Dennis, 1969; Hess & Torney, 1967; and Dennis, Lindberg, McCrone, & Stiefbold, 1968). Even when government institutions themselves were the point of analytic focus, this focus was often on the popular legitimacy of government. Thus, Kingsley's book on *Representative Bureaucracy* (1944) emphasizes the importance within a democratic setting of recruiting administrative elites from less restricted social backgrounds.

Ironically, actual studies of American political processes that have been cited as examples of pluralist premises, such as Dahl's study of political leadership in New Haven (1961) or Bauer, Poole, and Dexter's study of interest group pressures on trade policy in Congress (1963), reveal, as in Dahl's study, a relatively powerful role for the political authorities in forging coalitions to support their programs or, as in Bauer, Poole, and Dexter's study (1963), a powerful ability of decision makers to resist strong interest group pressures (see also Nordlinger, 1981). Stephen Krasner's (1978) historical investigation of American foreign policy and business and investment interests also reveals the highly influential role of presidential leadership. Thus, studies of state influence in policy making, even in the American setting, seem to support an important role for the state (at least its leadership) in spite of intellectual premises that frequently envision state action as merely a result of the parallelogram of social forces. Yet at least until now, conceptualizing this influence using the language of the state (rather than political leadership or coalition formation) has been rare.

In part, of course, the state has become an appealing concept because it is now fashionable. But the conceptual attractiveness of the state stems from new concerns as well as a methodological rebellion against positivist premises and the belief that these have spun off only ahistorical contractarian and pluralist theories. Moreover, the literature of "ungovernability" and "overload" (King, 1975; Brittan, 1975; Crozier, Huntington, & Watanuki, 1975) which portrayed a state mired in political debt and overcommitment with diminished steering capacity also laid the basis for rethinking the relationship between the state and social organization.[1] In Britain and America, particularly, thinking about the capacities of the state stems, in significant degree, from this crisis. The state, ironically, has come into intellectual fashion, then, just as its legitimacy and competence have been called into question. In addition, its intellectual ascendance has corresponded to a time of interdependence in which the boundaries of the state, figuratively speaking, have become more permeable (Rosenau, 1988).

State and Society

Much of the contemporary resurgence of the state in political theory obviously is constructed around the connections between the organization of state authority and the organization of society, most especially the organization of collective action—social classes, the organization and mobilization of labor, the organization and mobilization of capital, and other forms of interest expression.

In this regard, Schmitter (1974) points to two strands of corporatist theory in thinking about state-society relations. He distinguishes between state corporatism and societal corporatism. The former emphasizes the creation and manipulation of societal groups from above; that is, through the state apparatus, yet absent total penetration and control. Its roots have been in Latin Europe (especially the Iberian peninsula) and in Latin America. Societal corporatism, alternatively, emphasizes the role of sectorally dominant (essentially noncompetitive) and hierarchically controlled societal groups with whom the state is functionally interdependent. This latter model is recognizable particularly in the context of Nordic Europe. Its key elements have been characterized by Heisler and Kvavik (1974) as the "European Polity" model. In a sentence, state corporatism structures domination (through the state) whereas societal corporatism structures accommodation (between the state and peak associations).

Alfred Stepan (1978) concludes here that corporatism (*organic statism*, in his language) as a construct for defining the relationship between the apparatus of the state and the organization of societal groups falls between a central command (totalitarian) model and a classical liberalism (market) model. This statist version of corporatism (organic statism) has authoritarian or state-directed political elements to it, yet lacks the command features of centralized economic planning—the latter being a form that is presently of declining attraction.

Whatever the state is as a concept, its ascendance has something to do with the fact that a conceptualization that encompasses the government, yet is broader and more abstract than it, is necessary to get at the mediating role of the state in structuring the formation and organization of societal pressures and in providing collective direction for public policy.

Conceptions of the State

Conceptions of the state are both abundant and varied. Their range encompasses very concrete institutional manifestations and highly abstracted normative conceptions of the structure of social relations. Dyson (1980), for example, deals with the state in an almost wholly Idealist fashion as essentially an intellectual tradition that gives meaning to a system of law and to a set of institutions (Kvistad, 1988). Clearly, in Dyson's conception, the concept of the state lends meaning to authority and gives it coherence—that is to say that it provides an underlying normative conception of the relations between authority and civil society. Dyson frames this stance in the following terms:

> The idea of the state stands in complete contrast to the notion of political institutions as neutral "transformatory" structures processing "inputs" (demands and supports) from the system's environment into "outputs" . . . . Such a perspective avoids the character of the ideas embedded in institutions and their influence on conduct. (1980:230)

Lentner, too, directly invokes a conception of the state "as the instrument for preserving the continuity of and formulating and executing community purposes." (1984:370) The state is decidedly not a thing or an actor, but instead a set of instruments with an inherited past. At this juncture, of course, the distinction between state institutions and culture becomes either a seamless web or, less charitably, simply enshrouded in intellectual mist.

At the opposite end of the range in conceptualizing the state is Krasner's (1978) use of the concept to describe the central governmental leadership (the American president and secretary of state) in contrast to both a set of societal interests (business investing interests) and bureaucrats, who, while also empowered by the state, are thought by him only to reflect parochial or subgovernmental bureaucratic interests. Although Krasner later broadens his notions about the state in both an interesting review article (1984) and a theoretical essay (1988), his operative definition of the state as its central leadership in his empirical study stands in startling contrast to the notion held by others that the bureaucratic apparatus of the state embodies its continuity and interests above and beyond the comings and goings of particular regimes.[2] In his earlier study, therefore, Krasner's conception of the state was really a subset of its temporary regime.

One of the difficulties with the state as an organizing concept is that its taxonomic possibilities seem virtually boundless. Different conceptions of the state are useful to shed light on particular theoretical and practical problems, though it is not always completely clear just precisely what comparative advantage the *state* as a concept provides. One problem around which these various conceptions of the state seem to converge, however, is that of state capability. Indeed, the logic of these various conceptions is implicitly that ideas reinforce institutions (Kvistad, 1988; Benjamin & Duvall, 1985)—or, to put it differently, institutional elites generate self-justifying ideologies—and that the nature of this interaction between institutions and ideas can influence the relative balance of policy capacity at any point in time. Who, in other words, is able to decide what for whom?

There are three conceptions of the state that I want to emphasize in the remainder of this paper that I think help address the issue of state capability. These are: (1) the role of the state as an authoritative policy-making system (the decision-making state); (2) the role of the state as a provider of collective and distributional goods (the production state); and (3) the role of the state as a repository, creator, and mediator of societal interests (the intermediary state). There is inherently some spillover in the reality of these state functions. The relationship between the first and third functions of the state is especially notable because the organization of state authority also influences the organization of private interests (Wilson, 1976). And, each of these conceptions, in turn, is related to how it is the state supplies goods—and to whom (Malloy & Parodi, 1988).

The first conception of the state, which Karl Deutsch (1986) calls the enforcement/decision state, has to do with the internal configuration of authority relations between the agents of the state—its decision-making capability. This capability we may think of as the political capability of the state, and it most obviously reflects the formal constitutional order and the organization of institutions and behavior that develops around it. Richard Rose's article (1969), on "The Variability of Party Government," illustrates handsomely how structures for the mobilization of political capacity can differ.

It is often believed, if not necessarily conclusively shown, that the greater the structural unity in the state apparatus for making decisions, the more conclusive such decisions will be for the society. Whether or not this proposition is true is debatable, but its logic is twofold: (1) a unified state purportedly can arrive at decisions more rapidly, and (2) a unified state also will have fewer possibilities for the losers in any given situation to appeal the decision (Rockman, 1988). In this respect, Wilsford (1988) notes that the French state enjoys particular tactical advantages and yet, precisely because opportunities for institutional appeal are limited, disagreement with decisions frequently leads to street protests.

The constituted structures of political authority are a better place to begin than to end, however. For these provide a frame for the exercise of political authority, but the frame itself lacks a dynamic. For as Malloy and Parodi

(1988) aptly point out "One task in the analysis of statecraft is to chart how the capacity moves over time and develop explanations as to how and why it is concentrated or dispersed, where it is lodged, the consequences of particular patterns, etc." (1988:5).

The second conception of the state has to do with its commitments—its scope, functions, size, activities, and the way these are organized. It is precisely this aspect of the state that is at the heart of the belief that the state is receding; that is, the notion that the scope of the state in producing societal goods has reached an upper limit. The issue of the size of the state and the activities it is engaged in is thought to be, in some sense, also related to the scope of the state. Free market liberals, for instance, have seen in the expansion of state production insidious encroachments on the sphere of society by the state. And certainly, states with centrally controlled economies also usually have centrally controlled organizations reputing to speak for a conflictless (and thus libertyless) society. A distinctly alternate perception sees the expansion of state policies as proliferating social organizations, which then create new interdependencies between state and society, and ultimately shift decision capacity from its initial point of origin (Malloy & Parodi, 1988). This particular condition is often characterized as the bloated state—big, but incapable of system-wide direction.

Yet a small state also can be a powerful one if it is able to monopolize the instruments of coercion—not merely legally, but actually. The hangman's noose may be the major production function of a state with few other goods to produce. (One might consider Haiti, for example.) But that is entirely sufficient to make for a powerful state.

The third conception of the state, the intermediary function, defines the bargaining and control milieu for state/society relations. There are interlocking, yet causally ambiguous, linkages between the first two functions of the state and this third one. Only certain arrangements of political authority appear to be compatible with a system-wide organization of societal interests, and, thus, can accommodate system-wide bargaining such as that posed in the model of societal corporatism. These organizational relationships also can influence the character of the state's production functions—how, for example, it is that social policy is organized; what instruments are available for forging "social contracts" and for managing the economy (Katzenstein, 1985; Hall, 1986); or even what incentives exist to oversupply public goods (Niskanen, 1971; Fiorina, 1977). These state/societal relationships can be shaped and sometimes created, in turn, by the production functions of the state, as Theodore Lowi (1972) noted in setting forth his famous typology of policies and politics.

One of the key questions certainly that remains ambiguous is the nature, if any, of the relationship between the internal decision-making configuration of the state and the nature and scope of its impact on society. What is the relationship (if any) between the decisiveness of the state and its authority over society? These relationships are, as mentioned, causally ambiguous and indeterminate. The Pinochet regime in Chile, for instance, brought together for a period a high degree of political repression with a strong emphasis on liberal market economics (Borzutsky, 1983). Obviously, variables exogenous to the state, yet relevant to its functioning are a part of any effort to fully draw links between these various functions of the state. The relative development of organized interests in society, the culture and style of the political class, and the dependence on international capital and economic conditions are necessary elements of the total picture. Yet, adding them also blurs further any theoretical, generalizable, and determinate links that can be made between the decision-making, production, and intermediating functions of the state.

In the pages that follow, I explore some of the aspects of each functional dimension of the state, and raise some issues pertaining to their linkage. A theoretical specification of these linkages, while beyond my ken here, obviously is a goal worth striving for. It is by no means clear, however, that we have even a firm descriptive grasp on the range of elements within each dimension.

The Decision-Making State

How diffuse or concentrated is the decision-making capability of the state? This is an important question (at least constitution makers think so), but it is not equivalent to asking what is the power of the state to mold society, or even how large and varied is the state's production function? Obviously, in the extreme ranges, a state in which power is very concentrated (Stalinism, for instance) will have great impact over society if in no other way than in its repressive functions. Alternatively, a state in which the power to decide is rampantly diffused risks the prospect of stalemate and anarchy. Raymond Aron (1950:143) observed that unity in the rulership of the state created large dangers to the maintenance of civil freedom, whereas the absence of such unity brought risks to the maintenance of the state itself.

While the relative scope and penetration of the state into society and its ability to resist particular types of societal pressures may be connected to the political or decision-making capacities of the state, the issue here is how clearly can power be mobilized within government? What, in other words, are the relevant relations between the constituted agents of the state?

From a formal standpoint, two obvious dimensions define relationships between agents of the state. The first is the territorial or spatial dimension of power resources; the second is the interinstitutional and intrainstitutional organization of power. The most obvious way of thinking about the vertical arrangement of power is the federalism/unitary state distinction. In theory, the former creates diversity while the latter imposes uniformity. Certainly, the potential for different units of government to be operating at cross-purposes is considerably greater under federal than unitary systems.

In the first years of the Reagan administration in the U.S., for instance, it busily cut taxes and social programs administered by the Federal government. The tax cuts, in part, were done for macroeconomic reasons (so-called supply-side economics) but also because of Reagan's belief that the extractive arm of government should be lessened at all levels. Many states, in fact, faced dramatic cuts in programs maintained by Federal assistance, and, in the face of this, raised taxes. Unfortunately, there is no clear evidence on the macroeconomic effects of these counteractions for the supply-side strategy of freeing capital from the grasp of government, but it is clear that the President's ideological objectives of reducing government at all levels were not completely satisfied.

By way of contrast, in the British unitary state the Thatcher government has reached down into local government to uproot councils whose behavior struck the Prime Minister as unruly, frivolous and radical (Jones, 1988).

Although Sbragia's study of policy entrepreneurship in Milan (1979) and Milch's (1974) in two French cities also reveal that local leadership can operate around the constraints of the unitary state, overall, the legal structure of the unitary state dampens tendencies toward political (and policy) diffusion. Thus, despite the mediating role given to the Bonn government to provide for greater equalization of resources in the German Federal Republic, the relative independence of the *Laender* under a federal structure and their direct representation in the *Bundesrat* make for somewhat greater tendencies for diffusion than in unitary states—though, obviously less than in the two North American federal states (excluding Mexico).

Insofar as the resources commanded by the central government are concerned, Rose (1984a) demonstrates that ten European unitary states average approximately 85% of the total tax take at the center, whereas three federal states for which he has data (West Germany, the United States, and Switzerland) average only 66%. Income, and the ability to raise it, of course, represent political leverage, but this does not mean that regional or local officials in countries with federal systems are resistant to generating pressures for subsidies of various sorts from the center. At least in the American budgetary context in the 1980s, though, after a meteoric rise through the earlier decade, federal subsidies to other levels of government have become a declining component of Federal government expenditure. The ten unitary states, however, are themselves markedly varied in the extent to which financial resources are concentrated at the center. These range from a low of about 69% in Sweden to highs of about 99% in Italy and the Netherlands, which, in the latter case, is governed in Parliament through a national at-large system of representation.

At face value, the mechanisms for concerted action are assuredly weaker in federal than in unitary systems, and they are especially so in the American system of federalism where the American constitution provides for all nonspecified powers to reside at the state level (the so-called Doctrine of Residual Powers). The great growth in public employment in the United States also throughout recent decades has been at the state and local levels rather than the Federal government. Peters (1985) shows, for example, that during a 30-year period (1952-82), the percentage of government employees at the Federal level dropped from 57% of the total in 1952 to a mere 24% in 1982. Some of this decrease at the Federal level is reflected in the conversion of a previously direct and labor intensive function (postal services) to a public corporation.

Ultimately, though, the key resource commanded by the center is much less its percentage of state employment or even its percentage of the total tax take (though the latter is not to be discounted) than it is the ability to make national policy. There is no doubt that this has something to do with the leverage that local or regional governments can exert, and, also with the institutions at the national level through which interests are articulated.

Whatever else can be said about the state, it is clear that it is not a unified entity (Allison, 1969). Even when all or the bulk of policy capacity is lodged in instrumentalities of the state, such capacity may be dispersed among its various instrumentalities in such a way as to checkmate decisional power (Malloy & Parodi, 1988). The state, in other words, almost never is a coherent and encompassing unit of action. Instead, the governing bodies and authorities of the state represent a number of units of action—their relative autonomy or interdependence or dependence being shaped by constitutional law. Yet, actual behavior in the struggle between units of government to gain needed resources or fair share allotments, or simply to acquire freedom of action often rests upon factors outside of the purely legal domain, for example, elite networks, salient constituencies or interest organizations, entrepreneurial skills, and the principal values of the political culture.[3]

Within the central level of government as well, constituted relations between offices also shape the extent to which power within government can be relatively unified. Even here, of course, these constituted relations are forcefully influenced by the rise of extraconstitutional institutions. Parliamentary supremacy in Britain, in reality, now means party supremacy and that, in turn, therefore, has come to mean the supremacy of the reigning government. When combined with a party system that normally produces a majority result, this concentrates pure political power greatly, though that power mostly exists in the form of potential energy. In brief, the power to expedite authoritative decisions of government is remarkably strong in Britain—putting off to one side, of course, issues raised by the civil service in implementing those decisions and in following through. The British political system, however, unlike that of, say, France or Japan or, from a different perspective, the United States, is remarkably self-contained. Both British politicians and civil servants live in a rather more enclosed world than their counterparts in these other settings. Their environment also is one that probably is more obsessed with secrecy than is any other political democracy. The dependence of political leaders upon civil servants who, themselves, have limited exposure to other spheres and channels of activity means, as Peter Hall (1986) puts it, that "power is concentrated in the hands of those with the greatest interest in longstanding approaches to policy" (1986:62).

In these respects, it appears to be the case that the government of the British state has great decision-making or political capacity, yet relatively modest steering or guidance capacity toward society overall. Writing, for example, in the context of environmental and industrial regulatory policies in Britain, David Vogel (1986) observes that "The government is unable to implement policies in either area without securing the consent and cooperation of the companies affected by their decisions" (1986:284). In other words, while central authority in British government "is more powerful than that of any other democracy . . ., the relative power of the British state vis-à-vis British society is sharply limited" (1986:287).

The American system of dispersing political authority is nearly at the other extreme to the British case. The American system is purposefully designed as a form of government to be in perpetual conflict with itself. The design of American political structure is to inhibit the possibilities for decision making in the absence of transinstitutional agreements. The nature of British political organization, alternatively, reinforces centrism. American political organization, however, has made authority even more diffuse in the United States. Lowi points out that American political parties represent a case of incomplete development; their prime organizational moment (outside of the legislative body) came in the latter part of the nineteenth and early twentieth centuries when American politics was denationalized and the influx of new populations into urban centers made the party organizations into little more than effective patronage dispensing machines. Thus, American political organization traditionally has catered to the already ample centrifugal tendencies of American government. Over the years, these tendencies changed from local and often corrupt mechanisms of political control to providing virtually no mechanisms for such control. The advent of mass political processes in the selection of a party's candidates to stand for office has produced an especially individualistic form of politics. This often exacerbates the problem of decision making in American government, by promoting the independence of officeholders, and makes resisting constituent and group pressures on the part of officeholders particularly difficult.

This view of the American state as lacking an authoritative center is one of the reasons that it is referred to as a *weak state* (Krasner, 1978; Nordlinger, 1981). The wide dispersion of authority also is thought to make it easier for private interests to colonize sectors of the state (McConnell, 1967; Lowi, 1979). In Richard Rose's (1980) phrase, in Europe there are governments, while in the United States there are subgovernments.

In this regard, the national legislative body because of its district winner-take-all elections and its weak party organization represents local constituencies particularly well but often is unable to aggregate effectively these interests to a broader arena for bargaining or national policy determination (Huntington, 1965; Fenno, 1978). Similarly, the bureaucracy, because it too is pulled partly toward Congress and not exclusively toward the Executive, is often viewed as a functionally parochial resister to decision-making clarity (Aberbach & Rockman, 1977). Because of this level of disaggregation, it is not surprising that Krasner (1978) falls into equating the will of the president with the identity of the state. Indeed, of late, American presidents also have fallen into this habit.

The centrifugal combination of vertical decentralization and horizontal noncentralization makes government in the United States peculiarly sensitive to momentary rushes of popular sentiment. Christopher Leman (1980) shows that in the Canadian federal system popular backlashes to social welfare spending were unable to influence public policy as deeply as in the United States. Leman suggests that the reasons for the relatively greater insulation of the authorities in Canada had to do with, first, the relative concentration of authority within each of the Canadian provinces where party-cabinet government prevailed and, also, the existence of linking mechanisms between bureaucrats at the provincial and Federal levels of government. In the United States, on the other hand, popular sparks of resentment could catch somewhere in a system in which at each level of government the power to create agendas was far more dispersed and where vertical networks between state and Federal bureaucrats were more loosely connected.

Only a part of the story of decision-making capability, however, can be rendered through the formal arrangements of majoritarian (or for that matter, authoritarian) governments. Thus, it is possible for "strong states to make weak policies and for weak states to make strong policies"—the notion that broader agreements provide the basis for effective policy. Authoritative decisional capability, in fact, may reduce the need to test and learn about policies being adopted or to subject policy ideas to the review of policy networks inside and outside of government. Policies may be produced without necessarily having had to be forged through a substantive intellectual and political consensus. Thus, it is conceivable that where decision-making networks are more complex, where external interests more intrusively invade government, and where agreements have to be forged to carry out policy decisions, the results may have broader support and will ultimately prove to be less contentious.

This kind of analysis suggests that beyond very broad categories of governmental and political structure, we need to know a great deal more about political style and culture and the organization of society (the intermediary state). Sweden, after all, has centralized structures but policy making has generally avoided strict majoritarian formulas. Its centralization enables bargains to be reached or accommodated in ways that are hard to imagine, for instance, in the United States. The structure of American government (all other things aside) clearly sets limits to what is possible here. But British government is not so limited structurally. Rather, its limitations derive, in comparison to Sweden, for instance, from political culture, and the organization of the society it governs. These differences are exemplified in the role of adversarial parties and majoritarianism in the British case in contrast to the accommodationist and syndicating style of Swedish decision making, in the structure of social aggregates with which the state authorities deal and the accustomed pattern of these relations, and, also, in the instruments available to the state (which ironically are extensively a function of social organization) for influencing social outcomes.

In other words, the structure of decision making is itself only partly revealed by institutional frameworks. The problem is akin to inferring physiology from anatomy. Even within this limitation, the structure of relations between the agents of the state are as much influenced by the organization of informal organizations (such as parties) that have wrapped themselves around the state as they are a product of the formally constituted structures. The joint effect of both formal and informal organizational structures still does not explain many of the important ways in which the state connects to society. The sociocultural elements of politics, the implicit and tacit understandings that permeate its operations, as well as the historical development of social organization are essential ingredients for comprehending the forms this connection takes. Yet, a theory of incentives also is necessary for understanding the strategic choices that are available in these relations.

The Production State

One of the major themes about the state emanating particularly from the literature of the 1970s and early 1980s is that of the *overburdened state*. Following upon the great prosperity of the 1960s in Western Europe and the expansion of programs and public expenditure commitments made then, the economic stagflation that arose by the end of the 1970s coincided with a realization that an ever more vast set of spending pressures on governments would be created by the logic of these expanded commitments and of the demographic tendencies spurring the demand for pensions and medical care.

Three sets of explanations for this alleged overburden can be readily identified. Behind at least two of them is the idea that the state oversupplies public goods because of systematic biases in the way in which demands for these goods are represented in the polity.

At the most microcosmic level Niskanen's effort (1971) to apply the theory of the firm to the bureau stipulates that public goods are oversupplied because both their supply and the demand for them are monopolized. This monopoly conceals a true aggregate demand function that, if known, would constrain supply. Thus, a noncompetitive bureau has incentives to maximize its budget resources, and clientele groups with intense preferences for the goods the bureau supplies demand their production while diverting their cost onto the general public. If the political representation of demands were as unbiased as the channeling of demands through a competitive market, supply inevitably would be more constrained because the true costs of the good would have to be met by each taxpayer relative to the taxpayer's demand for the good. Governments, in short, are profligate precisely because, in the Weberian sense, the state monopolizes the production of certain goods. Inevitably, in this formulation, governments will overspend and overtax until market constraints are imposed.

Implicit also in Niskanen's theory is the notion that the demand function is distorted because the state is colonized by special interest groups, each of whom claims a special parcel of state authority. Also employing the analytic tools of microeconomic theory. Mancur Olson extended his earlier theory of incentives for interest group behavior presented in *The Logic of Collective Action* (1968) to the level of the macroeconomic fate of nations in his book, *The Rise and Decline of Nations* (1982). Olson's theory is disarmingly simple, and, as we shall later note, he comes at least to a partial recognition of that. Essentially, Olson's theory is that the older and more continuous the political structure of democracy, the more established the interest group linkages are, and, thus, the more intense are the biases toward inefficiencies and subsidies. The relatively high productivity of the Japanese and German economies is, therefore, explainable mainly from the postwar reorganization of the political system, rather than as merely a consequence of the wartime destruction of the productive infrastructure. In this conception, the new or reconstructed political order has yet to suffer the fate of interest group colonization, which seems, however, to be an outcome of the more continuous political orders.

A rather different kind of argument, represented in the early literature on "overload,' emphasized the declining capabilities for governance as more and more interests acquired a stake in public policy. Whereas the theory of oversupply emphasizes the symbiotic relationship (stemming from matched incentives) between subgovernmental elites and interest group elites, the syndrome of "overload" explanations stresses the role of public demand. To put it in slightly different language, *oversupply* is a supply-side argument, whereas *overload* is a demand-side argument. The logic of demand-side politics, in this view, stemmed from an apparently insatiable appetite for the supply of public goods that would outstrip the capacity of governments to generate policies with short-term costs. Much (though by no means all) of this literature is British-based (King, 1975; Brittan, 1975) as it was the British economy that seemed most under siege during this period. During a period of sluggish economic growth, of course, even relatively incremental increases in the absolute growth of public expenditure will usually produce a greater increase in the proportion of GNP devoted to public sector expenditures (Cameron, 1978). The denominator (GNP) is more apt to fluctuate, in other words, than the numerator (public expenditure).

In any event, the clear supposition behind this literature and the concern it expresses for the legitimacy of public authority is that more demands are being put on government than governments can deliver. Given the constraints of democratic politics, more expenditure demands are made on government than governments are willing to pay for. This is presumably because citizens are tax minimizers and politicians are vote maximizers.

Yet a third emphasis on the "overburdened state," though not necessarily inconsistent with the other two, focuses on the steady accretion of past commitments as being chiefly responsible for the growth in public expenditure (Rose & Peters, 1978; Rose, 1984b). The truly large and accumulating expenditures with nearly untouchable political status are principally the consequence of relatively early commitments to social welfare, such as pensions and medical care which, however, also were adjusted upward through the 1970s. Left undisturbed, the inertial effects of these commitments produce what Rose and Peters (1979) call *the juggernaut of incrementalism.*

The consequences of all of these notions about the overburdened state is that in the end the oversupply of public goods and the undersupply of public authority and state capacity will lead either to an erosion in standards of living and, hence, a crisis of legitimacy or, in the shorter term, a crisis of capital accumulation (O'Connor, 1973). Depending upon how indebtedness is financed, the state may be rendered increasingly vulnerable to international capital flows or, at considerable political cost, must impose policies of domestic austerity.

These conceptions of the overburdened state, however differently conceived, give little emphasis or even possibility to the role of political leadership and the active role of statecraft in rearranging priorities. In the United States, for example, growth in the rate of increase in domestic expenditure had peaked by the mid-1970s, and by the end of the Carter presidency, growth in domestic expenditures had come to a virtual halt, averaging only about ¼ of 1% a year (Aberbach & Rockman, 1985). Spearheaded by the new market-oriented regimes in Britain and the U.S., governments also moved to privatize state assets. Additionally, caps have been imposed on such highly popular programs as health care resulting both in some decrease of supply and increased absolute costs. In short, the 1980s has been the decade for thinking about rolling back the state. In actual fact, the rolling back usually has been more of a redistribution to the extent that it has occurred (Campbell, 1985). Particularly in the U.S. and Britain, the conservative regimes of Reagan and Thatcher have re-sorted the bundle of expenditures in ways more favorable to their ideas of what the principal responsibilities of government should be. Yet, this revision itself potentially testifies to the imapct of statecraft on expectations (Wildavsky, 1988; Clarke, Stewart, & Zuk, 1988). These expectations affect the tide and character of expenditure dynamics, and as Christopher Hood's (1988) analysis of cutbacks of the state in Britain and Australia shows, where cuts are levied is not simply a product of immutable forces.

A further conception of the production function of the state, emphasizing the role of statecraft, is that of the *expert state*. Expertise presumably is agnostic about ideological presuppositions. It may be interventionist or market focused, but state guidance on the part of a technocratic elite with accessibility to political and economic power is the essential characteristic of the expert state. The administrative elites in France (Suleiman, 1974; 1978), Japan (Johnson, 1975; 1982), and Sweden (Anton, Linde, & Melbourn, 1973), among others, are reputed to be a strategically located elite of this sort.

In this regard, Birnbaum (1982) notes that the logic of the state lies in the institutionalization of its administration, and, therefore, in the ability of the administration "to elaborate national policy by itself, without interference from either elected representatives or interest groups (Birnbaum, 1982: 142)." Thus, it is the administration of the state as an institution, rather than as an actor, that is crucial to conceptualizing the functional autonomy of the state. In the case of France, in particular, Birnbaum (1982:129-130) concludes that Gaullist interventionism simultaneously strengthened the independence and unity of the state, while it laid the basis for a collaboration with key industrial interests by also unifying them. Technocratic guidance under Giscardism, however, was transformed from planning and interventionism to the approach of liberal market economics. The latter, of course, meant also the solidification of large industrial and financial organization. The political-sociological implication of the liberal economic course, according to Birnbaum (1982:125-137), is the creation of a state-centered elite of bureaucrats, management experts, business elites and economists with pervasive penetration over a more large-scale and centrally organized political, economic, and administrative sphere. Technocratic domination and centralized administration, thus, can coexist with liberal economic policies. Yet, in this process of the joint solidification and centralization of society and state, the mutual absorption of leading personnel from the organizations of one to the other diminishes the independence of the state from society.

Indeed, this argument has been made by scholars of Latin American developments—the growth of a centralizing technocratic elite that helps to consolidate and to unify policy and, therefore, also to consolidate and unify domination through a strategic elite (Malloy & Borzutsky, 1984). Studies of the development of social security policy in Brazil and other Latin American countries, for example, strongly hint at the utility of developing centralized and uniform policy administration as a means of weakening traditional social aggregates that had controlled the administration of more segmented and sectorized social security systems (Malloy, 1979, 1984). Looked at in this fashion, technocratic guidance and rationalization also provide justification for delegitimizing interest-based politics and, indeed, delegitimizing politics itself. This claim, ironically, also was voiced in the United States by critics of the introduction of centralizing technocratic analytic instruments of administration such as PPBS (Program, Planning, Budgeting System), which were introduced briefly in the middle 1960s in the U.S. Federal government (Wildavsky, 1966, 1969).

A further conception of the production state that seems to be increasingly pertinent (and, to some extent, also connected to a particular mode of technocratic guidance) is the *financial control state*. Current tendencies among large business firms have been to move financial managers increasingly into the top positions. In some respects, the finance ministries and their equivalents have always held similarly hallowed positions within their governments. But the present emphasis on retrenchment, of course, greatly strengthens the role of the financial minister. Accordingly, the production link to society is being relatively deemphasized while the management of finances is being upgraded. This development gives rise to Cassese's argument (1986) that the state is no longer a viable concept for normative or analytic purposes because it has ceased to represent a unified conception, other than in its financial control aspect. This financial control function is, in Cassese's view, a wholly secondary element of the state, but it alone now constitutes the center and central purpose of the state.[4] In Cassese's view:

> For a long time the financial aspect of the state has been regarded as of secondary importance because it was held to be merely instrumental to the purposes of government. When government bodies have too many purposes, financing becomes important. If it is the laws that distribute areas of competence, it is the budgets that distribute powers. . . .
> In this way, financing takes on a dominant role, to the point at which government bodies are ruled by financing. This permits the reduction of all the

disparate government tasks to a common denominator, their monetary value. . . .

All this revitalizes the center, but not the state, because it turns to the advantage of only one part of it, the administration of finance, and to the detriment of those government bodies that up till now had held the reins (1986:127).

This struggle between the convoluted organization of the production functions of the state and its financial management is frequently defined in terms of a struggle between the whole and the parts of government. Increasingly, in times of fiscal stress (which are most times), the political leadership at the center identifies with the finance officer rather than the production line, whereas the political constituencies upon whom the central leadership depends identify with the production functions rather than their financial management. Cassese's analysis, thereby, reflects in some ways arguments put forth by Tarschys (1985) and by Aberbach and Rockman (1988, 1989) that the financial control function forces a rearrangement of roles and of relations between agents of the state—that is, it enhances centrism. Yet, centrism, by itself, as we discussed in the preceding section, does not necessarily fit a conception of the state as an institutionalized orchestrator of society.[5]

The irony here is that the greater the expanse of state functions, the greater the sprawl of its administrative apparatus, thus, the greater its proliferation of societal constituents, and the less able the state is to impose (except through financial management) a unified course or vision. An intriguing implication of this is that the state can retain such a unity only when its functions are relatively limited to the production of collective goods. If that is the case, then the irony is complete. For then, the real state-builders appear to be named Thatcher and Reagan each of whom, but especially Thatcher, is devoted to a leaner, yet morally purposeful state.

The Intermediary State

The major focus of state-centered theory lies in the relationship between the organizations and institutions of the state and those of society. The prevailing supposition of state-centered theory is that state organization influences the aggregation of social interests.

These relationships, however, Peter Hall (1986) and Esping-Andersen (1985) point out, are not static. When existing equilibria become unsatisfactory, the regime will seek to manipulate or counter the organization of relevant social aggregates. For example, the Reagan administration in 1981 successfully altered funding formulas of health and other assistance programs so as to decentralize the discretion for decision making. One key objective was to dissipate the influence of the interests who were organized around the existing administration of these programs.

Yet, the organization of social aggregates (especially as peak organizations) also is held together by some pattern of marginal benefit to the members. When such benefits decline, the stability of existing organization also comes under pressure. Thus, there is a dual dynamic—an internal organizational one, and one that exists between the organization of the state and the social aggregates.

What instruments are available to whom in this interaction is, however, the interesting question. As ideal types, Stepan (1978) draws sharply the conceptions of "command socialism" under which the state dominates both the economy and the organization of society and that of classical liberalism under which a market economy exists and the state, more or less, is merely an impartial equilibrator of social conflicts. In ideal form, then, under the command socialism model no independent social organization exists, whereas under classical liberalism the only independent function of the state is the impartial umpiring of social interests. Obviously, no such societies or states exist anywhere. Increasingly, in the command economy states, market modes are assuming greater importance, and in some there also are independent social organizations (the Catholic Church in Poland, for example). Similarly, the state is nowhere simply a passive repository of social demands nor merely their impartial arbitrator.

Rather, the modern state through its empowered agents is a player. And when it has internal unity, it has the potential to be the most powerful player. The instruments possessed by the state to steer society, however, differ across societies. The societal corporatist pattern, for example, is based on a framework of encompassing (or peak) groups with a stake in system-wide outcomes. This framework presumably makes for a bargaining game that is relatively more simplified and manageable for steering policy change.

These patterns, also, may not be constant over time. Disequilibrating pressures brought on by exogenous influences and events, most especially events in the international economy, are often present. Such pressures can lead to diverse outcomes, however—ones that, *inter alia*, lead to the destabilization of existing social aggregates, or ones that lead to greater concentrations of coercive state control, or ones that lead to greater concentrations of state sanctioned social power. In regard to the latter, the relative eclipse of American finance capital, for example, has led to proposals by the present Chairman of the Federal Reserve Board in the United States, Alan Greenspan, to allow the creation of massive concentrations of capital in American banks through deregulation of the banking system (meaning, of course, the elimination of many smaller banks). Such a proposal, as Skocpol's analysis (1980) of the failure of the National Recovery Administration to influence industrial organization in the 1930s suggests, probably tests the capacities of the American state to reconstruct the organization of finance capital.[6]

The link between state authority and social fabric, however, is frequently so tightly woven that it is difficult to extricate clear causal patterns. Indeed, the weave more nearly has the quality of a seamless web. The problem, as Peter Hall correctly argues, is that:

> The capacities of the state to implement a program tend to depend as much on the configuration of the society as of the state. . . . The state appears as a network of institutions, deeply embedded within a constellation of ancillary institutions associated with society and the economic system (1986:17).

It is certainly true, of course, that the configuration between state institutions and social organization helps determine the capabilities of the former and the methods of influence deployed by the latter. In this regard, Mancur Olson's analysis (1968) of the incentives for collective action emphasizes the redistributional benefits (in relation to costs) of narrowly organized and essentially single interest modes of organization. Such forms of organization are believed to hold maximum marginal benefits for the individual members of the groups, thus, enhancing the ability of such groups to obtain collective benefits through the mobilization of their membership. The second part of Olson's theory, which focuses on the redistributional payoff accruing to the group, emphasizes the relationship between narrowness of organizational purpose and influence over government. Such a mode of organization is particularly notable in the United States because of the fact that it provides a sensible fit to a state in which there are many pockets of political authority and where each may have a significant hold on a specific sector of policy.

Olson's theory also fits other types of redistributional coalitions such as parliaments in which at-large pure proportional representation systems produce a large number of parties (for instance, the Netherlands and Israel) and, thus, give vastly disproportionate benefits to the smallest but most pivotal members of a governing coalition. The general point, however, is clear and that is that from Olson's point of view, institutions do structure incentives, and institutions that stimulate groups to seek narrow redistributional benefits (because there is no advantage to not doing so) certainly will have great difficulty aggregating bargains to a system-wide level.

Olson attempts to salvage his theory of incentives by taking into consideration the encompassing forms of social organization prevalent in the societal corporate states of Europe. Olson's argument here (1986) is that encompassing groups, by reaping a larger share of the gain to society and also suffering a larger share of the loss, thus have a larger stake in the aggregate outcome to society. Because of this, Olson argues (1986:176-180) that encompassing and unified business and labor organizations have a large incentive to continue bargaining in order to achieve joint gains by maximizing output rather than, for example, passing on costs. However, internal contradictions, such as the potential for uneven distribution of marginal benefits within large social aggregates by industry, by class, or by blue-collar vs. white-collar work force pose the potential for disrupting this positive-sum equilibrium. As Esping-Andersen has said in respect to Scandinavia, "It seems quite inconceivable that all wage-earner strata are moving in the direction of a massive convergence of interests" (1985:322).

The shape of the state and its mechanisms for decision making clearly influence the structure and organization of societal interests. Not surprisingly, the American system which is predicated on the individualistic and institutionalized notion of countering ambition with ambition makes it difficult to organize cooperation system-wide and, thus, ultimately makes it easier to develop narrow distributional coalitions. These subgovernmental coalitions both reinforce the problem of aggregating decisions while potentially increasing the aggregative costs for the society of indecision.

To the extent that the central leadership of the state is able to shape the bargaining game, its interests lie in depoliticizing it. One of the elements of that strategy is the creation of large aggregates to displace a larger number of smaller ones so as to absorb parochial and less manageable interests into larger and presumably more manageable national ones. The latter condition conduces to providing the state leadership with more tools for the management of the economy and public finance. When, however, the institutions of the state and the organization of society are noncentralized and relatively mature (as in the United States), the prospects for producing this level of aggregation are highly improbable.

While under state corporatist conditions the penetration and organization of the state and society are only partial and heavily focused in urban areas, movement toward centralization and uniformity of social policy provides a means of eclipsing the sectoral modes of organization on which earlier and segmented policies were initially based. In addition, liberal economic policies can serve to eclipse smaller producers, thus concentrating industrial capital in a way that may be relatively more manageable for the state. From this perspective (as Greenspan's proposal, referred to earlier, suggests), the centralization of capital and the weakening of peripheral and sectoral interests rationalizes state functions and social organization.

Under societal corporatist conditions, finally, there are continuous pressures for the decomposition of encompassing interests as the distribution of benefits is altered and identifiable winners and losers appear. Thus, while the relationship between state organization and societal organization is vital in determining what tools the state has for steering, it is equally the case that the perceived successes or failures of the state in steering also influence the tools that it will possess in the future.

Conclusion

The state is a concept that is simultaneously alluring and protean. Part of its allure apparently rests on its protean character—the ability to be molded into whatever shape the analyst finds useful. Of the various ways in which the state can be conceptualized, I have focused in this paper on three: (1) the decision-making state; (2) the production state; and (3) the intermediary state. These conceptualizations of the state are all relevant to the even broader, if highly ambiguous, notion of state capacity.

Characterizing the state as a decisional entity helps us to focus on the bargaining (and command) relationships that exist among its officers. It helps to define the terms of the "game" that the agents of the state play. Whether the apparatus of the state has a center or not can suggest to us how complicated these bargains may be. They do not necessarily tell us how the state may influence society, but they may tell us how society organizes to try to influence the state.

Describing the state in the context of its production functions helps us to focus on its assets and liabilities and problems of liquidity. It also can lead us to focus on how these production functions are organized so as to enable a clearer understanding of the state as both decisional entity and as intermediary with society. The organization of these production functions, in fact, is very much linked to the decisional structure of the state and the organization of society. Rationalization of the production function typically is associated with centristic control which clearly represents a vital means of building state authority. Today, the financial management function seems to be ascendant, and its rationalization dictates both growing centrism within the state apparatus and growing insulation from demand-oriented societal groups.

Finally, analysis of the intermediary functions of the state necessarily leads us to focus on the organization of society and the opportunities thus given to state authorities to steer society. It is helpful to look at these relations in the form of a dynamic equilibrium. Thus, we need to know the terms of the "game" played between the state authorities and significant social aggregates. These, in turn, also help us to understand how some state actors must interact with others—for example, whether or not, and to what extent, public investment is dependent on private financial markets (Sbragia, 1986).

Overall, the state lacks uniqueness as a concept because it assumes so many definitions. It lacks, therefore, a universalized specificity of meaning. Rather, its meaning and utility appear to derive from different cultural, political, and developmental traditions. Particularly in Latin traditions, the state takes on the Hegelian conception of being the highest expression of the community over whom its authority is exercised. In theory, if not reality, this provides the logic for the so-called autonomous state, which expresses a unity that is greater than the sum of the constituent parts of the society it governs.

But this conception of the state, in spite of realities that often are in accord with it—the right of eminent domain, for instance—does not resonate in the Anglo cultures where historical developments limited the powers of rulership and stressed the separateness of society from the state.

A third conception, however, which has tended to characterize Nordic societies has stressed the organizational principles of society in the form of corporate aggregates, the influence of these aggregates over certain functions of the state, and also their cooptation into the state. The stark distinction of public vs. private that characterizes the Anglo cultures is not sharply drawn in notions of societal corporatism.

Cultural myths, of course, remain powerful even after the realities they purport to justify have been greatly altered. This is both the advantage and disadvantage of focusing on ideas or cultural mythologies of the state. The disadvantage is clear: the reality often is at odds with the mythology and when that occurs we may fail to see exactly how and why this disparity came into being. The problem with culture as an exclusive focus is that it implies a static equilibrium, and so a theory to explain disparities between realities and powerful myths is lacking. Alternatively, the advantage of focusing on myth is that ideas constitute a set of expectations that impose limits not only upon what the state should do but also essentially how it should do it (King, 1973; Sharpe, 1973; Wildavsky, 1985).

The trouble is that while ideas count, so also, and very importantly, do institutions and interests. Explaining, for example, why Mr. Greenspan's aforementioned ideas about the need to concentrate finance capital through the deregulation of the banking industry in the United States likely will fail makes use of all of these conceptions—ideas, interests, and institutions. Americans have been notoriously opposed to concentrations of either governmental or market power (though dominant views vary from time to time). Small bankers are important elites in their local communities and are thought to take a special influence in local development. Thus, they are apt to wield considerable influence especially by mobilizing other local business and political interests through Congress, a powerfully representative (and politically powerful) institution that is especially sensitized to the representation of local interests. Could we have done this analysis without use of the concept of the state? Surely I think so because obviously we just did.

If that is the case, then of what utility is the state as a concept? Because there are so many traditions, no single conception will be universally satisfactory, which is why, in David Easton's view (1981), the concept is rendered useless. In this regard, I have not even made mention of the vast and highly varied neo-Marxist literature on the state, much of which is maddeningly obscurantist and reductionist—even while focused on questions that are considerably better than the analysis it provides.

My own view as to why the state has been theoretically resurgent (even as it has in certain regards mildly receded) is that it brings together the most important macrolevel connections of the polity, the society, and the economy, which cannot be adequately analyzed in isolation from one another. The monopoly of legal authority gives the state (and statesmen) the responsibility for the maintenance of social peace and the production of collective goods. These, of course, may be operationalized in wildly different ways—the peace may be kept by the policeman's truncheon or it may be kept through the so-called social contract. The peace may be seen by Marxists as a means for the maintenance of a dominant (if not always ruling) class. Or it may be seen by social integration theorists, such as Talcott Parsons, as the most extraordinary outcome of complex social processes.

The state, above all, provides a means for the study of statecraft within a given constellation of institutional and interest formations and public cultures. Statecraft, in this conception, is more than the leadership of single individuals. It does and certainly must focus attention on the means of building political support within the state apparatus itself (the decision-making state), but it also must focus on the manipulations between the state (and its internal elements) and social aggregates (the intermediating state). Above all, it seems to me that a theory of the state also must provide for a dynamic—that is, a theory of equilibrium and disequilibrium. Ironically, both Marxists and the neoliberal market theorists share, at one level, similar theoretical premises about the internal contradictions of the capitalist-welfare state: the problem of its liquidity and its legitimation.

Of course, as Krasner (1988) properly points out, the state is not merely an arena through which strategic interactions take place. Its structural institutional characteristics and their normative overlay are not easily disturbed. Institutionalization and, above all, normative assimilation powerfully increase the transaction costs associated with change (Krasner, 1988; Rockman, 1984; Kumar, 1988). The sheer power of these forces increases the risks attached to seeking change; they also weaken the prospect that other possibilities will even be recognized, much less acted upon. To use rather different conceptual language, they inhibit search. Yet, change does occur, but, unlike Krasner, I find it difficult to account for that in the absence of a theory of incentives. For despite the vast gulf that separates macrolevel contemporary theories of the state from the long (and revived) tradition of rational choice deriving from Hobbes, the latter remains central to a consideration of available strategies—those within the ambit of the agents of state authority as well as to those acting in the name of social associations.

Within the context, then, of a theoretical dynamic that provides for an inner logic of change, statecraft is vital. The role of statecraft is to manipulate the equilibrium to ensure (for a time) a favorable balance on behalf of the fundamental functions of the state. To achieve this, bargains are made with elements of civil society. From the perspective of the steering capacity of the state, some of these bargains are Machiavellian; others, it is later discovered, are Faustian.

Notes

1. For an analysis of much of this literature, see Birch (1984).
2. See Birnbaum (1982). His argument can be expressed thusly:

Under the Fifth Republic . . . senior civil servants took control of the executive and abandoned parliament to the professional politicians, who thereafter tended to express not national but local interests, while the executive took charge of the regulation of the social system. The partial unification of the executive and the bureaucracy . . . gave rise once again to a claim to independence on the part of the state. (1982:139).

3. The importance of elite networks is illustrated nicely in Sbragia's (1979) work on Milanese housing policy. For the relevance of entrepreneurship in leadership, see Putnam, Leonardi,

Nanetti, and Pavoncello (1983). In regard to the nonadversarial values associated
life in Sweden and Japan, for example, see Anton (1980), Kelman (1981), and Campl.
In both settings (Sweden and Japan), the main problem to be resolved before any o
be is that of politics, defined in terms of the resolution of interpersonal relations.

4. For a contrasting view that asks us to think about government chiefly as a financial institution, see Sbragia (1986).

5. Thus, Badie and Birnbaum (1983) distinguish between the gravitational pull of a strong
center to the political system and the institutionalization of the state itself. It is possible for
there to be a strong center (our first conception of the state) but a weak orchestrating capacity
vis-à-vis society (our third conception of the state).

6. For the impact of state institutions in transforming (expanding and limiting) policy ideas,
see Weir and Skocpol (1985). My reading of their analysis, however, is that, whether in-
advertently or not, their interpretation places as much emphasis on the values and cultures
of elites as on the organization of state institutions.

References

Aberbach, J. D. & Rockman, B. A. (1977). The overlapping worlds of American federal
executives and congressmen. *British Journal of Political Science, 7* (January), 23-47.

_____ (1985). Governmental responses to budget scarcity—the United States. *Policy Studies
Journal, 13* (March), 494-505.

_____ (1988). Political and bureaucratic roles in public service reorganization, pp. 79-98.
In C. Campbell & B. G. Peters (Eds.) *Organizing governance: Governing organizations.*
Pittsburgh: University of Pittsburgh Press.

_____ (1989). On the rise, transformation, and decline of analysis in government. *Governance, 2* (July), 293-314.

Allison, G. T. (1969). Conceptual models and the Cuban missile crisis. *American Political
Science Review, 63* (September), 689-718.

Anton, T. J. (1980). *Administered politics: Elite political culture in Sweden* Boston: Martinus
Nijhoff.

Anton, T. J., Linde, C., and Melbourne, A. (1973). Bureaucrats in politics: A profile of the
Swedish administrative elite. *Canadian Public Administration, 16,* 627-651.

Aron, R. (1950). Social structure and the ruling class. *British Journal of Sociology* (Parts
1 and 2), *1* (March and June), 1-16; 126-143.

Badie, B. & Birnbaum, P. (1983). *The sociology of the state.* Chicago: University of Chicago
Press.

Bauer, R. A., de Sola Pool, I. & Dexter, L. A. (1963). *American business and public policy.*
New York: Atherton Press.

Benjamin, R. and Duvall, R. (1985). The capitalist state in context, pp. 19-58. In R. Benjamin & S. L. Elkin (Eds.) *The democratic state.* Lawrence, KS: University Press of Kansas.

Birch, A. H. (1984). Overload, ungovernability and delegitimization: The theories and the
British case. *British Journal of Political Science, 14* (April), 136-160.

Birnbaum, P. (1982). *The heights of power: An essay on the power elite in France.* Chicago:
University of Chicago Press.

Borzutsky, S. (1983). *Chilean politics and social security policies.* Ph.D. dissertation. Pittsburgh: University of Pittsburgh.

Brittan, S. (1975). The economic contradictions of democracy. *British Journal of Political Science, 5* (April), 129-159.

Cameron, D. H. (1978). The expansion of the public economy: A comparative analysis. *American Political Science Review, 72* (December), 1243-1261.

Campbell, J. C. (Ed.) (1985). Research roundtable: Government responses to budget scarcity. *Policy Studies Journal, 13* (March), 471-547.

Campbell, J. C. (1989). Democracy and bureaucracy in Japan. In T. Ishida & E. S. Krauss (Eds.) *Democracy in Japan* (pp. 113-137). Pittsburgh: University of Pittsburgh Press.

Cassese, S. (1986). The rise and decline of the notion of the state. *International Political Science Review, 7* (2), 120-130.

Clarke, H. D., Stewart, M. C. & Zuk, G. (1988). Not for turning: Beliefs about the role of government in contemporary Britain. *Governance, 1* (July), 271-287.

Crozier, M., Huntington, S. and Watanuki, J. (1975). *The crisis of democracy.* New York: New York University Press.

Dahl, R. A. (1961). *Who governs? Democracy and power in an American city.* New Haven, CT: Yale University Press.

Dennis, J., Lindberg, L., McCrone, D., & Stiefbold, R. (1968). Political socialization to democratic orientations in four western systems. *Comparative Political Studies, 1* (April), 71-101.

Deutsch, K. W. (1986). State functions and the future of the state. *International Political Science Review, 7* (2), 209-222.

Dyson, K. (1980). *The state tradition in western Europe.* New York: Oxford University Press.

Easton, D. (1981). The political system besieged by the state. *Political Theory, 9* (August), 303-325.

Easton, D. and Dennis, J. (1969). *Children in the political system: Origins of political legitimacy.* New York: McGraw-Hill.

Esping-Andersen, G. (1985). *Politics against markets: The social democratic road to power.* Princeton, NJ: Princeton University Press.

Fenno, R. F., Jr. (1978). *Home style: House members in their districts.* Boston: Little, Brown.

Fiorina, M. P. (1977). *Congress: Keystone of the Washington establishment.* New Haven, CT: Yale University Press.

Hall, P. (1986). *Governing the economy: The economics of state intervention in Britain and France.* New York: Oxford University Press.

Heisler, M. with Kvavik, R. B. (1974). Patterns of European politics--the 'European polity' model, pp. 27-89. In M. O. Heisler (Ed.) *Politics in Europe: Structures and processes in some postindustrial democracies.* New York: David McKay.

Hess, R. D. and Torney, J. V. (1967). *The development of political attitudes in children.* Chicago: Aldine.

Hood, C. with Dunsire, A. and Thomson, L. (1988). Rolling back the state: Thatcherism, Fraserism and bureaucracy. *Governance, 1* (July), 243-270.

Huntington, S. P. (1965). Congressional responses to the twentieth century, pp. 5-31. In D. B. Truman (Ed.) *The congress and America's future.* Englewood-Cliffs, NJ: Prentice-Hall.

Johnson, C. (1975). Japan: Who governs? An essay on official bureaucracy. *Journal of Japanese Studies, 2* (Autumn), 1-28.

_____ (1982). *MITI and the Japanese miracle: The growth of industrial policy, 1925-1975.* Stanford, CA: Stanford University Press.

Jones, G. (1988). The crisis in British central-local government relationships. *Governance, 1* (April), 162-183.

Katzenstein, P. (1985). *Small states in world markets: Industrial policy in Europe.* Ithaca, NY: Cornell University Press.

Kelman, S. (1981). *Regulating America, regulating Sweden: A comparative study of occupational safety and health policy.* Cambridge, MA: MIT Press.

King, A. (1973). Ideas, institutions, and policies—Parts I and III. *British Journal of Political Science, 3* (July and October), 291-313; 409-423.

———— (1975). Overload: Problems of governing in the 1970s. *Political Studies, 23* (June-September), 284-296.

Kingsley, J. D. (1944). *Representative bureaucracy.* Yellow Springs, OH: Antioch University Press.

Krasner, S. D. (1978). *Defending the national interest: Raw materials investments and U.S. foreign policy.* Princeton, NJ: Princeton University Press.

———— (1984). Approaches to the state: Alternative conceptions and historical dynamics. *Comparative Politics, 16* (January), 223-247.

———— (1988). Sovereignty: An institutional perspective. *Comparative Political Studies, 21* (April), 66-94.

Kumar, K. (1988). *Social thought and social action: The 'dicey' problem and the curious strength of individualism in English social policy.* Paper presented at the Conference on Policy and Politics, University of Pittsburgh, Pittsburgh, Pennsylvania.

Kvistad, G. O. (1988). Radicals and the state: The political demands on west German civil servants. *Comparative Political Studies, 21* (April), 95-125.

Leman, C. (1980). *The collapse of welfare reform: Political institutions, policy, and the poor in Canada and the United States.* Cambridge, MA: MIT Press.

Lentner, H. H. (1984). The concept of the state: A response to Stephen Krasner. *Comparative Politics, 16* (April), 367-377.

Lowi, T. J. (1972). Four systems of policy, politics and choice. *Public Administration Review, 32* (July/August), 298-310.

———— (1979). *The end of liberalism* (2nd ed.). New York: W. W. Norton.

Malloy, J. M. (1979). *The politics of social security in Brazil.* Pittsburgh: University of Pittsburgh Press.

———— (1984). *Politics, fiscal crisis and social security reform in Brazil.* Paper presented at the annual meeting of the American Political Science Association, Washington, D.C.

Malloy, J. M. & Borzutsky, S. (1984). *Authoritarian statecraft in South America: The reform of social security in Brazil and Chile.* Unpublished paper.

Malloy, J. M. & Parodi, C. A. (1988). *Statecraft, social policy and regime transition in Brazil.* Paper presented at the 14th International Congress of the Latin American Studies Association, New Orleans, Louisiana.

McConnell, G. (1967). *Private power and American democracy.* New York: Alfred A. Knopf.

Milch, J. (1974). Influence as power: French local government reconsidered. *British Journal of Political Science, 4* (April), 139-161.

Niskanen, W. A., Jr. (1971). *Bureaucracy and representative government.* Chicago: Aldine-Atherton.

Nordlinger, E. (1981). *On the autonomy of the democratic state.* Cambridge, MA: Harvard University Press.

O'Connor, J. (1973). *The fiscal crisis of the state.* New York: St. Martin's Press.

Olson, M. (1968). *The logic of collective action.* New York: Schocken Books edition.

———— (1982). *The rise and decline of nations: Economic growth, stagflation, and social rigidities.* New Haven, CT: Yale University Press.

———— (1986). A theory of the incentives facing political organizations: Neo corporatism and the hegemonic state. *International Political Science Review, 7* (2), 165-189.

Peters, B. G. (1985). The United States: Absolute change and relative stability, pp. 228-261. In R. Rose (Ed.) *Public employment in western nations.* Cambridge: Cambridge University Press.

Putnam, R. D., Leonardi, R., Nanetti, R. Y., and Pavoncello, F. (1983). Explaining institutional success: The case of Italian regional government. *American Political Science Review, 77* (March), 55-74.

Rockman, B. A. (1984). *The leadership question: The presidency and the American system.* New York: Praeger.

———— (1988). *Centrism without a center—The development of American presidentialism.* Paper prepared for the Roundtable on L'Etat aux Etats Unis, Chantilly, France.

Rose, R. (1969). The variability of party government. *Political Studies, 17* (December), 413-445.

———— (1980). Government against sub-governments: A European perspective on Washington, pp. 284-347. In R. Rose & E. N. Suleiman (Eds.) *Presidents and prime ministers.* Washington, D.C.: American Enterprise Institute.

———— (1984a). *The capacity of the president: A comparative analysis* (Studies in Public Policy, #130). Glasgow: Center for the Study of Public Policy, University of Strathclyde.

———— (1984b). *Understanding big government: The program approach.* London: Sage Publications.

Rose, R. & Peters, G. (1978). *Can governments go bankrupt?* New York: Basic Books.

———— (1979). The juggernaut of incrementalism (Studies in Public Policy, #63). Glasgow: Center for the Study of Public Policy, University of Strathclyde.

Rosenau, J. N. (1988). The state in an era of cascading politics: Wavering concept, widening competence, withering colossus, or weathering change? *Comparative Political Studies, 21* (April), 13-44.

Sbragia, A. (1979). Not all roads lead to Rome: Local housing policy in the unitary Italian state. *British Journal of Political Science, 9* (July), 315-339.

———— (1986). Capital markets and central-local politics in Britain. *British Journal of Political Science, 16* (July), 311-339.

Schmitter, P. C. (1974). Still the century of corporatism? pp. 85-131. In F. B. Pike & T. Stritch (Eds.) *The new corporatism: Social-political structures in the Iberian world.* Notre Dame, IN: University of Notre Dame Press.

Sharpe, L. J. (1973). American democracy reconsidered, Parts I, II, and Conclusions. *British Journal of Political Science, 3* (January and April), 1-28; 129-167.

Skocpol, T. (1980). Political response to capitalist crisis: Neo-Marxist theories of the state and the case of the new deal. *Politics and Society, 10* (2), 155-202.

Stepan, A. (1978). *The state and society: Peru in comparative perspective.* Princeton, NJ: Princeton University Press.

Suleiman, E. N. (1974). *Politics, power, and bureaucracy in France: The administrative elite.* Princeton, NJ: Princeton University Press.

———— (1978). *Elites in French society: The politics of survival.* Princeton, NJ: Princeton University Press.

Tarschys, D. (1985). Curbing public expenditure: Current trends. *Journal of Public Policy, 5* (February), 23-67.

Vogel, D. (1986). *National styles of regulation: Environmental policy in Great Britain and the United States.* Ithaca, NY: Cornell University Press.

Weir, M. & Skocpol, T. (1985). State structures and the possibilities for 'Keynesian' responses to the great depression in Sweden, Britain, and the United States, pp. 107-163. In P. B. Evans, D. Rueschemeyer, and T. Skocpol (Eds.) *Bringing the state back in.* Cambridge: Cambridge University Press.

Wildavsky, A. (1966). The political economy of efficiency: Cost-benefit analysis, systems analysis, and program budgeting. *Public Administration Review, 26* (December), 292-310.

_____ (1969). Rescuing policy analysis from PPBS. *Public Administration Review, 29* (March/April), 189-202.

_____ (1985). The logic of public sector growth, pp. 231-270. In J.-E. Lane (Ed.) *State and market: The politics of the public and the private.* London: Sage Publications.

_____ (1988). President Reagan as a political strategist, pp. 289-305. In C. O. Jones (Ed.) *The Reagan legacy: Promise and performance.* Chatham, NJ: Chatham House.

Wilsford, D. (1988). Tactical advantages versus administrative heterogeneity: The strengths and the limits of the French state. *Comparative Political Studies, 21* (April), 126-168.

Wilson, J. Q. (1976). The rise of the bureaucratic state, pp. 77-103. In N. Glazer & I. Kristol (Eds.) *The American commonwealth—1976.* New York: Basic Books.

This chapter provides a critique of contemporary state theory for being teleological and ahistorical. It argues that the process of constructing the modern state has involved the displacement of power upwards, away from fragmented localities and into the orbit of the state apparatus. In Lowi's words, the conquest is thought incomplete, insofar as local political arrangements still maintain, and their existence constitutes a significant tension within the political system. The chapter reviews the recent literature dealing with the existence of the "local state," and concludes that although the state apparatus possesses much greater legal and fiscal power, political issues can develop and survive within the locality and may become part of the national political discourse. The implications of this interpretation for the development of future state theory are also examined.

8

State, Local State, Context, and Spatiality: A Reappraisal of State Theory

ANDREW KIRBY

Introduction

The purpose of this paper is to sketch out an approach to the state that is quite different from that which is dominant within the literature of sociology, political science, and other disciplines. The assertion that there currently exists a dominant approach may seem immediately surprising and will be addressed head on. Rather than admit to some dominant or consensual view of the state, it is more usual for commentators to identify a plethora of

Author's Note: This essay was produced within the Program on Political and Economic Change at the University of Colorado, Boulder, and helpful comments were received from my erstwhile colleagues. The paper was also presented verbally in a number of settings, including the Annual Meeting of the American Political Science Association in 1987, the Department of Geography, University of Southern California, and the Sixth Conference of Europeanists, where Bruno Dente acted as a stimulating discussant. Thanks to all those who engaged with the paper in some way, and in particular to Jim Caporaso for his help and encouragement. The usual disclaimers apply.

perspectives. Alford and Friedland, for instance, in their massive overview of capitalism, the state, and democracy, suggest that there are three quite distinct ways of approaching the state—the pluralist, the managerial, and the class perspective (Alford & Friedland, 1985). Indeed, they go much further by suggesting that this taxonomy is composed of "incompatible world views" (1985: xiii). In part, this is correct, although to take this at face value would be seriously misleading. The studies that go to make up the substance of this taxonomy have a very great deal in common, and this commodity transcends the dissimilarities of method and assumption.[1] It is a commonality rooted in a particular set of interpretations and emphases, which serve, ultimately, to reduce many of our views of the state to little more than a cartoon version of reality.

The most serious failing displayed by this body of research is its assumption that the state is a single monolithic enterprise. This problem is implicit in almost all efforts to understand the state, for if a space is to be made for the latter within the lexicon of social science, if the state is indeed to be "brought back in," then this must be justified. And the most salient justification rests upon demonstrations of the power, sovereignty, and centrality of the state apparatus within contemporary social affairs. Now, this must be qualified. Clearly, the pluralist interpretations of the roles and functions of the state are different from those of the Marxist functionalist; Parsons does not lie down with O'Connor, so to speak.[2] But this is to ignore the very basic similarities of these views, which, to reiterate, elevate the state-as-object to a place of some privilege. Nor, to extend this argument, are the methods of analysis so very different: teleological explanation and ahistoricism go hand in hand and are not the monopoly of any particular approach or school.

In the remainder of this paper, my task is to develop the argument that these superficial dissimilarities of approach mask a single, fundamental flaw in the way in which the state is characterized. The paper is divided into four sections. The first begins to map out a new terrain, which starts with the premise that political analysis should be situated or contextual. Such a starting point embraces very different methodological assumptions, insofar as our aim is shifted from reductionism, toward a more sensitive understanding of processes operating across time and space, and the interrelations between them and their outcomes. As we shall see, such a contextual focus moves us toward an historical interpretation of state creation and the recognition that the emergence of the state apparatus has involved a radical displacement of power from dispersed locations toward some more central locus. As the second section indicates however, this project of state formation is unfinished, as there remain large vestiges of power outside the state. Despite legal claims of sovereignty, plus for the future the rise of new surveillance technologies, the state still faces political resistance to its efforts. The third section begins to codify this argument, by setting out the existence of what is identified as the local state: the local bases of power, which are associated with, but not restricted to, local government, are recast using some aspects of state theory. The aim of the paper—that is, the recreation of the state as something that is neither monolithic nor functionalistic—is then evaluated in the conclusions.

In this examination, the focus will be consistent with a loosely knit body of research—it is certainly too soon to call it a school of thought—which draws on a broad mix of ideas: some anthropology, some historical sociology, some geography, some political science. The research in question is united in its concern for the complexity of social organization, an understanding of historical evolution, the singularities of place, and the potential of human agency. It is a perspective that rejects the extremes of behavioralism and structuralism, of materialism and idealism, and narrow disciplinary boundaries. I will refer to this work as possessing a *contextual* focus.

Context and Spatiality

In arguing for the importance of taking context seriously, we should be aware that most social science research already possesses an inbuilt contextual content: most research is actively shaped by its temporal and geographical origins. American social science reflects, for the most part, the pervasive ideology of possessive-individualism, and, thus, focuses upon individuals and individual behavior (Steinberger, 1985). Much European research, in contradistinction, reflects the prevailing importance of class conflicts, and in so doing employs typically some form of structural analysis. To be sure, this distinction is unacknowledged and nonapparent to most researchers. Indeed, most social and behavioral scientists believe mistakenly in the possibility of ubiquitous statements—timeless questions and answers— that transcend both material dimensions: that is, explanations without regard for the specifics of particular moments or particular locations (Skinner, 1969). For the social scientist, these specifics are simply noise factors, which can be reduced to an error term within the linear model of explanation. To the political scientist, the consideration of context is frequently little more than an attempt to increase an R^2 value.[3] The use of the analogy of the linear model is intentional, for it is the principle of regression that has driven much of the progress made in sociology, political science, and other quantitative studies in recent decades. In other words, it is the reduction of a spread of data to some mean characteristics, which has characterized the process of inference.

This process only makes sense if we possess a priori theories that allow us to undertake such reductionist thinking; unfortunately, theory is more usually the logical outcome of empiricist analysis, rather than vice versa.[4] Without such theoretical statements, it can be asserted that the methods of regression—or indeed, of any parsimonious manipulation—destroy some of the implications of our data. The most important element within a data set may be its diversity, a richness that is destroyed in the creation of mean values. Once more, the opposition of terms such as *richness* and *meanness* is intentional and apposite, for it *is* possible to turn to recent examples of research that are able to confront the variation extant within reality and that do not descend into triviality; nor is such analysis necessarily nonquantitative. Such research deals with the details *and* the larger picture, and in so doing finds material that is highly charged with significance. The most obvious example in this case is the work of the French *Annales* school, of which the monumental histories of Fernand Braudel are perhaps the best known. His last completed work, the trilogy of *Civilization and Capitalism*, specifically deals with the creation of a global system of mercantilism, and the ways in which that system had impacts on the day-to-day lives of "ordinary people" (Braudel, 1981, 1984). The creativity of Braudel's insights relate to the manner in which he juggles both time *and* space. His analysis is ever-conscious of the ways in which the general processes of capitalism were resolved in a multitude of different ways in different localities at different moments. This is of some importance, of course, because it is the manner in which general processes resolve themselves in specific cases, which accounts for further processes of change. To take a particular example: mercantile capitalism established itself in very different ways throughout India in the sixteenth and seventeenth centuries: there emerged something akin to a mosaic, with some localities maintaining and others relinquishing their traditional economic and social practices. It was this mosaic that was then the setting for the highly uneven unrest of the Indian Mutiny of 1857, which ultimately failed because it was unable to spread ubiquitously through the subcontinent. In such an instance, it would be inadequate to write simply of a struggle between colonialism and feudalism, or some such general statement; the Indian Mutiny was—despite its name—a highly localized instance of collective action.[5]

This kind of perspective may not at first pass appear to offer major challenges to contemporary research practice; it does, however, take us to the heart of a complex methodological problem. Of particular importance within the views of Braudel and others, such as Abrams, is the recognition of a relationship between the extremes of structure and agency. Both would argue that it is not possible to prise this dualism apart and to privilege one above the other. Structure determines the ways in which human agents act; but those agents are responsible for recreating the structure, and they do this task in subtly different ways. As a result, they frequently change the structure in some manner. The usual example here is of language: we inherit its structure, and must operate within it to be understood: in recreating it, we do individually change the terms and shades of language, such that each generation is continually presented with a subtly changed text from that which went before it. In consequence, it is now seen to be not possible to break apart the big picture and the small details; resorting to our previous example, human agents recreate capitalism in specific ways, and in so doing they create tensions that have impacts upon the system as a whole. Specific localities inherit the blueprints of a structure such as industrialism in different ways; agents impose upon it particular cultural meanings and particular priorities, with the result that there emerge different types of labor relations, different forms of legal practice, and different social relations. Nor do these exist in isolation, for all parts of a complex economic system have some impact upon the whole; capital and labor are both mobile, and may move to take advantage of such variations. Once more, the whole is continually reinterpreted and changed by individual and local collective action.

The identification of the specifics of a particular narrative is, thus, of theoretical importance, because without knowledge of such instances, we cannot understand realistically the creation and recreation of the whole—a process variously called *structuring* or *structuration* (Abrams, 1982; Giddens, 1981). Attempts to comprehend structuring will necessarily pay attention to moments of time and the variations of place. We are, typically, aware of the historical dimension, but are less conscious of the spatial dimension. It is common to assume that society is a monolithic structure, undifferentiated from locality to locality. This, though, ignores the historical reality of the ways in which social practices have resolved themselves. During long periods of human history, behavior has been circumscribed within particular localities and limited to certain small-scale political forms. This reflected, in some measure, the problems of interaction across long distances, and the way in which power was rooted in locally specific phenomena such as cities and land. That is why, for Braudel, the "structures of everyday life" are so important, because it was the realities of diet and lodging, not the ideologies of capitalism or religion, that until relatively recently determined the paths of political quiescence or rebellion. As Tilly observes, it took the attacks by employers upon craft associations to force the concerns of local collective action outside the local political arena, although some have observed that even in England, which of course went through this process first, "electoral politics would essentially be local politics" into the 1880s (Tilly, 1986b; Urwin, 1982: 40).

It is only in recent periods that the fragmentation of existence has diminished, as power has been "displaced upwards," to use Perry Anderson's phrase (1974). This is though not to argue that localities, and their styles of life, are now of little importance. As Foucault observes, this progressive coalescence of the fragmented bases of human organization has posed particular problems for the political organization of society (Foucault, in Rabinow, 1984). This, which he relates to the *spatiality* of society, is fundamentally a question of integrating complex styles of life—typically though not exclusively manifest in different locales—within the grip of the state. Time and space are clearly central to this concern, for it is the diminution of the importance of these material bases that permits the state to override the localized practices of its internal units. Put most simply, the consolidation of the state apparatus was very much dependent upon the latter's ability to gather information quickly and move things—taxes, armies, proclamations—rapidly about the country. Spatial integration can be achieved, *inter alia*, via transportation change and other forms of technological innovation, including the construction of state subsidized highways; localized measures of time can be standardized via changed economic practices (the creation of the factory system) and the incorporation of uniform measures of clock time. The alteration of conceptions of time and space remains a key component of the movement toward the modern state; as Giddens notes, the breaking down of temporal and spatial barriers continues to be instrumental in the creation of state institutions, which can now intrude virtually instantaneously into every home, meeting, and educational establishment (Giddens, 1985). Equally, similar changes have been manifested throughout civil society; as Kern has shown in some detail, changing views of time and space have occurred in the spheres of art, religion, architecture, and politics (Kern, 1983), and others have argued that a shift in conceptions of space was even a prerequisite for the scientific revolution of the seventeenth century (Heelan, 1983).

While the process of creating what we recognize as the contemporary national state continued—albeit at different speeds in different locations—there remained a vivid set of interactions at the local level, akin to what Locke identified as a *political society*, and in themselves a coherent and replicated set of political practices (Crenson, 1983). These did not rival the political practices of the state, which typically maintains the ultimate control of coercion, but they did nonetheless have a specific and important purpose: local politics were defined, in a patriarchal society, by men . . .

> agreeing with other men to join and unite into a community for their comfortable, safe and peaceable living one amongst another, in a secure enjoyment of their properties and a greater security against any that are not of it (Locke, quoted in Crenson, 1983, p. 17).

In short the maintenance of personal, religious and use values were all achieved at the local level, and via a localized political tradition.

What is particularly interesting about this tradition is the way it has been replicated—as an identifiable activity as opposed to a set of specific practices—from society to society and the way in which local political traditions have survived—one is tempted to say via a process of structuration—from period to period. Small political jurisdictions have permitted the maintenance of minute variations in the structures of everyday life, legal practice, religious behavior, and economic activity over long periods of time. Of interest too is the fact that this form of political organization was not simply a continuation of what had preceded it: when *new* societies were developed—as in North America—they immediately began to establish themselves via systems of local organization. In turn, these political units have, in the case of the original colonies, been reproduced over successive centuries.

The most convincing evidence that points to the importance residing in local political structures is the extremely slow evolution of what we might identify today as *national* political parties. The latter do indicate the existence of issues that exist at a national scale and that require resolution and perhaps some standardization of action. This notwithstanding, they have typically evolved as coalitions of small local interests, as Taylor and Johnston indicate successfully in their book on *The Geography of Elections* (1979). More importantly, that evolution was itself delayed by the late integration of most nation states. Long after there existed national bureaucracies, legal codes, and national armies, it was difficult to move capital from one locality to another and difficult to determine what might constitute a political issue on which scattered delegates might reasonably agree. To reiterate then, the politics of everyday life were rooted in local structures, and the forging of national political parties was very much in distinction to the latter (Archer & Taylor, 1981).[6]

This is not to argue that an increase in state power has diminished entirely the intrinsic importance of specific contexts—spatial or temporal. It is clear that spatiality, to return to Foucault's means of describing fragmentation, remains important within American society, to take but one example. Whilst the United States, as an urban society, has lost contact with its local rhythms, thus, has little distinct sense of *time* and is essentially existential—or now-oriented—it is also the case that there is little indication of a *spatial* unity within that society. Geographical fragmentation is reified by the legal and political system: the locality is still of some importance within human affairs. The neighborhood, the political jurisdiction, and the city are all real objects within American society, in a way that they are not, within, for example, most European countries (Lowi, 1976).

If we bring together the strands that we have unravelled this far, we have a concern for space, time, agents, and structures. To reiterate, these dimensions go some way toward explicating the use of the term *contextual*. The refusal to eliminate any aspect of reality from consideration on an a priori basis is central to this concern. In the next section, this principle is extended to the question of relations between the state and civil society.

State and Civil Society

If at the outset we reintroduce the metrics of time and space to our discussion, this immediately reminds us that bold assertions concerning the state cannot claim any universality. In most cases, analysis is restricted to a tiny proportion of the global system of states; those that never experienced nineteenth-century colonialism, those that never experienced twentieth-century communist revolutions. Just as studies of political behavior have concentrated on voting, and in so doing have chosen to ignore the majority of the globe's political acts, so too the study of the state has managed to exclude the majority of state forms (Thrift & Forbes, 1983). This is, to say the least, unfortunate, for the isolated studies that have been undertaken beyond the advanced capitalist societies are enormously provocative (Anderson, 1983; Krasner, 1984). We find ourselves in a political terrain where many of the usual assumptions bear no fruit. Geertz's studies of Bali, for instance, reveal in the immediate precolonial period—not a century ago—state institutions so utterly different from those with which we are accustomed to deal, that it would be hard to use the same vocabulary in order to discuss them (Geertz, 1980).[7] Now, the Balinese example of *negara* may seem remote and strange to us, but it reminds us quite clearly of two basic tenets: first, that different societies and states evolve along different trajectories; and second, that no society reshapes itself anew with each generation—it will be recreated, but it does not alter precipitately. Aspects of the Balinese state and culture remain—and thus any interpretation of the *contemporary* situation would, necessarily, invoke Geertz's historical insights. For these reasons, there are very real attractions in trying to undertake "an ethnography of the state" in a contemporary society, for we can be sure that such an effort would reinforce two points: first, that the form of *any* state apparatus is only to be understood in relation to the society within which it is locked; and second, that society is essentially a palimpsest of many layers, each a particular form of organization that itself reflects specific historical circumstances. Nor is this solely true for nonadvanced societies: aspects of the premodern state are reflected within the United States, insofar as the electoral college, and other components of the state's formal organization, reflect compromises made two centuries ago. In short, to understand the state in the advanced society, we once again need a long lens. In fact, a rather different historical method may be more useful: to draw once again on Foucault, an "archaeology of the state" may pay large dividends in revealing the present to us.

In contrast, most recent studies of the state have been driven by materialist analyses, which posit a simplistic relation between capital and the institutions of the state.[8] Whilst these studies have redressed a prior imbalance, they do in themselves negate most of the principles already introduced in this essay. In the first instance, such studies are typically ahistorical. The presentist examination of an apparatus as complex as the state must lead us into the trap of teleological explanation—into the assumption that the state has emerged with the purpose of doing what it currently does. As Bryan Jones has observed, we thus often find that in such studies, the state is capable of taking on a "subjunctive mood" (Jones, 1986: 285). Second, in its rush to identify the controlling interests behind the state, materialist analyses have emphasized conflicts between *vertical interests*—such as classes, or fractions of capital.[9] They have though neglected one basic issue: namely, that these vertical coalitions are at best only that: they are amalgamations of interests that also have *horizontal*, or spatial expression. Classes do not exist as national entities: they are divided both geographically and by industrial sector. The working class in one region has interests that are analogous to, but hardly identical to the working class in another region;

the same is true of a capitalist class. Indeed, in situations of capital mobility, there is likely to be antagonism between different regional groups within the same class, as they implicitly compete for employment or profit.

This rejection of a simple interest-group view of the state rests upon the recognition of a long-standing localism within a nation: in the United States, for instance, a tradition of localism can be traced back to the settlement of the Thirteen Colonies. As Steinberger has indicated with enormous insight and economy, the ideology of *communalism*, developed at that time, remains a powerful strand within the skein of American political development and can still be identified within political discourse (Steinberger, 1985). This commitment to local practices, and its political expression, has already been linked with the overarching concept of spatiality. And as already noted, the tension between local practices and the authority of the state is important to an understanding of both entities: taking this logic a little further, we can argue that an understanding of the contemporary state must rest upon a recognition of this tension. The mechanism of state formation has involved overcoming what Katznelson calls a *parcelization of sovereignty,* that is, the entropic dispersal of power and privilege, both political and economic, across numerous localities, and this process has left its imprint on what has emerged.

At this juncture, it will be useful to pose two questions: why did this process of change take place, and how complete has it been? So far as the first question is concerned, we can see the displacement of power as a response to continual crises, both fiscal and political. As Braudel points out, the changing scale of mercantile operation far outstripped the political stability extant within Europe during the sixteenth and seventeenth centuries, such that the economic sphere was often instrumental in shoring up the political sphere. Indeed, it is a reasonable generalization that a broadened scale of political action was inevitable once the economic system began to move toward a global reach. The rise of the state is intimately bound up with increases in transactions of all types—within countries, within continents, beyond continents. Such materialism necessitates a certain set of state structures and is dependent upon and encourages a very specific type of internationalism—one that emphasizes domination of other economic or military rivals, and hence, national prestige. The process did not occur in a linear fashion, with some goal clearly in view. However, there has been something like a ratchet effect, and as each displacement of power has occurred, it has rarely been reversed (see for instance Tilly, 1985).

The more recent aspects of this narrative—at least for the United States—have been fleshed out by Skowronek, whose book is a remarkably detailed study of the origins of the American state, and its evolution up until the end of the First World War (Skowronek, 1982). He shows clearly enough that both as a set of institutions, and as an intellectual construct, the nineteenth-century state in the United States was relatively weak, in contrast to the legal and procedural powers rooted at state and local levels. It was strong enough to undertake the tasks for which it was responsible, but still weak by contemporary standards. It was only as industrialization increased in importance that new tensions revealed themselves, and the increase in Federal authority grew. That growth was however slow, and unsure—Skowronek likens it to a patchwork expansion. Political parties continued to have direct ties to particular locations, and decision makers in those locations maintained close control of privilege. Attempts to expand and professionalize the Army were opposed by the locally based National Guard network. The development of the Interstate Commerce Commission was beset continually by contradictory geographical interests. In the end, it was a series of contingent factors—the collapse of the Democratic party between 1896 and 1910, the seriousness of labor unrest, and the need to mobilize national resources during the First World War—which allowed a central bureaucracy to push against local interests. As Skowronek observes, the change was never a smooth one:

> administrative expansion accompanied by a withering of party machinery and judicial restrictions on state action has defined America's peculiar approach to modernity (Skowronek, 1982, p. 288).

This account of political struggle takes us to the heart of the process of state evolution. It reveals quite clearly a conflict between two ideologies: on the one hand, the traditions of localism, and on the other the notion of a national state, the existence of which is based upon an assumption of values and priorities which transcend sectional and local concerns. As Skowronek's argument indicates, one of the roles of the state apparatus has been, historically, the resolution of diverse sectional interests, in both a vertical *and* a horizontal sense. Nor is this process at an end: returning to our second question, we may note that the process of state formation is incomplete. Indeed, the single-most intriguing aspect of the rise of the modern state is the veritable slowness of the process of political domination. The Hobbesian Leviathan—which was to strangle all it touched—takes a long time to emerge. This may seem a paradoxical statement, if the rudimentary institutions of the eighteenth and nineteenth centuries are contrasted with those of the age of Kafka and Koestler, and this assertion will be elaborated at greater length.

It is usual to describe the emergence of the modern state as a displacement of power relations away from multiple locations—such as cities—until authority rests in some central locus, itself often reified by the construction of some symbolic capital city (see for instance Giddens, 1981, 1985). This perspective emphasizes a concentration of what Miliband identified as *the legitimate means of violence* within the institutions of the state (Miliband, 1969). It should be noted at this point that this confuses the relative and absolute strengths of the state. In absolute terms, the state institutions are more powerful than before, with respect to surveillance, weaponry and personnel. Conversely, society itself is more complex, more diverse, and more populous, and as a result contains more interests and possesses more ways to press for them. In consequence, the relative power of the state is not necessarily greater than it was decades ago. Indeed, it is central to the argument being developed here that the relative power of the state is not as great as is frequently supposed; and most importantly, that the process of power displacement is not in fact complete. In the remainder of this section I want to argue that our concern for the sheer power of the contemporary state is such that we have lost the recognition that there still exists significant opposition to that apparatus. This premise involves the analysis of a number of issues, and this section will continue with the question of sovereignty, focusing particularly upon the possibility of formal political opposition to the state.

Such a premise confronts a large literature that deals with the nature of sovereignty within the American system. Therein, we find some consensus that local forms of government are not only weak in practical terms, but are lacking in sovereign power, and cannot therefore initiate meaningful opposition to the state. This kind of interpretation is however weighed down by its teleological emphasis, manifested as the need to produce a balance sheet of respective strengths and weaknesses, powers and vetoes enjoyed by different layers of government (Johnston, 1984). These inductive examinations have been paralleled by theoretical and historical examinations, particularly of a constitutional nature. Although there have been occasional expressions of the communalist ideal within legal theory (see for instance the writings of Judge Thomas Cooley [Syed, 1966]), these have been superseded as the ultimate statement on the autonomy of local government. By invoking Dillon's Rule, most commentators feel able to argue that such autonomy is extremely circumscribed.[10]

The central problem in such questions, and the manner in which they are cast as constitutional issues, is the way in which the legal system is invoked as an autonomous realm, when of course it is part of social and political discourse. Indeed, it is difficult to think of a legal system without introducing the notion of a state apparatus attempting to impose its standards upon local practice. Thus, discussions of the long run diminution of local autonomy should not surprise us: few states can maintain claim to a monopoly of power if they possess constituent parts which can challenge each other and the state itself.[11] This does not mean, however, that we can then interpret the vexed question of "local autonomy" in terms of some balance of power as it prevails at any moment. No analyst would wipe from consideration the existence of a particular class, for instance, simply because that class lacked actual power in assemblies or on the streets: *potential* or *behavioral* power must be taken into consideration too.[12] Thus, the fact that we can often fail to identify powers of autonomy or initiation within local political units hardly allows us to diminish the existence of those same units or to imply that they can only ever be addressed via the study of national systems of government.

Implicit then in these remarks is an assertion that the locality can be examined as a realm in which political and social life has its own trajectory: social relations can be identified at this scale, rather than at, solely, the national level. The locality is the scale at which people reproduce themselves and their "local knowledge" (Geertz, 1983), and is the scale at which reality is experienced. All events, however large in a global sense, are ultimately transformed into a local issue. The changes in the world economy result in unemployment in the local plant; famine in India becomes represented as a fund-raising event on local television. In short, the locality is a filter through which we deal with the realities of existence. This is true of all affairs, be they expressed in the struggles of women, of gays, or of ethnic groups, defined within the sphere of reproduction, or of groups defined within the sphere of production. Even class struggles, typically expressed as national or even international conflicts, are spatially fragmented and locally expressed via industrial or political action.[13] In turn, the locality determines the options available for individuals to create collectivities, to exert political pressure, and to recreate themselves, both individually and as groups. It is my contention that such action takes place continually at the local level, and is much less frequently displaced upwards into the higher realms of judicial and political debate. This notwithstanding, displacement can and does occur, and when this happens, it poses specific challenges to state authority. Recent examples include the increasing instability of the British contribution to NATO, due to efforts of communities to declare themselves nuclear-free zones, thus weakening the state's control of nuclear rhetoric; and the success of fundamental religious groups in the United States, which have moved out of local political contexts and are now influencing State and Federal discussion on abortion rights, prayer, and similar matters.[14]

With regard to such interpretations, there have of course been numerous critiques of localism, which has been seen to rest on a romantic image, derived from de Tocqueville's naturalistic images of the community. It can be argued that the latter descended into a naturalistic evocation of the splendors of local association, which was an ideological fabrication that has colored subsequent perspectives on the locality. This way of approaching the question of relations between forms of government does though tend to create an alternate fabrication, which rests upon the sovereignty of the state and an implicit assumption that it is the state alone that can guarantee individual rights. By arguing that only the state can permit heterogeneous behavior and, thus, guarantee civil liberties, because local communities cannot sustain variations in belief or action, the state becomes elevated to a position of morality. This position is one which lies beneath the extension of the legal process and the increase in state power, despite the fact that it rests upon dubious premises. It is not greatly dissimilar to the Aristotelean position, which regarded the *city* as a natural organ of government because it was the most complete, more mature than both the village and the household. It also suffers the same problems as does the Aristotelean thesis, namely that it necessarily evokes a state which itself rests upon some naturalistic principles: the state is, in other words, the logical extension of incomplete, localized forms of association. The problem here is as follows: if the state (or in its original form, the city-state), is so much more of a complete form of organization, why then do other subsidiary, localized forms of government remain in existence? We witness local organization in virtually every nation state, for it is central to both these arguments that the immature forms (localism, or in Aristotle's case, the household), resist their eclipse for explicit social reasons (Ambler, 1985).[15]

From this discussion, it should be clear that the sovereignty question is somewhat of a red herring, because it suggests that there can be no meaningful political struggle initiated at the lowest political levels of government. Essentially, this is because sovereignty is a concept open to critical analysis, insofar as it is defined by the state. State institutions have continually appropriated powers to themselves, in order to exclude other institutions from the exercise of that power, and have cloaked this within the ideology of sovereignty. Consequently, a strict reading of the latter (which will tell us that local government, as a part of the state apparatus, is relatively weak) is to misread the question.

Nor is this the only implication of this line of inquiry. What this argument has done is to come close to falling into the trap of specifying all political action within the confines of the state, which is a problem inherent in the state-centered approach. In addition, we must take into account the fact that not all political struggles are found within the confines of the formal political system. Important elements of struggle are located within civil society, and not within the state per se. This assertion—and the implications of that insight—will be explored in the next section.

State and Local State

Access to the state's institutions is defined by the state itself. This leaves much political struggle to take place at the organizational frontiers of that apparatus. There are instances where such struggles are expressed elsewhere: questions of civil rights for example, are often, in the American case, fought out through the courts, rather than the streets. More usually, though, political acts are expressed first through the local medium of organization: diverse political struggles are manifested in the sphere of local government. This is revealed most clearly in the work of Manuel Castells, whose *City and the Grassroots* is a compendium of a number of very different social movements. What all of these have in common (an insight that is explicit within Castells' broader theoretical framework), is the manner in which the struggles are pitched in the first instance against the organizational structure of local government (Castells, 1983). This unites a number of singular struggles, which have otherwise in common only the fact that they are expressed in the realm of consumption and not production. Castells' examples include the struggles of gay men to gain some political representation within the city of San Francisco; the urban riots in black inner city areas throughout the United States in the 1960s; the Glasgow Rent Strike in Scotland in 1915; and the Citizen Movement in Madrid at the end of the Franquist era. In each case, the struggles were in part successful because they were expressed in the first instance within the confines of the locality, a fact which allowed these diverse groups to become established in a manner that would not have been possible had they confronted the state more explicitly. This insight is in conflict with a number of studies that have reexamined the operation of local government using the rubric of state theory. This literature has coined the phrase *the local state*, to discuss the workings of local government as an explicit arm of the state. Although misconceived according to the arguments outlined here, this perspective is nonetheless of some importance and will be discussed briefly below.

The term *local state* was first used consistently by Cynthia Cockburn in a study of the workings of Lambeth borough council (Cockburn, 1977). In developing her theoretical perspective, she argued that the local state is made up of local government per se, plus a range of other organizations: bodies dealing with water supply, education, sport and recreation, employment, and so on.

> . . . local authorities, including local health, water and transport authorities as well as local education, housing and planning authorities, are aspects of the national state and share its work. When I refer to Lambeth borough council as 'local state' it is to say neither that it is something distinct from 'national state' nor that it alone represents the state locally. It is to indicate that it is part of a whole. (Cockburn, 1977: 46-47)

The terminology of the local state was broadened by Saunders, who emphasized the way in which the local state is responsible for the reproduction of social practices, whilst the central state is responsible for the nature of production, an insight which Saunders has since called the *dual state thesis*. In turn, Dear produced a theory of the local state that both follows Cockburn in denying the local state any autonomy, yet self-evidently regards it as an object of theoretical interest, not least in the way in which its relations with the central state are repeated in different political contexts (Dear, 1981). In particular, tensions between the levels of the state apparatus are examined, as are the ways in which crises at one level of administration may be passed down to other levels (see for example Clark and Dear, 1984).

A confusion of Marxist and Weberian concepts exists beneath the surface of this literature, and the reader will probably recognize the way in which the *local state* literature has gone through many of the redefinitions that we have noted with respect to *state* theory. This is revealed clearly in Fincher's critique of what she calls "the local level capitalist state" (1981). She argues that the local state is not a theoretically-distinct phenomenon, and that there is no theoretically-distinct status for the functions that are presently in the hands of local government agencies (1981:26). Rather, the local state simply reflects the manner in which the state continually attempts to reconcile contradictions within capitalism, and in consequence the nature of the local state will shift as those contradictions themselves shift. In other words, the manifestations of the state are only a window to the crises of capitalism, and not derivable as theoretical propositions; conversely, the prising apart of central and local is "fetishistic." It cannot though be enough to suggest that the state is indivisible, a mere window (or mirror, at a different point in Fincher's text) to the totality of the mode of production. It may well be important to underline the fact that the state cannot be theorized without recourse to the economy or civil society, but this does not then permit the assertion that the historical transience of local jurisdictional activity makes a theoretical analysis impossible.

As we have seen, the historical evolution of state structures remains as the insight to the relationship between the state (and other political forms), and civil society as a whole. Let me make this argument specific. The local state—and we are correct in using this term because it emphasizes both the similarities, and the conflicts with, the national state—maintains a political life. More than that, it is the normal scale at which individuals undertake their political actions. As Castells reminds us, revolutionary socialism of the Parisian commune variety grew from specific community issues, and was in consequence exhibited in the same arena (Harvey, 1985). The development of ward machines and of ethnic politics in United States cities was another explicit example of the structures of everyday life being imposed upon the struggle for personal and class advancement (Katznelson, 1981). Even where political conflict was constrained to the workplace, as in Britain, it was the case that syndicalism was locally rooted; more than that, it was the case too that the Labour Party originally, and naturally, focused its attention upon taking control of local government structures (Buck, 1981). It is rare for the politics of what we may call ordinary people to be other than locally based, and the failures of the various Internationals only underlines this basic point.

Here then is the basic material that we require for an understanding of the local state. It represents a fundamental expression of political organization and outlook: some have called this *territoriality* (Sack, 1986). The state uses many devices to inhibit and weaken these long-standing forms. Fiscal constraints are the most usual, but control may take the form of destroying the jurisdictional unit (as occurred in the UK in 1974, and once again in 1986), or creating new, artificial units which serve to break up extant loyalties (Kirby, 1983). In consequence, in some social contexts the local state has effectively been destroyed, and its political reality is evident to only a tiny minority of residents.[16] In other instances, and here the United States is a good example, local political forms are vibrant and the total spatial integration alluded to by Clark, Lowi, and others, is still being resisted.

Now, this logic involves a particular insight, namely the specificity of the locality as a political unit. The term *local state* clearly places the latter in the realm of the state apparatus, even though these local units may be disbanded by state fiat. This could not, though, imply that the dismemberment of the local state would spell the conclusion of local political action. In consequence, we are left to explore the curious political position occupied by the local state. On the one hand, it is part of the institutions of the state; on the other, it is also a component of civil society, where political actions opposing the state apparatus may be found. This interpretation may seem antithetical to our interpretations of the structures of the state, although this once more leads us to examine the obfuscations that surround the whole question of local government. Magnusson, for instance, has argued that there exist a number of what he calls *bourgeois ideologies* surrounding the latter, and as he notes, "in any form . . . [these] . . . condemn the local polity to a tenuous existence" (1986:2). These ideologies have tended to mask a clear, historically determined role for local governments, and particularly municipalities, to act as a component of civil society, in resistance to the state. This position is clearly spelled out by Hegel (writing of course at a time when state control was increasing), who recognized that the specificities of local organization necessarily placed them in conflict with the state, the residue of "absolutely universal interest" (Magnusson, 1986:5).

Magnusson's statements bring us toward a key idea, one that must be placed centrally within any understanding of the state. That idea revolves around the importance of local governments as local polities, rather than as extended instruments of the state. As polities, they are at a crucial position between civil society on the one hand, and the state on the other. Expressed within the language of contemporary state theory, the local state is both part of that apparatus, but also in conflict with the institutional arrangements of the latter. This is no ritualistic competition with respect to fiscal propriety, but is seen realistically as an elemental struggle between groups within civil society and the state. The most clearly defined case of this is to be found in the recent political history of the UK, where a dramatic manifestation of this process of opposition and alternative policy development has been played out in the recent past with respect to styles of production and reproduction. Various local administrative units—notably those in London and Liverpool—have consistently opposed the state with respect to levels of local taxation, the organization of public housing, and levels of municipal employment. This is a fundamental attack on the ideology of the state's ability to control domestic policy, which has resulted in the most direct means of counterattack available. The state has dismantled the most vigorous sources of opposition: Metropolitan Counties and the Greater London Council have been dismembered by state fiat, in the most recent expression of a continual movement toward increased centralist penetration of the local arena (Kirby, 1982). This has been going on for some years in urban policy, but can also be traced in Northern Ireland, where the apotheosive case of "direct rule" has been perfected (Evans, 1986). At stake in this situation is, therefore, not simply the manner in which local government is organized, but rather the possibility of maintaining certain forms of local social and political relations, on the one hand, or state control, on the other. In order to maintain a particular form of state direction that is committed to recapitalization, a dismemberment of local government has begun, with the result that class, gender, or ethnically distinct politics, in the forms that are currently visible in parts of Britain, are all threatened with something close to extinction.[17]

Summary and Conclusions

At this point, it becomes necessary to summarize the complexities of this argument. So far, we have argued that society is fragmented, and in consequence its contextual bases are of importance. This implies that localities possess important political concerns, which reflect the needs and intentions of those collectivities that are represented in such localities. This fragmentation—also called here *communalism*—poses specific challenges to the state apparatus, which has continually sought to increase its control of diversity within the nation state. Indeed, we may continue by arguing that this entropy is in fact an important determinant of state actions; that is, there exists a continual tension between the state and the complexities of its internal organization. In some instances, this complexity remains powerful and is clearly expressed within the realm of local political action; in others, the state has gone further in imposing uniformity upon localities. In either instance, however, the manner in which local issues are resolved is of importance. The local state, as we have called these political units, represents an interface between the structures of the state apparatus, on the one hand, and the structures of civil society, on the other.

It is the tension explored here that is crucial to an understanding of state development. This is an important point of difference between the current argument, and those which take a solely state-centered approach to analysis. This interpretation of the state is, therefore, entirely consistent with the contextual theme outlined above. It portrays a situation in which the complexity of localist interests can only be resolved by the imposition of some external direction—namely, state policies. Moreover, it shows that the state cannot be separated from civil society for analytical purposes, insofar as there necessarily exists some tension between the two for as long as there exists a recognition of local interests.

In consequence, this perspective permits us to introduce a number of intriguing questions into the analysis of state forms. In the first instance, to repeat, we are necessarily rejecting a state-centered view: which means that we must reject simplistic and automatic notions such as the burden of legitimacy, which is often placed upon teleological interpretations of the state apparatus. Second, it brings us back to a reconsideration of the arguments of those, like Wallerstein, who would taxonomize the world into global, national, and local spheres, with that particular ordering in importance (Wallerstein, 1984). Without questioning the importance of the world economy, from the present analysis, local matters are of political (and economic) import, while it is also demonstrated that neither national nor local politics can be privileged, one above the other, for they are part of a peculiar antinomy which must be examined intact.

There is little question that this type of analysis takes us down a rather different route toward an understanding of the state. It is clearly difficult to generate broad interpretations when faced by the complexities of state evolution in both the historical *and* the spatial dimensions. As we have seen here, though, it is the complexity and fragmentation of social, political and economic organization that have such profound influence upon the evolution of state forms, state power, and state performance. To theorize the state apparatus without recourse to this reality is to set up a normative model, lacking in insight. In short, the problem has long moved beyond the necessity of bringing the state back into the picture. The question now revolves around some specification of the state, its relations with economy and civil society, and an understanding of the ways in which these structures have evolved *qua* structures, and the ways in which they have been shaped, from context to context, by human struggle. The problem is, thus, now one of *taking context seriously.*

Notes

1. Alford and Friedland cite Wildavsky's *The Politics of the Budgetary Process* as being representative of the pluralist perspective; Dahrendorf's *Class and Class Conflict in Industrial Society* as an examplar of the managerial view; and in relation to the third category of class perspectives obvious examples include: Giddens' (1985) *The Nation State and Violence;* Clark and Dear's (1984) *State Apparatus;* Skocpol's (1979) *States and Social Revolutions.*

2. Talcott Parsons, *The Social System;* James O'Connor, *The Fiscal Crisis of the State.*

3. See for example: Huckfeldt R. and Sprague J. (1986) *Networks in context*. Paper #120, Department of Political Science, Washington University, St. Louis.

4. This is not to argue of course that statistical analysis necessarily takes us down this path of reasoning. Exploratory data analysis, pioneered by Tukey, emphasizes the close scrutiny of data and encourages the researcher to make executive decisions concerning the inclusion or exclusion of specific data cases (Tukey, 1977).

5. As is normally the case, of course: the French Revolution was strongly resisted in a number of parts of France, for instance: see Tilly, 1986a.

6. Space does not permit the introduction of the related topic of political culture, although this is important: see for instance Richard Bensel (1984) *Sectionalism and American Political Development*, Madison, University of Wisconsin Press.

7. Geertz describes *negara* as a *theater state*, which was fashioned to recreate the timeless world of the deities, and which had as its goal the demonstration of ceremony; in consequence, "power served pomp, not policy making power" (1980:13).

8. See for instance Poulantzas N. (1973), *Political Power and Social Classes*; Althusser L. (1969), *For Marx*; for further examples, see Peter Saunders, 1983, "On the shoulders of which giant?" *Social Process and the City*, Sydney, George Allen and Unwin.

9. By "vertical interests," I mean components of the social structure that reinforce the notion of heterogeneity: that is to say, the concepts of class and status invoke a richness, implying as they do many strata within a society. In contrast, "horizontal interests" are used here to refer to components that have geographic expression: such as ethnic-regional minorities.

10. See for instance Syed, 1966; Clark, 1981, Clark, 1985. Dillon's Rule: an instrumental definition of local legal powers; see Clark, 1985:77.

11. Note the work of Smith (1984) on the British case. He points out that the legal system in medieval England moved gradually from a fragmented system toward a unified common law. The locality remained important, and lower courts were able to interpret some particular issues to their advantage. Simultaneously, these same courts had a role to play in the election of parliamentary representatives, which emphasized their relation with the highest levels of government. This example of gradual state domination was in contrast to the situation to be noted in many European countries, where the very different Roman law system was used by absolute rulers to remove local discretion and to create a large legal bureaucracy (Smith, 1984:171).

12. Ward argues that salience may distort the power—or lack of it—possessed by a protagonist. A simple example is the power of a small child to disrupt the lives of her parents. See Ward M. D. and House L. (1988) "A theory of the behavioral power of nations," *Journal of Conflict Resolution 32*(1), 3-36.

13. The example of the national miners' strike in the United Kingdom in 1984 is a case in point, for the strike ultimately collapsed due to regional conflicts within the Union.

14. Interesting examples are discussed by Alger C. F. and Mendlovitz S. H. (1987) "Grassroots initiatives: The challenge of linkages," in Mendlovitz S. H. and Walker R. (Eds.) *Towards a Just World Peace*, London, Butterworths, pp. 333-62.

15. Much of this argument is explicitly a response to Gordon Clark's extended essay on the interpretation of local autonomy (Clark, 1985). Whilst disagreeing with some of his interpretations, I am of course in absolute agreement with his emphasis upon the importance of examining local complexity and the ideologies that surround it.

16. Peter Saunders, University of Sussex, personal communication.

17. Nor should it be assumed that this principle is limited to the case of Great Britain. The position of the Communist Party in Italy within certain cities has been documented (see, *inter*

alia, Castells, 1983, although not without criticism: Bruno Dente, personal communication). Similarly, we can find a flurry of books in the United States that focus upon a specific type of political consciousness within (typically urban) places. Clavel (1986) has written about the progressive political movement in Hartford and Santa Monica, which has developed out of old-fashioned populism based within city neighborhoods. Similar moves are well discussed by Swanstrom (1985), vis-à-vis Cleveland.

References

Abrams, P. (1982). *Historical sociology.* Ithaca, NY: Cornell University Press.

Alford, R. & Friedland, R. (1985). *Powers of theory.* Cambridge: Cambridge University Press.

Ambler, W. H. (1985). Aristotle's understanding of the naturalness of the city. *The Review of Politics, 47*(2), 163-185.

Anderson, B. (1983). *Imagined communities.* London: Verso Press.

Anderson, P. (1974). *The lineages of the absolute state.* London: New Left Books.

Archer, J. C. & Taylor, P. J. (1981). *Section and party.* Chichester: Wiley.

Braudel, F. (1981, 1984). *Civilization and capitalism.* New York: Harper and Row.

Buck, N. (1981). The analysis of state intervention in nineteenth century cities, pp. 501-534. In M. J. Dear & A. Scott, (Eds.), *Urbanization and urban planning in capitalist societies.* New York: Methuen.

Castells, M. (1983). *The city and the grassroots.* London: Arnold.

Clark, G. L. (1981). Law, the state and the spatial integration of the United States. *Environment and Planning, A. 13*, 1197-1232.

Clark, G. L. (1984). A theory of local autonomy. *Annals of the Association of American Geographers, 74*(2), 195-208.

Clark, G. L. (1985). *Judges and the cities.* Chicago: Chicago University Press.

Clark, G. L. & Dear, M. J. (1984). *State apparatus.* Boston: Allen and Unwin.

Clavel, P. (1986). *The progressive city.* New Brunswick: Rutgers University Press.

Cockburn, C. (1977). *The local state.* London: Pluto Press.

Crenson, M. (1983). *Neighborhood politics.* Princeton: Princeton University Press.

Dear, M. J. (1981). A theory of the local state, pp. 183-200. In A. D. Burnett & P. J. Taylor, (Eds.), *Political studies from spatial perspectives.* Chichester: Wiley.

Evans, R. W. (1986). Could direct rule work for Britain? *Town and Country Planning*, April, 120-122.

Fincher, R. (1981). Analysis of the local level capitalist state. *Antipode, 13* 25-30.

Foucault, M. (1984). In Rabinow H. *The Foucault reader.* New York: Pantheon.

Geertz, C. (1980). *Negara: The theater state of Bali.* Princeton, NJ: Princeton University Press.

Geertz, C. (1983). *Local knowledge.* New York: Basic Books.

Giddens, A. (1981). *A contemporary critique of historical materialism.* London: Macmillan.

Giddens, A. (1985). *The nation state and violence.* Cambridge: Polity.

Harvey, D. W. (1985). *Consciousness and the urban experience.* Baltimore: Johns Hopkins University Press.

Heelan, P. A. (1983). *Space-perception and the philosophy of science.* Berkeley, CA: UC Press.

Johnston, R. J. (1984). *Residential segregation, the state and constitutional conflict in American urban areas.* London: Academic Press.

Jones, B. D. (1986). Political geography and the law: Banishing space from geography. *Political Geography Quarterly, 5*(3), 283-287.

Katznelson, I. (1981). *City trenches*. Chicago: Chicago University Press.

Kern, S. (1983). *The culture of time and space 1880-1918*. Cambridge, MA: Harvard University Press.

Kirby, A. M. (1982). The external relations of the local state, pp. 88-104. In K. R. Cox & R. J. Johnston (Eds.) *Conflict, politics and the urban scene*. London: Longman.

Kirby, A. M. (1983). A public city: Concepts of space and the local state. *Urban Geography, 4*(3), 191-202.

Krasner, S. D. (1984). Approaches to the state: Alternative conceptions and historical dynamics. *Comparative Politics, 16,* 223-246.

Lowi, T. (1976). *American government: Incomplete conquest*. Hinsdale, IL: Dryden.

Magnusson, W. (1986). Bourgeois theories of local government. *Political Studies, 34*(1), 1-18.

Miliband, R. (1969). *The state in capitalist society*. London: Quartet.

Sack, R. D. (1986). *Human territoriality*. Cambridge: Cambridge University Press.

Skinner, Q. (1969). Meaning and understanding in the history of ideas. *History and Theory, 8,* 3-53.

Skocpol, T. (1979). *States and social revolutions*. Cambridge: Cambridge University Press.

Skowronek, S. (1982). *Building a new American state: The expansion of national administrative capacities*. New York: Cambridge University Press.

Smith, R. M. (1984). "Modernization" and the corporate medieval village community in England: Some sceptical reflections, pp. 240-79. In A. R. H. Baker & D. Gregory (Eds.) *Exploration in historical geography: Interpretive essays*. Cambridge: Cambridge University Press.

Steinberger, P. J. (1985). *Ideology and the urban crisis*. Albany, NY: State University of New York Press.

Swanstrom, T. (1985). *The crisis of growth politics*. Philadelphia: Temple University Press.

Syed, A. (1966). *The political theory of American local government*. New York: Random House.

Taylor, P. J. & Johnston, R. J. (1979). *The geography of elections*. Beckenham: Croom Helm.

Thrift, N. & Forbes D. (1983). A landscape with figures. *Political Geography Quarterly, 2,* 247-264.

Tilly, C. (1985). *Space for capital, space for states*. Working Paper 17, CSSC. New York: New School for Social Research.

Tilly, C. (1986a). *The contentious French*. Cambridge, MA: Harvard University Press.

Tilly, C. (1986b). *Structural change and contention in Great Britain, 1758-1834*. Working Paper 36, CSSC, New York: New School for Social Research.

Tukey, J. (1977). *Exploratory data analysis*. Reading, Mass.: Addison Wesley.

Urwin, D. (1982). Territorial structures and political developments in the UK, pp. 19-74. In S. Rokkan & D. Urwin, (Eds.) *The politics of territorial identity*. Beverly Hills, CA: Sage.

Wallerstein, I. (1984). *Politics in the world-economy*. Cambridge: Cambridge University Press.

This chapter examines the process through which states achieved control over the exercise of violence on the high seas. This process entailed the politicization and delegitimation of two forms of nonstate, extraterritorial violence—privateering and piracy—and the development of new norms of sovereign control. Privateering was abolished through an international agreement, while piracy was eliminated through a much more complex process involving the use of force, domestic legal reforms, and the extension of European norms of state control to regions outside the European state system.

9

Sovereignty in Historical Perspective: The Evolution of State Control Over Extraterritorial Violence

JANICE E. THOMSON

Despite their debate over whether the state is a withering colossus or a highly adaptive entity (Rosenau, this volume), international relations theorists agree on an even more fundamental point. Both liberal interdependence and realist theories rest on the assumption that the state controls at least the principal means of coercion. It is this factor that distinguishes the state from other actors and institutions and ultimately justifies our treating the state as *the* actor in international relations.

Both empirically and for purposes of theorizing about the modern state system, this assumption seems justified. Contemporary states generally do have a monopoly on at least the major forces of coercion. It is important to recognize, however, that this is a quite recent development. Nonstate violence played a significant role in the international system as late as the mid-nineteenth century. States suffered, exploited, and sometimes ignored the violent activities of such actors as mercantile companies, pirates, and

Author's Note: I would like to thank Rick Ashley, Jim Caporaso, Steve Krasner, and John Meyer for helpful comments on earlier drafts of this chapter. Funding for this research was provided by the MacArthur Foundation and Stanford University.

227

mercenaries (Thomson & Krasner, 1989). For several centuries, states did not exert the kind of control over extraterritorial violence that they have in the twentieth century.

A more historical perspective on state control raises challenges to both liberal and realist theories. Increasing interdependence did not result in the erosion of state control, as liberal theory might predict. At the same time, it is clearly incorrect to treat state control as unproblematic and static, as at least some realist theorists do. Empirically, state control of violence in the international system has varied across both states and time. Diachronically, the variation has been in the direction of increasing state control.

This chapter examines the political process through which two related forms of nonstate violence—piracy and privateering—were eliminated. Of course, an increase in the state's capacity to project coercive power beyond its borders was a necessary precondition for their demise. However, the achievement of state control over violence in the international system was preceded by a complex political process. Traditional practices such as piracy and privateering had to first be politicized and delegitimated; they had to be defined as a problem with which states should deal.

My argument is that the elimination of these two forms of nonstate violence hinged on the resolution of three prior political issues. One concerned the question of establishing sovereignty on the high seas. This was not resolved until the turn of the nineteenth century, when it became clear that no one could exert effective sovereignty over the high seas. The seas would not be subject to sovereign control.

This raised the question of how order could be maintained on the high seas. If the high seas were beyond the pale of sovereignty, who was responsible or accountable for nonstate violence directed against a state or its subjects at sea? The third issue was how to distinguish a legitimate form of nonstate violence (privateering) from an illegitimate one (piracy).

Ultimately, these issues were resolved so that states ceased to authorize nonstate violence and therefore disclaimed responsibility for it. Because it proved impractical to enforce a distinction between legitimate and illegitimate nonstate violence, states eliminated it altogether, abandoning the practice of exploiting nonstate violence.

International and domestic politics and political institutions played an important role in this process. States did not eliminate nonstate violence by simply applying brute force. Privateering was abolished through an international agreement, while piracy was eliminated through a much more complex process involving the use of force, domestic legal reforms, and the extension of European norms of state control to regions outside the European state system.

Nonstate Violence and Sovereignty

Three solutions to the problem of nonstate violence on the high seas were possible. One was for a single state to claim sovereignty over broad stretches of the sea. Spain attempted this when the papal bull granted it sovereignty beyond a line "west of the Azores and north of the Tropic of Capricorn." Spain defined anyone trespassing this line as a pirate (Williams, 1962:117). This extraordinary claim to sovereignty failed for the simple reason that Spain could not enforce it. If even "legitimate" agents of other European states (e.g., privateers) were deemed pirates, then bona fide pirates could not even be identified. This produced a veritable "state of nature" in which Spain was at war with all outsiders. Ultimately, Spain was forced to recognize the legitimacy of other states' claims in the New World in exchange for the latter's agreement to control their subjects' violence against Spain.

The issue of establishing sovereignty over the high seas was not resolved until the turn of the nineteenth century. In other words, the absence of sovereignty over the oceans is not a timeless feature of the international system, but something which emerged in the course of the eighteenth century:

> Down to the beginning of the nineteenth century then, the course of opinion and practice with respect to the sea had been as follows. Originally it was taken for granted that the sea could be appropriated. It was effectively appropriated in some instances; and in others extravagant pretensions were put forward, supported by wholly insufficient acts. Gradually, as appropriation of the larger areas was found to be generally unreal, to be burdensome to strangers, and to be unattended by compensating advantages, a disinclination to submit to it arose, and partly through insensible abandonment, partly through opposition to the exercise of inadequate or intermittent control, the larger claims disappeared, and those only continued at last to be recognized which affected waters the possession of which was supposed to be necessary to the safety of a state, or which were thought to be within its power to command (Hall, 1924:189).

Until the middle of the seventeenth century, states generally considered the seas as objects for appropriation. By the turn of the nineteenth century, however, all but a handful of claims to sovereignty had been abandoned (Hall, 1924:180-187).

Once the extension of sovereignty to the high seas proved to be ineffective in controlling nonstate violence, two alternative solutions were attempted. One of these was to charge the responsibility to the home state of the perpetrators. The Mogul of India pursued this strategy. In his view, because the pirates who attacked his ships were white Europeans who spoke English, then they were English nationals whose activities were the responsibility of the English East India Company. He held the company's employees accountable for violence perpetrated by their fellow countrymen. This approach was successful insofar as it provoked Britain to enforce antipiracy laws within its empire. By rooting out corruption within its own territories and offering both positive and negative inducements to pirates operating from within its sovereign jurisdiction, Britain did much to suppress piracy in the East.

The Mogul's approach was based on the premise that the national origin of the pirate should determine which state was responsible for his acts in the international system. In practice, however, state sovereignty and nationality could be entirely divorced. For example, despite the fact that a ship flew the flag and carried the official documents of the British state (meaning the British state exerted sovereign authority over it) the crew might not include a single British national. Non-Europeans assumed that if the crew were Italian the ship was Italian, fraudulently claiming to be British.

Moreover, large numbers of European pirates, the so-called deep-sea marauders, expressly rejected any ties to their home states and gave their allegiance to pirate "commonwealths." These quasistates were based on a common interest in piracy, a rejection of European society, and a refusal to recognize themselves as being subject to the sovereign authority of any state. Nationality was irrelevant.

So neither claiming sovereignty over sections of the high seas nor charging the state with responsibility for its nationals produced an effective norm against piracy. European states refused to recognize a claim to sovereignty on the high seas because it could not be enforced. They also refused to accept responsibility for piratical acts based on the nationality of the perpetrators, because there was no firm link between nationality and state sovereignty. According to the norm that did develop, no state is responsible for the acts of pirates, and, therefore, no state can be held accountable for them. Pirates are stateless individuals. States are left with the discretion to prosecute pirates if they choose to outlaw piratical acts in their municipal law. In practice, however, effective enforcement of antipiracy norms depended on the ability to distinguish a pirate from a privateer.

In international law, privateers are defined as "vessels belonging to private owners, and sailing under a commission of war empowering the person to whom it is granted to carry on all forms of hostility which are permissible at sea by the usages of war." Privateers are usually required to post a bond to ensure their compliance with the government's instructions and their commissions are subject to inspection by public war-ships (Hall, 1924:620-621). In contrast, piracy consists "in acts of violence done upon the ocean or unappropriated lands, or within the territory of a state through descent from the sea, by a body of men acting independently of any politically organized society" (Hall, 1924:314).[1]

Acts of piracy are distinguished from other acts of violence on or emanating from the high seas by the fact that "they are done under conditions which render it impossible or unfair to hold any state responsible for their commission." Though "the absence of competent authority is the test of piracy, its essence consists in the pursuit of private, as contrasted with public, ends" (Hall, 1924:310-312). Thus, the distinction between a privateer and a pirate is twofold. The privateer acts under the authority of a state which accepts or is charged with responsibility for his acts, while the pirate acts on his own authority. Moreover, the privateer is regarded as pursuing the public interest and the pirate, his own private interest. In theory, these criteria provide a clear distinction between the legitimate practice of privateering and the illegitimate practice of piracy. While the activities of pirates and privateers are virtually identical, privateering is legitimate because it is authorized by a state and conducted only during wartime.

In practice, however, such clear-cut distinctions were not so easily made. Disputes among the members of the European state system centered on the question of whether or not an individual had been duly authorized by a state to engage in violence. For example, Spain and Britain on more than one occasion argued over whether various British adventurers were pirates or agents of the British crown. This problem was exacerbated by the fact that individuals slid easily from privateering into piracy and back to privateering. At the conclusion of a war, scores of unemployed privateers turned to piracy only to be granted amnesty and new privateering commissions in the next war.

Outside the European system, however, defining even the state and war could prove difficult. A case in point is the Barbary and Maltese corsairs. These corsairs, who attacked Mediterranean shipping, did not fit well into the category of pirates or of privateers.

While privateers were licensed only in time of war to capture or destroy enemy shipping, the situation of the corsairs was more complex. Moslems and Christians were in a virtually permanent state of war in the Mediterranean until the nineteenth century. Moreover, the designated "enemies" varied across countries and over time. From the 1620s on, victims of the

Barbary corsairs could change their status as enemies through treaties with the Barbary states, in which the latter agreed to prevent attacks on another state's commerce in exchange for the payment of protection money, frequently in the form of naval stores and other armaments. Yet "even after specific treaties had been signed in the 1620s, the question of whether Turkish and Algerine ships should be treated as pirates or public ships of a sovereign power was still undecided. Such attitudes lingered on until the early eighteenth century" (Earle, 1970:10, 34). Meanwhile, the Maltese corsairs, as Christians, were supposed to confine their attacks to Moslem shipping, but frequently targeted Greek Christian ships (Earle, 1970: 115-120).

Determining whether or not a state of war existed was only part of the problem. The corsairs, like privateers, were duly authorized by public officials to engage in their activities. However, the form of political authority under which the corsairs operated was unconventional by European state standards. The Barbary states, as part of the Ottoman Empire, were ostensibly ruled by the Sultan's appointees, the Pashas. Yet in reality, by the turn of the seventeenth century, these states were under the control of senior military officers acting through their elected leaders, the Beys and Deys. "Barbary and Turkey acted independently," so that "states which were at peace with Turkey were not necessarily at peace with Barbary, and vice versa" (Earle, 1970:24-26). Malta was ruled by the military order of the Knights of the Order of St. John of Jerusalem, who elected their leader, the Grand Master. But "the Grand Master owed feudal vassalage to whoever should be the ruler of Sicily, the King of Spain and later the Bourbon Kings." He was also subject to the authority of the Pope, and later to that of the king of France (Earle, 1970:101-102).

So, despite their being referred to as "military republics" (Earle, 1970:102, note), there are serious problems in determining who was really sovereign in these lands, and therefore, whether the authority under which their privateers operated met the conventional legal requirements of European privateering. Resolution of these issues came only with the end of European privateering. Once European states stopped authorizing nonstate violence, all nonstate violence on the high seas became piracy.

A key element in the modern definition of piracy is that it must emanate from the sea. Implicit in this notion is that piracy does not emanate from territories over which states exert sovereign control and authority. Historically, however, pirates were based in regions over which states did claim sovereignty, as well as in areas to which state sovereignty had not yet been extended. As a practical matter, states had to exert greater control over individuals within their sovereign jurisdictions. A state could not disclaim all responsibility for its subjects' activities even if it had not authorized them.

According to the practically derived norm of sovereign control, the state is responsible for quashing piracy within its own territorial waters, i.e., where it claims sovereignty. Evidence for the existence of this norm in Europe can be found as early as the beginning of the seventeenth century. In 1611, the Dutch asked for and were granted permission to send warships into English and Irish harbors "to capture pirates of any nationality" (Williams, 1962:91). In asking for permission, the Dutch were acknowledging the English state's sovereignty in its own territorial waters. In granting its permission, the English state conceded that it lacked the capacity to meet its sovereign obligations.

By the early nineteenth century, this antipiracy norm was clearly in place. When piracy broke out in Greece, the Persian Gulf, and China, European states charged the local sovereign with responsibility for controlling piracy in its own territorial waters. Backed with the threat of coercion, European states charged that non-Europeans could not simply disclaim responsibility for piracy in their territorial waters, regardless of who its victims were or how much those states might profit from it. To be recognized as sovereign a state had to control piracy within its jurisdiction.

By the mid-nineteenth century, then, several crucial issues had been resolved. States could not disclaim responsibility for violence emanating from their sovereign jurisdictions. States could disclaim responsibility for nonstate violence on the high seas since they agreed to stop authorizing it. They recognized that no one could establish effective sovereignty on the high seas, and developed the notion that each state would be free to deal with piracy as it saw fit.

The question is: How was all of this accomplished? How was piracy transformed from an "honorable crime" (Gosse, 1946:104) to a crime against the human race (Hall, 1924:312). Through what process was privateering converted from "patriotic piracy" (Lydon, 1970:28) to "a Kind of Piracy which disgraces our Civilisation . . ." (Malkin, 1927:30)? To shed some light on these questions, the following sections trace the processes through which piracy and privateering were politicized, delegitimated and finally eliminated.

Delegitimating Privateering

Privateering was an important and legitimate practice in the European state system for several centuries.[2] The practice apparently began in the 1200s when the English king ordered private vessels in English Channel ports to attack France (Sherry, 1986:57). Privateering proved to be a useful way for a state to raise a navy on short notice and at little cost.

Still, privateers caused problems for their sponsoring states. As we have seen, the end of a war and wartime privateering was always followed by a wave of piracy. But even during wartime, states had difficulty controlling privateers. States attempted to control privateers by requiring them to post bond or some form of "surety." This gave privateers an incentive to bring their prizes before a court which would rule on the legality of the capture. The problem with this mode of control was that the size of the bond, the need to share part of the prize with state officials, and the court-induced delay in actually receiving the prize money reduced the attractiveness of privateering. To maximize its gains from privateering, the state had to minimize the restrictions, but this reduced state control and inevitably led to abuses. Privateers attacked neutral and even their fellow-countrymen's shipping. Nevertheless, up until the mid-eighteenth century, states did little to control privateers. As major beneficiaries of privateering, states encouraged it.

Spain lodged perhaps the first major protest against privateering which produced real results. British privateers known as Sea Dogs, acting in collusion with the British crown, plundered and extorted money from Spanish ships and settlements in the New World. Britain rewarded two of these individuals, Drake and Raleigh, with knighthood (Stark, 1897:61-64; Lydon, 1970:27-28; Rankin, 1969:3-5).[3] When Spain and Britain's James I made peace, but Raleigh continued his depredations in Spanish America, the Spanish ambassador protested to the British government, which arrested and later executed Raleigh. After 1744, however, British merchants became major investors in privateering (Stark, 1897:66-70) and this led to the same old abuses.

The next major protest came from Prussia, another victim of British privateers. In response to a British privateer attack on one of his subject's ships, Frederick used the interest on money loaned him by English subjects (the Silesian loan) to indemnify the injured merchants (Hall, 1924:521).

Another source of protest was English insurance companies. When Britain lost control of its privateers in the mid-eighteenth century, English commercial interests suffered. The government responded by placing a minimal size on privateering vessels and requiring that privateers post a proper security. This eliminated the "little fishermen-privateers" who were most out of control, and improved the conduct of the larger ones (Stark, 1897:74-75). Moreover, the British government itself suffered from its privateers' attacks on neutral and even British commerce. A British naval historian has remarked that during the Seven Years War, "the action of our privateers was outrageous beyond endurance." Some of these "went so far as to capture vessels which had just been released by our own prize-courts" (Corbett, 1907:6). It seems that "nothing but the most strenuous exertions, penalties by Act of Parliament, cajolery by Government, pay in return for submission to naval discipline, restoration of prizes, enabled Britain to pacify the neutrals" (Piggott, 1919:147).

Yet another challenge to the practice of privateering came with the Armed Neutralities of 1780 and 1800. When two Russian ships carrying hemp and flax were seized by the British and detained for a year, Catherine II issued a document on February 26, 1780 "which declared that all neutral vessels might, of right, navigate freely from port to port and along the coasts of nations at war . . ." Other neutral powers adopted the Russian declaration and agreed to defend the principles with force if necessary. The second Armed Neutrality, which grew out of the renewal of this agreement in 1800, resulted in the 1801 Anglo-Russian convention in which Britain conceded "the immunity of convoyed vessels from search by privateers" (Stark, 1897:77-82).

So while friendly states, neutrals and insurance companies periodically defined privateering as a problem, their protests only resulted in the imposition of tighter controls on privateering. It was only when the greatest commercial and military naval power—Great Britain—defined privateering as a problem that it was permanently abolished. Yet, the prohibition on privateering was not simply imposed by Britain through the exercise of superior military power. Rather, the end of privateering was the result of an international agreement reached through bargaining between weak and strong naval powers.

The Abolition of Privateering

On April 16, 1856, the governments of France, Britain, Russia, Prussia, Austria, Sardinia, and Turkey signed the Treaty of Paris. Attached to this document was the Declaration of Paris whose intent was "to establish a uniform doctrine" on "Maritime Law in time of War." With this, the signatories declared that:

1. Privateering is, and remains abolished;
2. The Neutral Flag covers Enemy's Goods, with the exception of Contraband of War;

3. Neutral Goods, with the exception of Contraband of War, are not liable to capture under Enemy's Flag;

4. Blockades, in order to be binding, must be effective, that is to say, maintained by a force sufficient really to prevent access to the coast of the enemy.[4]

The agreement provided that states not attending the Congress of Paris be invited to accede to the Declaration, and that the provisions would be binding only on those states that signed or acceded to it. The agreement also specified that the four principles would be indivisible.

The Declaration's third and fourth principles were well established in international law and "perfectly settled" in prior practice (Stark, 1897: 143-144; Malkin, 1927:37). In other words, these two were simply declarations of what was already embodied in international law. In contrast, the first two principles *created* new international law.

While all but two states accepted the principle that neutral flags protect enemy goods (Principle 2), one of those two states was Britain (Stark, 1897:144).[5] Britain had traditionally exerted its right as a belligerent to make prize of enemy goods on neutral ships, regarding it as a mainstay of its naval supremacy. During the House of Lords' debate on the British government's decision to sign the Declaration of Paris, one critic stated that the government proposed to

surrender a right [i.e., to seize enemy goods on neutral ships] which belonged to us, which was established as a right by all jurists of earlier days, which was recognized by all jurists of modern times, which has been upheld by every statesman of importance in this country down to the latest, and which it was reserved for the present Government to throw away, although Pitt and Grenville and Canning successively declared it to be the mainstay of the naval power of England (UK, 1856:539).

Thus, the second provision of the Declaration could hardly be regarded as an established element of international law when the world's most powerful naval power regularly asserted its right to the contrary.

Even more controversial was the statement that "privateering is and remains abolished." As the U.S. State Department put it,

The right to resort to privateers is as clear as the right to use public armed ships, and as uncontestable as any other right appertaining to belligerents. The policy of that law has been occasionally questioned, not, however, by the best authorities; but the law itself has been universally admitted, and most nations have not hesitated to avail themselves of it; it is as well sustained by practice and public opinion as any other to be found in the Maritime Code.[6]

France and Britain had not issued letters of marque during the Crimean War. This meant that they had not authorized privateering since the Napoleonic Wars—a period of more than 40 years (Piggott, 1919:241). But of course this voluntary decision on the part of only two states to not engage in privateering in one war was not sufficient to make privateering a violation of international law.

The reason for linking the two well-established principles with the two new and controversial ones is simple: The Declaration of Paris was the result of a political deal. On one side were all the lesser and usually neutral naval powers whose main interest was to end the British practice of interdicting neutral ships in search of contraband. With no international agreement on what constituted contraband, British admiralty courts, in accordance with the government's policy of harassing neutral commerce, tended to apply a rather broad definition of contraband (Stark, 1897:70-71).[7] It was this practice which provoked the two Armed Neutralities.

On the other side was the British government whose principal interest was the abolition of privateering. As Lord Palmerston argued in a letter to the Queen:

> With regard to the proposal for an engagement against privateering, it seems to the Cabinet that as Great Britain is the Power which has the most extensive commerce by sea all over the world, which Privateers might attack, and has on the other Hand the largest Royal Navy which can do that which Privateers would perform, Great Britain would find it for her Interest to join in an agreement to abolish Privateering. In Fact during the last war with France though the French Navy was cooped up in its Ports British Commerce suffered very materially from French Privateers fitted out in Foreign Ports. . . .[8]

Not only had French privateers inflicted considerable damage on British commerce during the Napoleonic Wars, but at the outbreak of the Crimean War, Britain learned that the Russians were seeking U.S. permission to issue letters of marque to U.S. citizens (Piggott, 1919:8). Privateering was the weapon of the weak but Britain's global commerce made it most vulnerable to attack by privateers.

The Declaration offered a package which addressed the major concerns of both sides. None of the seven powers was averse to the prohibition on privateering. France's naval power was second only to that of Britain, so its reliance on privateering was diminishing.[9] The other European states had never been privateering states so they had no objection to ending the practice. Turkey, as a sort of junior member of the European state system, was not in a position to object to what the "Powers" decided (Stark,

1897:144). The ban on privateering was apparently a price worth paying for Britain's abandoning the right to interdict neutral ships in search of enemy contraband.

One state which did not share this view was the United States. It would agree to a ban on privateering only if states agreed to exempt from seizure the private property of a belligerent's subjects.[10] Britain counselled other states to reject such an agreement, hoping to isolate the United States in its defense of privateering. As Britain's Secretary of War put it, "If the Americans stood out on a question of privateering against a Resolution adopted by the Congress, they will be isolated on a point in which the whole civilized world will be against them" (Malkin, 1927:27).

Within two years, 42 of the 45 states invited to accede to the Declaration of Paris had done so (see Table 9.1). When invited to accede, the United States declined.[11]

Nevertheless, neither the United States nor Spain authorized privateering during the Spanish-American War, the first major maritime conflict after the Declaration of Paris.[12] On the whole, compliance with the ban on privateering was such that by 1874 the right to use them had "almost disappeared from the world" (Hall, 1924:621). Extending this norm beyond the European state system was another matter—a subject to which we turn now.

The Mediterranean Corsairs

As we saw earlier, the practices of the Mediterranean corsairs fell somewhere between privateering and piracy. The ambiguity of the distinction between the privateer and the pirate was dramatically revealed in Europe's encounter with the corsairs of Malta and the Barbary Coast. Because this region lay beyond the confines of the European state system, basic questions about sovereign authority and of war and peace were difficult to answer.

The Barbary Coast

Europeans tried three approaches to dealing with the Barbary corsairs. Many states negotiated treaties with the individual Barbary states, securing protection from corsair attacks with the payment of cash and/or commodities. As England, France, Spain, Holland, and Sweden did during the

TABLE 9.1 Accessions to the Declaration of Paris

State	Year
Anhalt-Dessau-Coethen	1856
Argentine Confederation	1856
Baden	1856
Bavaria	1856
Belgium	1856
Brazil	1858
Bremen	1856
Brunswick	1857
Chile	1856
Denmark	1856
Ecuador	1856
Frankfort	1856
Germanic Confederation	1856
Greece	1856
Guatemala	1856
Hamburgh	1856
Hanover	1856
Haiti	1856
Hesse-Cassel	1856
Hesse-Darmstadt	1856
Lubeck	1856
Mecklenburg-Schwerin	1856
Mecklenburg-Strelitz	1856
Mexico	—
Modena	1856
Uruguay	—[1]
Nassau	1856
Netherlands	1856
New Grenada	1856
Oldenburg	1856
Parma	1856
Peru	1857
Portugal	1856
Roman States	1856
Saxe-Altenburg	1856
Saxe-Coburg-Gotha	1856
Saxe-Meiningen	1856
Saxe-Weimar	1856
Saxony	1856
Sicilies	1856
Spain	—
Sweden and Norway	1856
Switzerland	1856
Tuscany	1856
United States	—
Wurtemberg	1856

1. Uruguay assented, subject to ratification by its legislature.
SOURCE: Hertslet (1875: 1284).

seventeenth century, the United States signed such agreements in the eighteenth century (Gosse, 1946:58-59, 63).[13]

These treaties were not easily enforced, in part because of the difficulty of establishing the national identity of European ships. Many of the Barbary corsair crewmen could not speak or read English or French, so it was difficult for them to verify the passports carried by European vessels. In addition, English ships employed Spanish and Italian crews while the French used Genoese crews. Barbary officials found it difficult to believe that a ship flying the French flag but whose crew couldn't speak French was really French, or that a ship with an Italian-speaking crew was really English (Wolf, 1979:311-317).

"Had all, or even three or four, of the wronged powers agreed to combine their forces, they could at any time have wiped out the North African pirates" (Gosse, 1946:58; Earle, 1970:15). Three factors prevented this.

First, European states viewed the Barbary corsairs as an opportunity to gain advantage in their competition with other European states—in war or in commerce. By paying protection money, a European state could dominate Mediterranean trade while its rivals would be open to attack by the corsairs (Gosse, 1946:58-59; Earle, 1970:15, 266). Second, European state leaders must have had a somewhat ambivalent attitude toward corsair activities since the people who purchased their prizes were "those same English, French or Dutch merchants who had sailed to buy just these goods in the normal run of commerce." Only it was much cheaper to purchase these goods in prize auctions than at their point of origin (Earle, 1970:16).

The third factor inhibiting European cooperation was related to the second strategy for dealing with the corsairs: the application of brute force. Though states repeatedly took unilateral military action against the corsairs' port bases (Gosse, 1946:59-62), these were not successful.[14] For example, a joint Anglo-Dutch naval force destroyed the Algerian navy in 1816 (Wolf, 1979:331). However, "scarcely was the fleet out of sight of the Mediterranean than the pirates were at their old ways again" (Gosse, 1946:66-67; Earle, 1970:267). Proposals for concerted action made at the Congress of Vienna (Earle, 1970:267) and the Congress of Aix-la-Chapelle came to naught, probably because "Britain feared the presence of Russian warships in the Mediterranean . . ." (Williams, 1962:195).

The third and ultimately successful approach to eliminating the corsairs was to threaten to revoke recognition of Barbary state sovereignty. In 1830, a French army of 37,000 men invaded and captured Algiers (Gosse, 1946:69).[15] The French occupation of Algiers led Tripoli and Tunis to suppress their corsairs and thus "to retain their independence for a further 50 and 80 years respectively'' (Earle, 1970:267). So, in the end, it was only through the imposition of European norms of sovereign control that the Barbary corsairs were eliminated.

Malta

The Europeans were also responsible for the demise of the Maltese corsairs, despite the fact that the latter's attacks were directed at Moslems. Europeans had three ways of exerting influence on the Maltese. First, since the Order of St. John was originally "created during the Crusades with charters from the Pope,'' the Pope exerted considerable influence, backed by the threat of excommunication. Second, due to its dependence on Sicily for corn, Malta was susceptible to threats of a Sicilian grain embargo. Finally, the Order, in its war against the Moslems, depended on contributions from the European faithful which were often in the form of land. Since these lands "were scattered all over Europe, the Order depended on the goodwill of European sovereigns . . .'' (Earle, 1970:101-104). Pressure from these sources eventually squeezed the Maltese corsairs out of business.

These corsairs got into trouble on three counts. First, though they were supposed to attack only Moslems, many persisted in capturing Christian—mainly Greek—ships. This led to repeated conflicts with the Pope whose mandate against attacking Greek Christians ended the practice in 1732 (Earle, 1970:109, 119). A second set of problems stemmed from the fact that the Maltese were Frenchmen. On the one hand, this meant that France was susceptible to reprisals by the corsairs' victims. On the other, when France was allied with Turkey, the Maltese were effectively prohibited from attacking Turkish ships, their principal targets. These concerns led France to consistently narrow the Maltese corsairs' range of targets.

The third problem was that the French, who wanted to dominate Mediterranean trade themselves, became major carriers of Moslem goods. Maltese corsairs were thus deprived of a major source of booty. Though the corsairs asserted the right to search friendly (i.e., French) ships for enemy (i.e., Moslem) goods, the French king prevailed in ordering a stop to this practice (Earle, 1970:109-120). As a result of all these restrictions, no corsair licenses were issued between 1749 and 1751 (Earle, 1970:268).[16]

As in the case of the Barbary corsairs, however, it was the extension of European norms of sovereign control to the island which put a permanent end to Maltese corsairing activity. In 1798, Napoleon took over Malta and abolished privateering (Earle, 1970:268-270).

The corsairs—whether privateers or pirates—were eliminated only with Europe's actual or threatened revocation of these military republics' sovereignty. It was difficult to assess the legitimacy of the corsairs when sovereignty and the existence of a state of war were themselves in dispute. Ultimately, all nonstate violence was defined as illegitimate. Thereafter, all violence committed by nonstate actors on the high seas was by definition piracy. In the next section we turn to the politicization and delegitimation of piracy.

European Piracy

Buccaneers

In the seventeenth century, French political and religious refugees settled on Hispaniola, providing supplies to visiting ships in exchange for guns and ammunition. Spain, which regarded these activities as illegal, expelled these buccaneers who turned to attacking Spanish shipping from the island of Tortuga.[17] This new base attracted adventurers of several nationalities, especially English and French, whose governments were enemies of Spain (Rankin, 1969:7-9; Sherry, 1986:59). "From about 1630, and for the next eighty years despite Spanish efforts to dislodge them, the people of Tortuga lived in something akin to a pirate 'republic' known as the Brethren of the Coast" (Rankin, 1969:8-9).

English buccaneering flourished after Britain seized Jamaica from Spain in 1655. To defend this colonial outpost from recapture by Spain, "the governor freely issued letters of marque to 'Frenchmen' from Tortuga, Dutch adventurers, and then, increasingly, to English rovers" (Williams, 1962:124). It was from Jamaica that Henry Morgan launched his 1671 attack on Panama. While Spain charged that Morgan was a pirate, "the English agreed with Morgan that he and his buccaneers were legal privateers" (Sherry, 1986:60). However, in 1670 Britain and Spain signed the Treaty of America by which Spain recognized British sovereignty in Jamaica[18] in exchange for British agreement to restrain its subjects' depredations on Spanish possessions (Kemp & Lloyd, 1960:29).

When news of Morgan's devastating attack on Panama reached Europe, Britain was forced to arrest the Jamaican governor and call Morgan home "to answer for his offences against the King, his crown and dignity" (Rankin, 1969:16). Neither man was punished.[19] Peace between William of Orange and Spain after 1689 led to a decline in buccaneering. The rich

Spanish shipping was no longer a legitimate target, and the brotherhood was shattered as "English and French buccaneers found themselves on opposite sides of the conflict" (Sherry, 1986:62; Rankin, 1969:18).

The Madagascar Pirate Commonwealth

European and American pirates poured into Madagascar after 1693, when a North American privateer captured a ship belonging to the Mogul of India. In addition to luxury goods, the ship carried £100,000 in gold and silver coins (Sherry, 1986:29, 91). While the ships of the Mogul and the East India Company provided the targets for the Madagascar pirates, North American merchants supplied the pirates with the economic infrastructure they needed (Williams, 1962:178). Some North American traders set up shop on Madagascar, exchanging colonial products for the luxury items captured through piracy. Corrupt colonial officials allowed the latter to enter their ports without customs inspections, and some even invested in pirate expeditions. North American shipbuilders could barely meet the demand for pirate trade vessels (Sherry, 1986:93).

The elimination of the Madagascar pirates was in part a function of eradicating piracy's base of support in the colonies, as we shall see in the next section. However, it also entailed the use of force against the pirates themselves.

A fundamental difference between the Madagascar pirates and others was that the former came close to constituting an independent nation.[20] Madagascar pirate ships operated under a consistent set of rules specifying the rights and duties of the crews. These rules more or less expressed the laws of the Madagascar "commonwealth." But there was more:

> Another strong sign of an evolving nationalism was the loyalty pirates showed to their fellow outlaws. In fact, pirates were more loyal to each other than they were to their country of origin or to their religion or even to their own race. The evidence for this abounds. English, American and French pirates sailed together and fought effectively together in Henry Every's crew, despite the fact that France was at war with England and her colonies. Irish Catholics and Protestant Scots worked alongside each other without friction aboard scores of pirate vessels, despite the religious antagonisms that divided their nonpirate countrymen.

These pirates also developed their own customs, language, cuisine, and flag. An East India Company petition to the British government noted that most of these pirates were English and warned "that if the present generation of pirates on Madagascar should become extinct, 'their Children will have the same Inclination to Madagascar, as these have to England, and will not have any such affection for England.' "

Clearly, Europeans viewed the Madagascar pirate "commonwealth" as a formidable quasistate. Their fears were not without foundation. In the words of one pirate captain, "*I am a free prince* and have as much authority to make war on the whole world as he who has a hundred sail of ships and an army of a hundred thousand men in the field."

East India Company complaints eventually drew the British government's attention to the Madagascar pirates. The company's problem was that since most of the pirates were English-speaking, the Mogul of India charged that they were acting in collusion with the company. When one of his ships was captured by an English pirate, the Mogul seized East India Company property and imprisoned 50 of its employees, including the manager. After this incident, the Mogul declared that Europeans trading with India would be responsible for the safety of his ships.

The company appealed to London for permission to prosecute pirates themselves and for help from the Royal Navy. Both of these requests were denied[21] so the company was forced to escort the Mogul's ships with its own armed merchant vessels. This led the pirates to attack the company's vessels, which they had previously avoided doing. Of course the company found it particularly galling that it was American colonial corruption that supported the Madagascar pirates.

In 1698 the Treaty of Ryswick produced a lull in the war between Britain and France, allowing the British government to send four naval vessels to Madagascar. Most of the pirates accepted the Royal Navy's offer of amnesty and within two years "the pirate nation had all but disappeared."

It was given new life, however, by the War of the Spanish Succession in which the British Crown authorized privateering against Spanish and French shipping. Madagascar pirates now became "lawful brigands of the queen of England." After the war, thousands of men with up to ten years' experience in sea raiding—and often in nothing else—turned to piracy. With the Royal Navy still patrolling the Madagascar area, many of them moved to the Bahamas.

North America

Suppressing piracy in the Americas entailed a two-pronged strategy: eliminating colonial participation in pirate trade and destroying the pirate stronghold in the Bahamas.[22]

Eliminating Colonial Support. A crucial problem for Britain in suppressing piracy in the Americas was the weak judicial system in the colonies. Under the system established in 1536 with the first Act of Piracy, piracy trials could be held only in England, necessitating the transport of the accused, evidence and witnesses from colonial areas to England. Time-consuming and expensive, this procedure led to "a general ignoring of the law, or the holding of what might be termed illegal trials for piracy in the colonies" (Rankin, 1969:76-77). Apparently, large numbers of captured pirates "escaped" from colonial prisons (Rankin, 1969:63), but those who did stand trial were often acquitted by colonial juries who were reluctant to impose the death penalty on the accused (Williams, 1962:141; Ritchie, 1986:144). Colonial magistrates and governors accepted bribes, or "exacted tribute," from pirates in exchange for the latter's freedom (Gosse, 1946:207-208, 321-322).

In 1699, Parliament passed the second Act of Piracy which provided for the establishment of vice-admiralty courts in the colonies. Thus, persons charged with piracy would no longer have to be taken to England for trial, and would be subject to admiralty laws rather than local, civil law. This act also provided that if a colony "refused to co-operate in working this system it would lose its charter. Another Act of the same sessions provided that each governor should be liable to punishment in England for offenses against the laws of the realm" (Williams, 1962:142).

In addition to these efforts at facilitating the prosecution of piracy, two other steps were taken. First, the crown replaced the corrupt governor of New York, Benjamin Fletcher, who "openly consorted with and entertained notorious pirates, some at his dinner table" (Rankin, 1969:57).[23] As Fletcher's replacement, the king selected the Earl of Bellomont, naming him "not only governor of New York, Massachusetts, and New Hampshire, but also captain-general of all the military and naval forces in Connecticut, Rhode Island, and New Jersey as well." Bellomont would be "the most powerful royal governor ever to serve in the colonies" (Sherry, 1986:147).

Arriving in 1698, Bellomont's first challenge was to overcome the pro-piracy sentiment, which pervaded both officialdom and the merchant community. Initially, the local customs collector, sheriff, and constables all refused to comply with Bellomont's orders to seize piratical goods, and the merchants resisted all his attempts to suppress the pirate trade. In response, Bellomont compiled such a mountain of evidence attesting to Fletcher's corruption that the latter was forced to defend himself in Britain against charges of piracy. Bellomont was then free to fire Fletcher's cronies from various public offices in New York. He forced New York pirate traders out of business by seizing their ships which were loaded with plunder purchased from pirates, and dismissed pirate traders from political appointments. The governor of Virginia and other colonial officials also joined in the antipiracy campaign so that by 1701 the pirate trade had "all but withered away . . ." (Sherry, 1986:197-198).

In 1721, when piracy threatened to revive in the East, the British parliament enacted a law which made trafficking with pirates or furnishing them with supplies crimes of piracy. Another law provided that merchant sailors who resisted pirate attacks would be rewarded and those who did not resist would be punished. Together with the suppression of markets for piratical goods, these laws contributed to the demise of eastern piracy. Unreformed pirates moved on to the western coast of Africa (Sherry, 1986:296-297).

Destroying the Pirate Base. Despite this successful suppression of the colonial supporters of piracy, there remained the problem of eliminating the pirates themselves. In 1716 the Bahamas was home to a 200-man "pirate republic" (Williams, 1962:149-150). These pirates preyed on shipping in the West Indies, Virginia and the Carolinas.

One strategy for dealing with piracy was to offer positive inducements for individuals to give up piracy. In 1717 a royal proclamation offering a pardon to those who would surrender prompted some 450 pirates to turn themselves in, but these small numbers indicated that further government action was required (Williams, 1962:158).

Royal Navy men-of-war were dispatched to the Caribbean and North America but proved ineffective. For one thing, the commanders refused to take orders from the colonial governors who were most familiar with the pirates' operations. Moreover, naval commanders found that they could make a great deal of money by charging a fee for either escorting merchant ships or transporting cargo themselves. When it became apparent that the Royal Navy was not up to the job, a group of English merchants leased the Bahamas from the crown and petitioned the crown to appoint Woodes Rogers as governor. The merchants planned to eradicate the pirates, and repopulate the islands with European farmers and artisans (Sherry, 1986:216-225; Rankin, 1969:20).

Meanwhile, Spain had driven English logwood cutters out of the Yucatan so that by the time Rogers arrived in July of 1718, nine out of ten of the 3000 pirates in New Providence were unemployed Englishmen (Rankin, 1969:91). With only 100 soldiers and four Royal Navy men-of-war under his command (Sherry, 1986:225-226), Rogers could hardly rely on force to suppress the pirate community. As an incentive for people to voluntarily give up piracy, he allowed those who would accept the government's pardon to keep their ill-gotten gains and offered free plots of land to those who had nothing. Perhaps Rogers' most successful action was to neutralize two of the best-known pirate captains by granting them pardons and issuing them privateering licenses to defend New Providence.[24]

The execution of two particularly famous pirates—Blackbeard and Bonnet—in the Carolinas, provided a new deterrent to piracy. At the same time, though he was not authorized by the crown to do so, Rogers decided to try piracy cases in his own court rather than send suspects to Jamaica (Sherry, 1986:253-256; Rankin, 1969:21).

Finally, when war broke out between Britain and Spain, the British crown offered a new amnesty to Caribbean pirates and induced them to enlist as privateers against Spain. During the war, Rogers rebuilt the island's defenses which, when no longer needed against the Spanish threat, were equally valuable against pirates. By mid-1729, piracy had been eradicated from the Bahamas. The remaining unreformed pirates moved to Jamaica and Hispaniola or to Madagascar (Sherry, 1986:264, 275).[25] Nevertheless, European piracy was effectively suppressed by 1730 (Sherry, 1986:358; Rediker, 1987:282; Ritchie, 1986:236).[26]

Piracy in the seventeenth and early eighteenth centuries was a European problem. British mercantile companies suffered from the actions of British pirates supported by subjects of the British empire. Institutional reforms within the empire were a major factor in quashing piracy. These reforms reflected the emerging norm that the state was responsible for controlling its own subjects.

Though the use of force against piracy was an important element in its suppression, it was not the only or even the most crucial method. The state's own coercive forces often proved ineffectual, as when Royal Navy personnel convoyed merchant ships for personal gain. States did not simply exterminate pirates, but attempted to reintegrate them into society or the armed forces. Independent pirate communities were not viewed simply as groups of bandits but as nationals of the several states who could be enticed back into society.

The antipiracy norm was clearly in place in the European state system by the early nineteenth century, when the powers agreed that the Barbary corsairs were pirates and that they should be eliminated. It remained for Europeans to spread the norm to areas outside of the European state system.

Non-European Piracy

In the Middle East, the most significant center of piracy was the southeast shore of the Persian Gulf. These pirates, the Joasmees, first began attacking English shipping in 1778. The King of Oman was quite effective in controlling piracy in this region, but with his death in 1804 came a resurgence in piracy. In 1806 an Arab fleet under British command secured the pirates' surrender and a treaty in which the Joasmees agreed to stop their attacks in exchange for the right to trade with English ports in India. The pirates shortly broke the treaty by attacking British ships, provoking the governor-general at Calcutta to send a fleet that destroyed the pirates' bases and most of their ships. Less than a year later, the Joasmees had not only regained control of the Gulf but began attacking trade in the Red Sea and along the Indian coast. The Joasmees were finally suppressed in 1819 when a large British-Omani naval fleet and 4000 soldiers effectively destroyed the Joasmees' bases and fleet (Gosse, 1946:254-264; Belgrave, 1966:135).

Another outbreak of piracy occurred during the Greek War for Independence (1821-1827) when major pirate bases were established in the North Aegean and in southern Crete. In 1826 alone there were 96 cases of Greek piracy. Again the line between acts of piracy and acts of war was blurred. Greek warships were so poorly provisioned that they seized what they needed from any ship unable to defend itself. After defeating the Turkish navy with an allied squadron of British, French, and Russian warships, the British admiral warned the Greek government that the forces used to destroy the Turkish navy could be turned against the Greeks unless their piracy were suppressed. Though both the Greek navy and the pirates seem to have taken the warning to heart, the British in 1828 destroyed the pirate base on Crete and large numbers of pirate vessels (Williams, 1962:195-197).

Borneo was a major base for piracy in the 1840s. After a successful British naval expedition against the pirates' inland bases, the Sultan of Brunei ceded to Britain the island of Labuan "for the suppression of piracy and the encouragement and extension of trade" (Williams, 1962:221-222). But as the Brunei state depended on the slave-trade and piracy for much of its revenues, the Sultan's opponents overthrew him and replaced him with "a puppet of the pirates" (Williams, 1962:222; Tarling, 1963:128). British naval forces sailed to the capital and, finding that the Sultan's court had fled,

(t)he Admiral issued a proclamation that "if the Sultan would return and govern his people justly, abstain from acts of piracy and keep his agreement with the British government, hostilities would cease," but "if the same atrocious system was again carried on when the ships left the Coast" he would burn Brunei to the ground (Williams, 1962:222-223).

This action was followed in 1849 by a final British naval operation in which more than 800 pirates were killed or drowned (Gosse, 1946:292). This expedition effectively put an end to Borneo piracy.[27]

Chinese pirates made costly attacks on British and Portuguese ships in the China Seas at the beginning of the nineteenth century. One pirate, at the peak of his career, employed 70,000 men organized in six large squadrons. The emperor's efforts to buy him off failed, and imperial fleets sent against him were defeated three times in two years. In 1810, the huge pirate fleet fell victim to a mutiny by its admirals. One squadron of 160 ships and 8000 men surrendered to the emperor who pardoned them. Eventually the leader of the pirate fleet took advantage of a general pardon and surrendered as well. "The government gave each pirate money for starting life ashore," gave the pirates two towns to live in, and bestowed an imperial commission as a major on the former second-in-command of the pirate fleet (Williams, 1962:207-210; Gosse, 1946:271-277).

Pirates based in Hong Kong also attacked European shipping. Initially the Chinese emperor forbade British gunboats from entering his territorial waters in pursuit of pirates. With the outbreak of civil strife in China in the 1850s, the British forced the Viceroy at Canton "to admit that he could not keep his own house in order" and secured his cooperation in suppressing the new outbreak of piracy.[28] Even while Britain and China were at war (1856-1860), Chinese mandarins continued to assist the Royal Navy in suppressing the pirates. Piracy in China was finally ended through a combination of international force, effective prosecution, and a new system of vessel-registration adopted by the Chinese at the behest of the British. After 1869, the Chinese themselves took responsibility for protecting local trade (Williams, 1962:215-218).

Just as in the corsairs case, the elimination of non-European piracy came with the extension of new norms of sovereign control to areas outside the European state system. Leaders of non-European states were expected to deal with piracy in their jurisdictions, despite the fact that many of them profited from it and Europeans were its major victims.

European states, usually Britain, first urged local rulers to take action against their pirates. Where they failed, as in Brunei and Greece, Europeans eliminated the pirates by force. In cases where local leaders were willing but unable to suppress piracy, as in Oman and China, Europeans joined them in taking military action against the pirates. Finally, a non-European state could develop independent enforcement capabilities by adopting European bureaucratic methods of control, as did China.

Conclusion

Findings from this analysis of the elimination of extraterritorial nonstate violence are inconsistent with notions that sovereignty is a static attribute of the state. This research suggests that the norms of sovereign control develop through the practical resolution of international issues which must first be politicized. Recognition that the high seas were beyond the pale of territorial sovereignty politicized nonstate violence. Questions of who was accountable for nonstate violence were forced onto the political agenda.

The attempt to maintain a distinction between legitimate and illegitimate forms of nonstate violence failed, as did the attempt to link state responsibility with the nationality of the perpetrators. Ultimately states agreed to give up the right to exploit nonstate violence through the practice of privateering. Only then could piracy be isolated. States agreed not to authorize nonstate violence so, by definition, all nonstate violence on the high seas was piracy. The elimination of European privateering was the prelude to the permanent elimination of piracy.

The key to eliminating piracy was a redefinition of the norms of sovereign control. Once Europeans had adopted this norm of expanded state control, they made it clear that states outside the system were expected to follow suit. States, like Algiers, which refused to go along, lost their sovereignty. Those who retained their sovereignty adopted the European norms of sovereign control as Tunisia and China did.

Notes

1. See also Harvard Law School Research in International Law (1932:739-1013) and Oppenheim (1955:609).

2. Privateers played a significant role in many eighteenth-century and early nineteenth-century conflicts, including the War of the Spanish Succession, the War of the Austrian Succession, the Seven Years War, and the French revolutionary wars. See Lydon (1970), Stark (1897), Swanson (1985), Sherry (1986), and Clowes (1898). French privateering was the main threat to eighteenth-century British trade in the Atlantic and Mediterranean (Crowhurst, 1977:15-17). In the mid-eighteenth century, French privateers nearly put an end to the slave trade between Africa and Britain's American colonies (Sherry, 1986:359). American privateers served both sides in the U.S. War for Independence. Rebel privateers even operated in British waters, forcing Britain to provide naval escort for shipping between Ireland and England. See Lydon (1970), Stark (1897), and Maclay (1899). In the War of 1812 American privateers captured prizes worth an estimated $39 million (Maclay, 1899:ix; Stark, 1897:135).

3. French privateers behaved similarly and were rewarded with letters of nobility (Stark, 1897:99-101).

4. Reprinted in Hertslet (1875:1282-1283). "Translation as laid before Parliament."

5. The other was Spain.

6. From the second Marcy note; reprinted in Piggott (1919:395). In fact, at about the same time as the Declaration was being formulated, a text on international law was published in France which declared that "the issuing of letters of marque, therefore, is a constantly customary belligerent act. Privateers are *bona-fide* war-vessels, manned by volunteers, to whom, by way of reward, the Sovereign resigns such prizes as they make, in the same manner as he sometimes assigns to the land forces a portion of the war contributions levied on the conquered enemy." Cited in Piggott (1919:397).

7. Hall (1924:770) says that Britain's views of its belligerent rights seem "to have permitted the list of contraband articles to be enlarged or restricted to suit the particular circumstances of the war."

8. Letter dated April 5, 1856. Quoted in Malkin (1927:30).

9. Moreover, the French privateer had always been of a "more uncontrollable and piratical type" than those of other states. It may be that "several decades of spoliation claims had suggested to the French nation that perhaps it was better to save the money which they would have to pay for his depredations, and use it toward carrying on the war." See Stark (1897:144).

10. The United States believed that there was no difference between a volunteer navy (privateers) and a volunteer army, so the attempt to ban one and not the other was illogical (Piggott, 1919:398). It also rejected the argument that privateering, because it was based on the profit motive, was more difficult to control than regular naval forces. In the United States view, this ignored the fact that sailors of regular navies also made prizes of private merchant ships and divided the prize money amongst themselves. See Bowles (1900:98-100) for this argument. Thus, the United States argued that there was only one logical basis for banning privateering: the protection of private commercial shipping—including that belonging to subjects of belligerent states—from attacks on the high seas.

11. The only other states which declined were Spain and Mexico. Spain acceded in 1908 and Mexico in 1909. Piggott (1919:138) also reports Venezuela as a non-signatory. The United States and Venezuela, it is believed, never acceded. See Hall (1924:621; Stark, 1897:147).

12. At the onset of the war the United States announced that it would abide by all the provisions of the Declaration of Paris, including the ban on privateering (Piggott, 1919:438). It is unclear why Spain and the United States decided not to use privateers. One source (Reuter, 1924:86-87) suggests it was the result of British pressure.

13. "Venice paid 22,000 gold sequines and an annual tribute of 12,000 gold sequines for peace; the young Republic of the United States paid $642,500 and an annual tribute of $21,600 in naval supplies; Hamburg, Sweden, Denmark and Naples also paid handsomely for protection." In its 1796 treaty, the United States also agreed to provide "the gift of a thirty-six-gun frigate." See Wolf (1979:311-313).

14. By the turn of the eighteenth century, French and English naval power in the Mediterranean was great enough to deter the corsairs from risking a war with either power by attacking its ships. Yet, the full force of these naval powers was not turned on the Barbary states, despite the pleas from Europe that the corsairs be destroyed. Though Britain and France surely enjoyed seeing their trading rivals bear the brunt of corsair attacks, it is also true that throughout the 18th century both powers devoted their resources to fighting each other. Moreover, it was not clear that the benefits of wiping out the corsairs would exceed the costs which would go far beyond the simple bombardment of coastal bases (Wolf, 1979:320).

15. What provoked the invasion was a dispute between the French government and the Dey over a debt owed the Dey by some French merchants. The French decision to invade

Algiers was approved by Russia and the two German powers, but was opposed by England and, of course, the Ottoman empire (Wolf, 1979:335).

16. The Maltese found various ways to "cheat" on these restrictions—such as sailing under the flag of the Prince of Monaco, or claiming that high winds had carried them into the restricted areas of the Mediterranean—so their activities continued through the 18th century (Earle, 1970).

17. Sovereignty over the island of Tortuga was disputed. In 1631, the English residents petitioned the Company of Providence Island "to take Tortuga under its protection." So Tortuga was technically British until Spain took it over in 1636 (Williams, 1962:123). Seeing Tortuga as a potentially valuable base, a group of Frenchmen from St. Christopher took possession of the island in 1640 and named one of their own governor (Rankin, 1969:9). Finally in 1659 Spain recognized Tortuga as part of the French empire (Williams, 1962:123).

18. Morgan's costly attacks were largely responsible for forcing Spain to deal with Britain (Rankin, 1969:15).

19. The governor was returned to Jamaica as Chief Justice and Morgan, a popular hero, was knighted and later named Lieutenant-Governor of Jamaica and a judge on its Vice-admiralty Court (Rankin, 1969:16; Williams, 1962:125).

20. The following account of the Madagascar pirates is taken from Sherry (1986:94-203).

21. Military assistance from Britain for the war against piracy came first in the form of Captain Kidd's privately financed privateering expedition (1696-99). His failed mission was not inconsequential since it demonstrated the futility of private efforts to suppress piracy and "helped to convince many of those in power that only a determined effort by the Royal Navy and an honest effort by colonial officials to enforce the king's writ at sea and ashore would eradicate piracy in the eastern seas" (Sherry, 1986:195).

22. Reasons for colonial support for piracy were numerous. Pirates supplied goods otherwise unobtainable under the Navigation Acts. Luxury goods, especially from the East, were made available at bargain prices. Trade in piratical goods helped the colonies maintain a balance of trade with England, and provisioning pirate ships was a thriving business. Financing pirate voyages provided an investment opportunity for wealthy individuals with excess capital. Bribes, gifts, and protection money obtained from pirates supplemented the rather meager incomes of colonial officials. See Rankin (1969:19, 43, 54-58), Sherry (1986:23-24, 116-118), Ritchie (1986:18-19, 36-39), and Gosse (1946:206-12).

23. Fletcher was actually removed from office for political corruption, not for collaboration with pirates. See Williams (1962:136) and Ritchie (1986:50).

24. His efforts suffered a serious setback, however, when an epidemic killed most of the settlers and drove the Royal Navy from Nassau. With the departure of the Royal Navy, many pirates returned to their old ways and Rogers faced the prospect that all his accomplishments would shortly come undone (Sherry, 1986:232-234).

25. Several successful pirates who departed the Bahamas upon learning of Rogers' appointment as governor had sailed to Madagascar and set up bases there (1718-1719) from which they attacked Indian and East India Company shipping. This time the British government responded quickly to East India Company appeals by sending four men-of-war to Madagascar. Though the navy did not capture a single pirate, its mere presence drove most of the pirates out of the region. See Sherry (1986:280-284, 293).

26. The abolition of slavery in the British empire in 1834 provided a major impetus for piracy. Since the demand for slaves in the Americas, India and the Arab World was unabated, the "illegal" trade in slaves continued. Those states which had outlawed slavery defined trading in slaves as piracy. Though the Royal Navy made a concerted effort to suppress the trade at its sources in West Africa, it was only with the abolition of slavery in the United States

that the trans-Atlantic slave trade ended (Williams, 1962:199-202; Gosse, 1946:296-297). The Arab slave trade was suppressed only with the policing of the Red Sea and Persian Gulf by France, Italy and Britain beginning with the turn of the nineteenth century (Williams, 1962:206).

27. This operation caused two problems for its commander. First, he employed "hundreds of native boats" whose sailors were motivated by the prospect of plunder. Questioning whether this expedition was directed only against pirates or against peaceful traders as well, the British government formed a commission to investigate the incident. The second problem was that according to an 1825 Act of Parliament, the government was to pay £25 for each captured or killed pirate. Thus, the Borneo expedition claimed a reward of nearly £21,000. Parliament was outraged that this amount of money should be paid "to those who destroyed primitive tribes, armed with spears and swords," when "men who captured vessels in actions against a national enemy" received one-fourth that amount. This outrage led to the repeal of the Act of 1825 (Williams, 1962:224-225).

28. The British forces were supplemented with one of the Viceroy's war junks, two steam ships supplied by a Chinese merchant, and aid from the American commodore and the Portuguese governor of Macao (Williams, 1962:215).

References

Belgrave, C. (1966). *The pirate coast*. New York: Roy.

Bowles, T. G. (1900). *The declaration of Paris of 1856*. London: Sampson Low, Marston.

Clowes, W. L. (1898). *The royal navy: A history from the earliest times to the present*. Vol. 3. Boston: Little, Brown.

Corbett, J. S. (1907). *England in the seven years' war*. (Vol. 2 of 2 vols.). London: Longmans, Green.

Crowhurst, P. (1977). *The defence of British trade, 1689-1815*. Folkestone, Kent, England: Dawson.

Earle, P. (1970). *Corsairs of Malta and Barbary*. London: Sidgwick & Jackson.

Gosse, P. (1946). *The history of piracy*. New York: Tudor.

Hall, W. E. (1924). *A treatise on international law*. (8th ed.). Edited by A. Pearce Higgins. Oxford: Clarendon Press.

Harvard Law School Research in International Law (1932). Draft convention on piracy. *American Journal of International Law, 26*. Special supplement, 739-1013.

Hertslet, E. (1875). *The map of Europe by treaty*. (Vol. 2 of 5 vols.). London: Butterworths.

Kemp, P. K. & Lloyd, C. (1960). *Brethren of the coast: Buccaneers of the south seas*. New York: St. Martin's.

Lydon, J. G. (1970). *Pirates, privateers and profits*. With an introduction by Richard B. Morris. Upper Saddle River, NJ: Gregg.

Maclay, E. S. (1899). *A history of American privateers*. New York: Appleton.

Malkin, H. W. (1927). The inner history of the Declaration of Paris. *British Yearbook of International Law, 8*, 1-44.

Oppenheim, L. (1955). *International law: A treatise*. (8th ed.). Edited by H. Lauterpacht. Vol. 1, *Peace*. New York: Longmans, Green.

Piggott, F. (1919). *The Declaration of Paris, 1856*. London: University of London Press.

Rankin, H. F. (1969). *The golden age of piracy*. New York: Holt, Rinehart & Winston.

Rediker, M. (1987). *Between the devil and the deep blue sea: Merchant seamen, pirates, and the Anglo-American maritime world, 1700-1750.* Cambridge, UK: Cambridge University Press.

Reuter, B. A. (1924). *Anglo-American relations during the Spanish-American war.* New York: Macmillan.

Ritchie, R. C. (1986). *Captain Kidd and the war against the pirates.* Cambridge, MA: Harvard University Press.

Sherry, F. (1986). *Raiders and rebels: The golden age of piracy.* New York: Hearst Marine Books.

Stark, F. R. (1897). The abolition of privateering and the Declaration of Paris. *Studies in history, economics and public law,* ed. Faculty of Political Science of Columbia University. (Vol. 8, no. 3.)

Swanson, C. E. (1985). American privateering and imperial warfare, 1739-1748. *William and Mary Quarterly.* (3d ser.) *42* (July), 357-382.

Tarling, N. (1963). *Piracy and politics in the Malay world.* Melbourne: F. W. Cheshire.

Thomson, J. E. and Krasner, S. D. (1989). Global transactions and the consolidation of sovereignty. In E. O. Czempiel & J. N. Rosenau, *Global changes and theoretical challenges: Approaches to world politics for the 1990s.* Lexington, MA: Heath.

U.K. (1856). *Hansard parliamentary debates.* (3d. ser., vol. 142, cols. 481-549).

Williams, N. (1962). *Captains outrageous: Seven centuries of piracy.* New York: Macmillan.

Wolf, J. B. (1979). *The Barbary Coast: Algiers under Turks, 1500-1830.* New York: Norton.

The article explores the prospects for market reforms within the Chinese state. It is argued that planned economies and market economies have incompatible state structures, one based on hierarchy and command, the other based on law and regulation. Law and private property are indispensible elements of market economies which exist in only rudimentary form in China. Where law and private property do not provide sufficient incentive for risk-taking in the market, entrepreneurs seek patrons within the state to improve the security of their profit-seeking activities. As patron-client relations preempt the universal application of law as well as the open competition of the market, the resulting bargaining system in China is neither a species of market system nor socialism, but might be compared to Mexico.

10

China: Mexicanization or Market Reform?

JEREMY T. PALTIEL

Introduction

A central focus in political economy is the relationship between states and markets. The Chinese economic reforms of the late 1970s and 1980s and Gorbachev's *perestroika* in the Soviet Union have revived interest in the possibilities of market socialism and the problems of combining plan and market. Much of the literature both in Marxist and non-Marxist political economy has been devoted to uncovering the functions of the state in the market economy and, conversely, the links between market position and state power. This article extends this discussion to socialist states. The revolutionary Chinese state administration that took power under Mao sought to suppress the social classes who dominated market relationships and to substitute the administration of the plan for the operations of market ex-

Author's Note: The author wishes to thank his colleague Alain Noël for his close reading of the drafts of this text and his many valuable suggestions. Prof. Caporaso's critical comments substantially clarified many aspects of the argument. Any remaining obscurities and involutions are the author's own.

change. The structure and ideology of this administration conflict with economic reform predicated on expanding the role of markets. The transition to capitalism is a two-hundred-year-old phenomenon in the west. By examining the transition to a market economy in China (albeit not yet an outright capitalist one), we can gain insight into the role of states in promoting and guaranteeing market exchange.

Market reforms in China and elsewhere in the socialist bloc have been introduced in order to raise the level of social productivity. Stalinist economic planning initially promoted industrialization by increasing the rate of social savings and channeling investment to key sectors. Demands for growth through greater factor productivity prompted communist authorities to experiment with market reforms, but these reforms raise intriguing questions: To what extent can the two conflicting systems of market and plan be juxtaposed without destroying the underlying basis and potential efficiencies of each? The study of the Chinese reforms may potentially reveal the political conditions underlying the economic efficiencies of capitalism. The anomalies of public administration that have arisen in China underscore the tension between conflicting models of administration and demonstrate the obstacles to the formation of a market system in a Leninist state.

Capitalist economies require state administrations of a particular kind. Similarly, planned economies require state administration of their own specific type. The inductive logic of a market system, where efficiencies of production and distribution are achieved by reference to flexible arrangement of factors of production and final goods, is contradicted by the logic of the planned economy, where deductive arrangements and administrative structures are required to coordinate the production and movement of factors of production and final goods according to a central plan. In the first case, state administration may be called upon to "referee" the application of rules ensuring the flow of goods and services in accordance with the "invisible hand" of the market, while in the second, state actors control those resources themselves. The first envisages a political system relying on a delicate balance of authoritative rules and the guarantee of autonomous action in the marketplace by nonstate actors, while the second has state actors exercise full rights of ownership with reference to the overall plan.

In this article, the *capitalist system* will be taken to mean an economic system where all factors of production—land, labor, and capital—can be exchanged in markets. By backing price-clearing markets and private property rights, the state facilitates the exchange of factors of production and final goods. By contrast, a planned economy entails the concentration of ownership in the hands of the state, which administratively allocates goods and services in order to coordinate production and distribution by reference to a central plan.

It remains to be seen whether absent property rights, mere devolution of management rights over state-owned enterprises, is sufficient to induce the microeconomic efficiencies of capitalism. I argue that the transition from plan to markets engenders clientelism as the functional substitute for property rights, and this has a profound impact on market efficiency as well as the political economy of the state. The newfound appetite of Chinese officials for the products and profits of private economic actors is complemented by the anxiety of those private actors to protect their market position. This has promoted the growth of particularistic alliances between state officials and entrepreneurs, a process we call *Mexicanization*. Entrepreneurs will not invest when their profits will be expropriated.

For the purposes of this article the term *Leninist* will refer to a public administrative system where property is state-owned, and all public institutions are penetrated by a centralized political party that holds a monopoly over personnel appointments.

A considerable literature has grown up around the state. Much of this has been devoted to the apparently increasing power of the state in advanced industrial societies. Neo-Marxists such as Poulantzas have emphasized the "relative autonomy" of the capitalist state vis-à-vis the ruling fractions of the dominant capitalist class.

In parallel fashion, there has been recognition that the socialist revolutions of the twentieth century have created even more powerful states than the ones which were overthrown (Skocpol, 1979). Yet, despite lingering belief in the monolithic character of Leninist states or equally wrongheaded convergence theories, there has been growing recognition of constraints to the exercise of state power specific to Leninist systems.

Most of the contemporary literature on the state remains focused on the theoretical and empirical relationship of the state to capitalism or market society. In neo-Marxist theory these relationships have been generalized in terms of the "functions" of accumulation, and legitimation, related to the operations of capitalism. However, these theories simply restate the base-superstructure argument in a different form. Attributing these functions to the *capitalist* state provides no guidance to how the state might relate to the market under a system of state socialism. Market relations do not develop in isolation from the socialist state, so that any attempt to understand the impact of markets on the state cannot be made simply in terms of the abstract model or ideal type of either socialism or capitalism. Because market socialism emerges from a process of reform and not a revolution where institutions are built from scratch, market relations evolve in interaction with an existing state administration. The hybrid system emerges from the interstices of state administration and entrepreneurial activity and is not created *ex-nihilo*.

> States are historical social constructs. Thus, When a state is founded the elements that have seized the political initiative can set the initial orientation of the state by devising an array of institutions embodying their ideological vision, by coalescing class alliances to form the social foundations of the state and by formulating legitimations to transform might into right. (Bennett & Sharpe, 1985:44).

By stressing the founding orientation we can address differential "capacities" of states and provide a framework for the scope of state action, for state projects under a given state administration. The institutional makeup and the ethos of the staff managing the state are historical developments that lend state administration continuity. The criteria by which the staff is trained, selected, and promoted form the basis of continuity, and through these criteria, the ideology and purposes of the founders are transmitted to succeeding generations of administrators. Any given state administration is, thus, "programmed" to handle different issues and social groups in a typical manner.

The degree of state autonomy is related to the ideology of the administrative staff. Nonstate actors have differential access to the administration, and that access is defined in part through the social make-up of the staff of the state and the ideological premises that inform state administration. The mode of production does not determine state strength and capacity. Instead, one must directly investigate the authorities sustaining state legitimacy. The ideologies of state personnel must be examined in relation to the ideology of the regime's social base. (Skocpol, 1986:171; Stinchcombe 1968:150).

State "strength" cannot be uniform across an unlimited range of policy issues, however closely any administration may approach Weberian rationality. Confronted by policy issues it was not designed to handle, policies state administrators have not been "programmed" to address, even the proverbially strong Leninist state will appear weak.

The administrative staff will adapt new policy orientations to its own conception of its status and place in the political system. The price of economic reform will be market distortions ingeniously conceived to preserve the power relationships and economic privileges that preceded the introduction of market reforms.

The Chinese State and the Economy

For thirty years the Chinese economy fitfully operated along a more or less Stalinist planned system. Prices were set administratively, and output was planned and distributed by administrative allocation. All enterprises had their production subordinated to the commands of administrative superiors, and until 1980 had no control over profits, which were automatically remitted to superordinate administrative units. Basically, the state decided what was to be produced, who was to produce it, and who the final consumers would be. By the mid-1970s even such consumer goods as cotton cloth, bicycles, and sewing machines were strictly rationed, as were basic staple foodstuffs.[1] Because of the difficulties of administering such a system in China, both because of periodic political turmoil and because of the weaknesses of China's communication system, the Chinese state early on decentralized administration over many enterprises and commodities to provincial and local authorities, creating a complex hierarchy of cellular autarkic units.

Under the command economy, nearly all economic intervention was microeconomic. There was no need for macro controls or regulatory mechanisms, as detailed administrative fiat was the normal coordinating mechanism of the economy. Administrative subordination of economic subunits ensured that detailed instructions would be kept, and an elaborate, if unsystematic web of sanctions was put into place to assure that administrative orders were conformed to. These sanctions took the form of formal and informal controls over the hiring, promotion, transfer, and punishment of personnel. Deviance would be punished, and conformity could be rewarded with promotion. Material incentives were frowned upon, but existed in the form of less conspicuous prerequisites of office, including access to better housing, food, hospital care, and schooling. To any extent possible the market was prohibited, enforced by draconian controls over illegal commerce, which effectively abolished any incentive to produce or allocate goods outside the channels provided for under the administrative plan.

The primary regulatory power exercised by the Chinese state came through the web of controls over personnel, which was largely but not exclusively controlled through the communist party. Since jobs were allocated and could not be changed without formal reassignment, and ration cards for daily necessities such as grain were issued by the workplace, the degree of control exercised by the workplace, or *danwei*, was extremely high. (Walder, 1986:23). Detailed regulation of administrative and productive performance was channeled through the formal communications channels of the administrative hierarchy *(xitong)* to which a particular work unit or enterprise belonged (usually a ministry) or the territorial unit (often through Party communications channels). Less binding, but significant nonetheless, were the instructions passed through the open media of the Party controlled press.

The strict relationship between administrative regulation and personnel control meant that valid regulations came through the channels of the administrative hierarchy and were *directly addressed* to subordinate units. Even regulations that were binding on everyone and decided upon at the highest levels of the Party and state had to be formally "transmitted" *(chuanda)* by superordinate agencies to their subunits together with the "red heading documents" *(hongtou wenjian)*, which contained the operative definition and interpretation of regulations.

Laws—administrative, criminal, civil, or commercial—were largely nonexistent until after the Third Plenum of the 11th Central Committee of the Chinese Communist Party took place in December 1978. Even since the regular introduction of new laws, there is no clear line of demarcation between formal legislation and the continuing powers of administrative regulation. In the absence of strong and consistent judicial independence, there are problems of enforcing even laws across administrative boundaries.

T. H. Rigby has rightly called the authority system of the communist system *goal rational* (Rigby, 1964, 1980) as opposed to the *legal-rational* procedure-based system of western market societies. Here the priority of the politically and administratively determined *task*, arithmetically subdivided and allocated to the subunits and subordinates constitutes the core of rational administrative behavior, substituting for and overriding any concept of procedure, contract, or law. The legal systems of market societies use public authority to guarantee the performance of privately decided ends. Legitimacy rests on following publicly decided rational rules. In the goal-rational system of Leninism, all goals are decided within the Party-state and agents are required to perform their given task, along the model of an army chain of command. Goals are allocated by reference to a central authority. Legitimacy derives from the source of the command not the process by which it is formulated. There is no role for privately decided ends.

These two systems can not only be regarded as mutually contradictory models of administrative behavior, but also as opposing paradigms or conceptual systems of administrative actors. While both legal-rational market systems and Leninist goal-rational systems presuppose administrative hierarchies and bureaucracies displaying many apparently similar organizational structures, structural similarities may conceal behavioral and cognitive dissimilarities of the first order.

The significance of Rigby's notion of goal rationality is that the task defines the official. It is important to note that all tasks are at least implicitly political. If the control system of the Leninist Party is based mainly on control over personnel, it is because there is a direct conceptual relationship between the ideas of democratic centralism and Party discipline, the political orientation of the task and control over personnel. In essence, party discipline means unconditional loyalty, and the control system of the Party is designed to ensure it. The stress on loyalty and task does promote effectiveness as an important advantage of Leninist organization, but only when the goal is concrete and explicit. More diffuse goals are more difficult to define and, consequently, make compliance difficult to monitor. Further, as Hirschman points out, the attachment of severe sanctions to questions of loyalty (thereby weakening both exit and voice) diminishes the amount of information available to the leaders and weakens the ability of the organization to react (Hirschman, 1970:97).

The universal guiding role of the Party undermines and preempts the establishment of an administrative system approaching Weberian rationality. As the former Premier and Chairman of the Communist Party put it in 1980: "Our government organs are improperly managing almost every aspect of social life by administrative methods, thereby burdening themselves with a complex, backbreaking and unparalleled job." At that time, he confessed: "there are no systematic and practicable administrative rules which define limits of power and responsibilities and lay down administrative procedure . . . from the State Council right down to the localities" (Hua, 1980). Since all organizational units are simultaneously social units, leaders are continually diverted from any functional task or role to dealing with the multitudinous social problems of the staff, including everything from housing to marriage and even funerals (Walder, 1983).

Given their diffuse responsibilities and singular control over subordinates' lives, it is not surprising that Chinese officials developed a *patriarchal* character (an epithet commonly attached to official behavior by the Chinese themselves). It is, therefore, fair to say that the outlook of the Chinese cadre resembles more closely the patrimonial type than the modern bureaucrat (Weber, 1964:148-149; 1947:346-358). Although subordinated to the formally impersonal system of the Party, the role of the cadre is not defined by his *office*.

The diffuse character of power relationships is needed to cement the hierarchy and unity of command required by the planned economy. There is a definite tension between specialization and Party authority. Planning creates a paradoxical coexistence of overspecialization and administrative bottlenecks, on the one hand, with insufficient technical specialization, on the other. Administrative decentralization simply displaces the problem of coordination. Under Mao, the resolution of this took the form of "putting politics in command" and favoring the "red" over the expert. Much of the thrust of the modernization and reform movements has been to overcome this exaggerated aberration and meet the demand for functional differentiation in an industrial economy. Yet widespread experience of administrative bottlenecks tempts political authorities to retain an ability to "trump" the administrative compartmentalization by political fiat.

Reforms in Chinese Economic Administration

For a variety of reasons, ranging from technological obsolescence to consumer dissatisfaction, which seriously affected both political morale as well as worker motivation, Chinese authorities began to loosen administrative controls and promote economic initiative beginning with the Third Plenum of the 11th Central Committee in December of 1978.

First, peasant producers were encouraged to produce for the open market, and gradually, enterprises were allowed to retain profits and produce "above plan" goods for the consumer market. A system of bonuses linked to productivity and profitability was put in place that gave all employees a stake in the profitability of the firm.

Gradually expanding the role of markets in the urban economy since 1979, the Chinese state progressively extended autonomy to enterprises in the control and distribution of profits, increasing discretion over wage scales and personnel, the power to enter into contracts and produce for the market, as well as some control over the assortment of production and pricing of products (Tidrick & Chen 1987:1-38).

These steps have succeeded in generating a consumer boom in China. Light industry has outstripped heavy industry's growth since 1978, and personal consumption has risen by almost 87% in real terms (*Renmin Ribao*, April 13, 1987). Remarkable rises in rural income and consumption have begun to fuel the growth of the industrial economy. Some idea of the shifting locus of economic decision making can be gauged by the fact that retained earnings by firms, localities and state organizations have nearly quadrupled since 1978, or at about four times the rate of increase of national income, reaching a figure now equivalent to 75% of state revenues (*Renmin Ribao*, April 13, 1987).

In October 1984, the Central Committee of the Chinese Communist Party defined the direction of China's economic reform as being "A Socialist

Planned Commodity Economy'' (Decision, 1984). This ambiguous term lightly camouflaged a full intention to move in the direction of market socialism despite uncertainties as to the degree of dominance to give to the market, or the nature of the ''indicative planning,'' which was to gradually displace the command-type administrative plan.

Conflicting Paradigms: Administration Under Plan and Market

When Party organization overlaps and penetrates all state institutions, defining goals in political terms, this creates conflicting values and goal orientations for administrative units and economic organizations. When faced by conflicting priorities, cadres have been enjoined to give priority to the political task, virtually ensuring suboptimal performance of economic enterprises. The official hierarchy of managerial values is set as: (1) State; (2) Collective (organization); and (3) individual, which inevitably weakens the competitive operation of the market and preempts the efficiencies that may be gained thereby. In other words, having first created the rudiments of markets, the state then turns around and asks managers (who are still state officials) to ignore its signals.

While the situation of consumers has been radically transformed, care has been taken in the urban industrial sector not to break the administrative subordination of enterprises to their supervising ministries and bureaus. Unlike the rural sector where the People's Communes were actually abolished and replaced by township governments, an equivalent separation of political and economic subordination has barely begun in the urban industrial sector. Rather than a reform of the industrial structure as such, reform thus far is more accurately seen as an expansion of managerial discretion within the old structure. We have the growth of a market within a state structure of the Leninist-Stalinist type.

It needs to be emphasized that the introduction of the market mechanism in China had nothing to do with the liberal ideology of laissez-faire and natural rights. The market was approved on purely instrumental pragmatic grounds, on the grounds of efficiency and not on the basis of property rights.

The call for the separation of the work of Party and government solemnly agreed to at the Thirteenth Party Congress of October 1987 is contradicted by the culture of administration and the realities of political life. Everything in the Leninist system, and the Chinese state in particular, militates against subsystem autonomy, and engenders capricious encroachment in the market.

Among the most important problems confronting a Leninist state attempting to establish a market system is the problem of releasing authority to societal actors. Under the planned economy, property belongs to the state and the authority to produce and allocate goods is in the hands of state actors. Regardless of the formal disposition of property, a market system presupposes at the minimum the devolution over actual powers of production and distribution to autonomous competing actors.

Market reform not only requires that prices be free. It means that private appropriation and contract be legally enforced by the state (North, 1981:42). A market system is not just an economic mechanism, it is a legal regime. Moreover, it is a historically exceptional type of regime (Polanyi, 1957:71).[2] This aspect of the market system is frequently ignored by the apostles of market socialism—for example, Alec Nove (1983). The transformation of a system that systematically limited private appropriation and exchange to monopolize production and allocation of consumer goods and "collective" goods by the state administration into a system where private appropriation or at least decentralized collective exchange and appropriation are the norm is more than a matter of laissez-faire. As Polanyi pointed out, the extraordinary feature of capitalism is that class pressure was used to "subordinate the substance of society itself to the laws of the market" (Polanyi 1957:71). The mere presence of markets is distinct from the formation of a market system. The former will arise whenever exchange is allowed under conditions of scarcity. The latter implies that all production and distribution be controlled by market supply and demand. Can state bureaucrats become entrepreneurs? If they do, how does one prevent them from using the public purse as risk capital, and abusing the coercive power of the state to extract economic rents?

Ironically, the assimilation of modern administrative theories and practices by the current Chinese leadership, appears to strengthen the practice of goal rationality over legal-rational procedure and preserve, rather than weaken the primary emphasis on loyalty of personnel in public administration. "Management by objectives" (MBO) has been adopted by Chinese state organizations. Significantly, MBO appears to have been adopted not as a criterion of budgetary performance as in PPBS in the United States, but rather, as a system of personnel control, promoted by the Party Organization Department (*Zhongong Haerbinishi Nangangqumei Zuzhibu Wenjian*, 1985).

Notwithstanding the enormous scope of reform in China, a Chinese textbook of public administration states very clearly: "Our country pursues a socialist system of the 'unity of legislation and administration' " (Xia, 1985:41). This is further contrasted with the capitalist system:

Capitalist administrative organs can directly control the state's political life, but cannot directly control social production. Our state administrative organs can issue policies and ordinances through the State plan and use various means to directly guide the state's economic activity and its various affairs, at the same time concretely organizing the implementation of these plans and policies (Xia, 1985:44).

All this has produced a number of unanticipated anomalies for the Chinese state.

To induce autonomous actors to produce public values under the new conditions, the state must move towards indirect methods of economic administration. There are two questions involved here: First, is the state willing to devolve the necessary authority in a manner which will allow enterprises to behave in a market competitive manner? Second, assuming that it does, does it have the awareness and capacity to induce autonomous actors to continue to produce public "collective goods" without undermining the autonomy upon which the market system stands?

These questions have vexed the Chinese regime throughout the reform process, and the effort to control the market and force the preservation of social values and the production of public goods has involved the Chinese administration in policies that tend to contradict the market principles they have espoused in the name of greater efficiency.

With regard to the second question, the introduction of profit incentives into the Chinese economic system has led to such familiar problems of early capitalism as uneven and declining quality standards, the introduction of counterfeit goods, quack medicines (*Renmin Ribao*, July 13, 1985), smuggling, trademark, copyright and patent infringements, disregard of public health standards in food processing, etc. These show the profit motive to be alive and well. However, while some of these phenomena can be constrained, if not controlled by competition, in the major capitalist countries the appearance of such phenomena has led to the growth and competence of government regulation. Often the pressure for regulation has come from private industry itself, railing against "unfair competition." Other instances show pressure from consumer and public advocates to narrow the purview of *caveat emptor*, or a combination of both of these in a competitive democratic system (Mitnick, 1980; Skorownek, 1982).

Regulation and the Chinese Administration

Sometimes, in an urge to condemn all infringements on property by the advocates of laissez faire, it is forgotten how important government regulation is to the smooth operation of the capitalist economy, and how its operation rests on a delicate balance between market principles of profit and the imposition of concerns of "public" interest mandated by law (Lindblom, 1977:172-176). The question is whether either law or the importance of the profit motive is sufficiently recognized in the Chinese system of public administration today.

For example, a Chinese textbook in public administration calls for "paying attention to the prevention both of "legal nihilism" and "legal universalism."

> Because of the influence of "leftist" thinking, administrative regulation went through two rises and two falls. Under the influence of legal nihilism, some people thought that administrative laws and regulations could be set aside, and even thought that more regulation simply mean binding one's own hands and feet. This type of thinking seriously hampered the development of administrative regulation and administrative effectiveness. On the other hand, some countries' administrative personnel have the notion legal universalism, and put the law above all else, which facts have shown to be extremely harmful. This type of viewpoint minimizes the guiding role of Party directives and policies and the authoritative power of political-ideological work and puts aside other methods of effective administration in favor of habitual use purely administrative orders and punitive administrative ideas, therefore in actuality harming socialist administrative construction (Xia, 1985:294).

Evidently, the uses of law are still extremely hazy to many Chinese officials. Note the apparent association of law with the notion of punishment, and even more important, the idea that the rule of law would somehow contradict the role of the Communist Party. The association of law with punishment can sometimes be expressed in a peculiar fashion. In an early draft of bankruptcy legislation, Chinese officials wanted to include a provision for punishing the managers of firms that had collapsed. They seemed genuinely surprised and puzzled that western bankruptcy laws contained no such provision (Chang, 1987:44).

The point is not that the Chinese government does not care whether firms produce substandard goods or quack medicines. Nor is the Chinese Communist Party, or even the "conservatives" opposed to the rule of law. When the matter of quack medicines sold by pyramid sales schemes was uncovered in 1985, the reaction was swift and harsh. However, the discipline was imposed by the Communist Party Discipline Inspection Commission (*Renmin Ribao*, August 5, 1985).[3] Individuals became the subjects of punishment, rather than firms. Firms were simply punished for violating regulations, yet there was little outcry about the inadequacy of licensing procedures and regulatory authorities. No account was taken of the drastically changed conditions and environment of firms. In contrast to conditions of perfect competition, when there is assumed to be unlimited information and unlimited opportunity for exit, in China there prevails the Gresham's law of the unregulated marketplace—shoddy or substandard goods drive out good ones because there is not the rapid exchange of information about quality goods, quality goods may be in restricted supply because of both artificial restrictions and distribution bottlenecks, and because trademark cannot be relied upon. Even decent firms will be reduced to shady practices when faced by competition from other firms. In the case of the quack medicines, there was an explosion of new enterprises dealing in counterfeit drugs when they saw how well their neighbors were doing.

The Chinese system lacks a consistent mechanism to enforce regulations across administrative boundaries (Lichtenstein, 1987; Eliasoph, 1986). The ministry in change of the pharmaceutical industry can issue instructions for the industries under its administrative control, but it has no means to enforce those regulations on firms that do not belong to its network and that sell their goods on the open market. Outside organizations have neither the competence nor the authority to do so. The Party and its associated disciplinary institutions are the exceptions to this rule. Thus, the regulatory reflex here is strong, but rather than stimulate the market by rational regulation, the heavy hand of the Party's disciplinary methods undermines contract, law, and property, thereby reducing calculability and adding an element of political risk to every business transaction.

> The province of Heilongjiang found it was losing money because milk delivered to plants processing it into milk powder have found it adulterated with salt and sugar water, soymilk, and other substances. Investigation showed that: (1) No standards for milk deliveries had been formulated; and (2) Laboratory tests at delivery points were totally inadequate. (*Heilongjiang Ribao* July 6, 1986)

Examples of such "incorrect practices" abound. Cumbersome and restrictive practices for state owned organizations involved in plan-sanctioned activities may be mirrored by complete absence of regulation for their private competitors, or even for the same firm engaged in "above plan" sideline activities. Sometimes when "regulations" are formulated these may as often as not be designed for predatory official "profit sharing" rather than the regulation of competition in the interests of the profitable firms. The result is opposite to that commonly prevailing in western societies where the regulated firms "colonize" the regulators. Unlike the situation of liberal capitalist democracy, Chinese "regulators" feel no obligation to ensure the profitability of the small competitive firm, but take a benign view of a profligate uncompetitive large firm. Large firms are well entrenched in the political system, both because of their economic importance and because of the size of their party membership.

Officials see the opportunity for profit as a privilege granted by state authority. It may be rescinded, and that obliges the entrepreneur to reward the benevolent official from the proceeds of the enterprise he has been "permitted" to run profitably. This has been called "red eye disease" the malady of cadre jealousy (*Toronto Globe and Mail*, February 20, 21, 22, 1984). A recent investigative reportage describes how a successful semiprivate firm was not only frustrated by regulation, but had its assets seized and personnel jailed, all because of vague suspicions on the part of someone in authority that such a successful enterprise *must* be involved in illegal dealings (Li & Lin 1987).

The central institution of the market system, the contract, is poorly understood and poorly enforced. In the context of a system still operating within a framework of hierarchic subordination, it is difficult to convey the message that a contract is a binding agreement between equal partners and it is even more difficult to get enforcement of contractual provisions (*Globe and Mail*, April 6, 1986). State officials may feel no obligation to enforce contractual obligations signed under their predecessors, even when a valid contract was signed by an office or organization and is still nominally in force.

The following examples illustrate the relationship between authority and contract in China: in recent years, in an effort to improve discipline and productivity in the workforce, workers have been given contracts by state enterprises. These specify pay and working conditions. Workers complain that these contracts are capriciously enforced by the management, and there is no forum in which they can seek redress.

A man who had leased a money-losing firm, and turned it around and was making profit, had his lease revoked when a new leadership team took over in his district. The man in question took the matter to court, which in fact decided in his favor. Yet the local government which revoked the lease refused to enforce the court order (*Heilongjiang Ribao*, July 12, 1986).

Another person, who leased a subdivision of a factory in return for fixed payment, found the locks changed on his warehouse and his equipment smashed. Upon discovering the lessee managed to turn a profit, the lessor wanted the facilities back. The lessee did not even bother applying to the court, though he did write the provincial newspaper (*Heilongjiang Ribao*, October 26, 1986).

It is not surprising litigants have little confidence in the courts. One business which took its case to court after repeated failure to enforce payment on an invoice had its case returned by the court with the following advice:

> it would be useless to take up your case. It would be better to (1) use your "connections" to persuade the invoicee to pay up, or (2) to find a high ranking "leader" to enforce payment . . ." (*Zhongguo Qingnianbao*, October 11, 1986).

The problem here is not simply one of an independent judiciary. For one thing, Chinese courts are ill equipped to handle business or commercial cases. Even when the legal mechanisms exist, Chinese courts have traditionally restricted themselves to "punishing criminals" and "enforcing the dictatorship of the proletariat." In effect, they decide on those cases that have been referred to them by other authorities for judgment. Moreover, they are often untrained in commercial matters, or anything outside the questions of stern retribution for moral wrongdoing. A chief of the traffic division of a municipal police force complained that most of their time was caught up in mediating and adjudicating questions of accident compensation. The courts would not intervene, but only punish those charged by the police with criminal negligence. Little wonder. There are only 76 judges for every million inhabitants in China. This figure compares with 50.5/0000 in England or 20.6/0000 in the United States. Even Japan, where recourse to the judiciary is traditionally frowned upon, there are more than three times the number of judges that China has on a per capita basis (*Heilongjiang Ribao*, October 24, 1986).

The Chinese authorities are well aware of the inadequacy of their legal infrastructure and the need to educate officials in the observance of the law (Qiao Shi, 1986). Over the last few years they have begun to set up separate "economic chambers" or courts to handle economic matters.

This is not simply a matter of technical competence or administrative development. As Lindblom points out:

> One of the great misconceptions of conventional economic theory is that business men are induced to perform their functions by purchases of their

goods and services, as though the vast productive tasks performed in market-oriented systems could be motivated solely by exchange relations between buyers and sellers. On so slender a foundation no great productive system can be established. What is required in addition is a set of governmentally provided inducements in the form of market and political benefits (Lindblom, 1977:172).

In the short term Chinese authorities are unlikely to realize that businessmen are not "simply . . . representatives of a special interest . . . [but] functionaries performing functions government officials regard as indispensable (Lindblom, 1977:175). Private businessmen may be tolerated in China, but there is abiding suspicion of them by Party officials. Party officials would prefer to monopolize profitable enterprise for themselves. To take advantage of the greater opportunities for acquiring wealth in private business, there has been phenomenal growth of businessmen cadres, despite the explicit prohibitions on cadres engaging in trade (Chen Yun, *Renmin Ribao*, September 27, 1985).

When public officials blatantly abuse their office to engage in trade for private gain, this diverts government public agencies from their public concerns and hurts government finances. But it is equally damaging to a market based system when nit-picking and uncomprehending officials make it impossible to turn a profit. Outlook or attitude are as important as competence. Regulations may be conceived on a reasonable basis but worded badly. In our system, courts can interpret the regulations in a manner consistent with public usage. The entire system of law, property and administration is in general harmony with the market system. The same cannot be said for China.

Sometimes the enabling regulations of guidelines drafted by central authorities may bear no relation to the original purpose of the regulation. Even if the affected individual can see the initial central regulation he has no one to appeal to other than the official who drafted the contradictory regulation in the first place. There are few lawyers supervising the drafting of regulations. Nor is there a tradition of common law to appeal to. Laws are themselves drafted in a way which preserves both the possibility of administrative intervention by higher authority and some manipulation in the name of higher moral purpose (Lichtenstein 1987; Cohen 1986). The most that can be hoped for is an individualized appeal based on "connection," which could grant a kind of personal exemption. Such exemptions however, defeat the purpose of regulation in the first place. This does not represent a common-sense interpretation of a rule that can be followed by everyone, but a side-deal between a conniving official and his personal client.

There is a recognition that the drafting of regulations results in irrationalities (*Heilongjiang Ribao*, July 4, 1986). An entrepreneur who appeals such regulation runs the risk of giving officials even more leverage over his private activities. To use Albert O. Hirschman's vocabulary, his preference may become that of "exit" over "voice" (Hirschman, 1970). On the other hand, managers of state-owned enterprises have the connections at their disposal to exercise "voice" and exempt their own firm from unfavorable regulations (Tidrick & Chen, 1987:203). The system as a whole suffers from high transactions costs (Williamson, 1975) and the market can never operate efficiently.[4]

As we have already seen, markets are not efficient allocators of goods in the absence of predictable enforcement of contracts or well-defined property rights over the means of production. This, in turn, implies what is commonly known as the rule of law, that is, the subordination of the behavior of state officials to rational, predictable, and publicly recognized procedures.

Despite the proclaimed objective of the Chinese Communist leadership to move toward the rule of law, demonstrated by a profusion of conferences and campaigns for mass legal education (*Zhongguo Fazhibao* December 22, 1986), the transformation of the Chinese state in such a direction is constrained, not just by the cultural orientation of the official stratum towards forms of patrimonial behavior sanctioned by tradition and habitual practice, but by the organizational code of the Communist Party—democratic centralism and party discipline. The leadership of the Communist Party is a basic principle written into the state constitution. Not only has the party no intention of giving up its monopoly over organization,[5] it has in recent years used this and attempted to strengthen it whenever confronted by any species of bureaupathology. Every official organization in the country has been "rectified" or "consolidated" in the past three years. Recently we have seen a move against "bourgeois liberalism" take hold. State organs are subordinated unconditionally to the political values of the party.

Therefore, whatever arrangement may be set out as the general case between enterprises and their superordinate administrative systems, is contingent on the general political climate set by the Chinese Communist Party. Instead of predictable and stable property relations, control over commercial assets is attendant on the political status of the nominal owner. While impossible to predict, state interventions must nevertheless be expected, and there is no guarantee that they will apply in an equal or fair manner.

To substitute for the protection of property based on law, the economic actor must seek the protection of political patrons. Uncertainty about potential Party intervention guarantees the persistence of clientelist *guanxi* or

connections. Clientelism in turn, not only subverts the impersonal operation of the competitive market place, but also subverts the operation of
predictable rational-legal norms within the state. Instead of the abstractions
of hierarchy and market human relations become the essential matrix of
economic behavior.

The veteran communist Chen Yun may offer this as the model of the
market as "the bird in the cage" of the planned economy, reality is not
nearly so coherent, since within such a cage neither the market nor the plan
operates according to their underlying rationales. Planning, even if it could
be consistently and effectively carried out is starved of information by the
operation of closed cliques, which also create monopolistic and monop-
sonistic conspiracies in the market.[6] Entrepreneurs, to protect their assets
and profits, seek allies within the state, and these cliques further distort
the bureaucratic rationality of the plan and state agencies.

Clientelism and Markets

All this does not mean that there cannot be a role for the market in China.
There will be many markets for many commodities. What exists or is likely
to be is not like a capitalist market system. Already, there have been
criticisms of China's mercantilist tendencies. (Yeung, 1986). But we should
not confuse the system that emerges with the theoretical constructions of
socialism, either. Socialism, like capitalism, is founded on universalistic
principles. Instead, what has emerged in China, and what is generally true
of most of the Leninist states, is the growth of particularistic relationships,
from *blat* in the USSR and its analogues in Eastern Europe (Jowitt, 1974,
1983), to *guanxi* in China. There is a multiplication of particularistic relationships hidden behind a facade of Leninist universalism in the name of
Marxist ideology and the monolithic Party. In China, the public affirma-
tion of mutually contradictory principles of plan and market economy, evident in the 1984 document on economic reform, merely expands the scope
for particularistic interpretation masked by dialectical reasoning.

It is not likely that the Chinese state, even under conditions of reform,
will attempt to institutionalize the only universal legal institution of
capitalism—private property. Yet this is the necessary institution for the
efficient operation of a market economy (North, 1974:21). The ideological
resistance to the institutionalization of private property, buttressed by the
strong personal inhibitions of cadres as state actors wishing to protect their
own power and privilege, is bound to increase "transactions costs" for the
entrepreneur (or in Weber's terms, to reduce the predictability of rational
economic calculation).

This is more than a sterile ideological debate: friction in the Chinese leadership long prevented the introduction of an "Enterprise Law" designed to entrench enterprise autonomy more effectively in the legal system and to clarify Party-enterprise relations (*Globe and Mail*, March 25, 1987). At the first session of the recently elected Seventh National People's Congress, a long-awaited "Socialist Enterprise Law" was finally enacted. This law for the first time attempts to define enterprises as legal persons and, recognizing that enterprises remain state property, to separate management rights from ownership. It has long been recognized that market reform required such a devolution of managerial rights. Yet, even a cursory look at this law finds the provisions dealing with managerial autonomy hedged in with deliberate and explicit loopholes designed to preserve a place for administrative intervention from higher authorities. Not only can managerial discretion be superseded by other legislation, but even by State Council regulations and by instructions from supervising bodies. Ironically, just about the only right managers have under these circumstances is that of "voice" (*Renmin Ribao*, April 18, 1988). Under this law, plan fulfillment is still mandatory and the State Council, the price control authorities and the supervising administrative bodies may control prices. Thus, there is no clear-cut grant of managerial authority to enterprises which would make them fully responsible for their own profits and losses. Therefore the new law will do little to change what Janos Kornai has called the *soft-budget constraint* inhibiting enterprise efficiency in socialist countries (Kornai, 1980; Tidrick & Chen, 1987:317-338).

The new law appears destined to perpetuate rather than eliminate the pattern of enterprise behavior noted by the author of a recent World Bank study:

> In China, the treatment of every enterprise and problem as a special case leads to collusion between the local government and enterprises, with the local governments acting as patrons rather than regulators. The lack of universally applicable rules divert the energies of enterprises to bargaining from improving efficiency and product quality. Enterprises seek rents rather than profits (Tidrick & Chen 1987:198-199).

The constraints on the growth of a market economy are a complex of interrelated factors. Party hegemony over public life is both structural and ideological. This not only inhibits autonomous economic activity in theory, but has created over time networks of state actors interested in perpetuating a modern form of bureaucratic patrimonialism. Party hegemony on the one hand encourages bureaucratic actors to resist legal limitations on their discretion, while on the other hand providing ideological justification for opposition to the distribution of property rights in the economy. This engenders the persistence of an unstable form of diffuse domination over economic activity. Cadres have both ideological and organizational grounds for this: first, because the Party cadre ideally embodies public interest in contrast to the selfish economic interest of the private or semiprivate enterprise—and second, on structural hierarchic grounds—ministries and bureaus exercise legal rights to intervene in the affairs of subordinate enterprises. Here again, hierarchic superiority is identified with a closer relationship to the public good. Any disruption in the economy, especially any disturbance that appears to benefit a few nonauthoritative actors at the expense of some publicly recognized social good, is likely to invite swift and massive intervention by Party-State actors, who use the opportunity to protect their legitimacy as guardians of the public interest by demonstrating the uncertain and contingent autonomy of the marketplace.

The result is a system considerably less efficient in its distribution of transaction costs than either a legal regulatory regime providing equal access to quasijudicial proceedings or the system of pluralist interest interaction, let alone the impersonality of the market. Hence, the market is unlikely to bring about efficient and impersonal allocation due to uncertain title and unstable control over assets in the first instance, and because the interventionist impulse will continually preempt market transactions. Since the justification for the market by the Party is instrumental and not ideological as in the West, the Party has every incentive to "prove" at various junctures that the market alone is an inadequate mechanism to produce and allocate public goods. Problems in the market will encourage administrative intervention which will in turn provide continual ideological justification for Party-patrimonialism.

What has emerged and seems destined to persist in China, is a kind of market plus particularism. The clearest example of the operation of such a system is in the Chinese countryside, where cadres have secured a position for themselves as patrons on market activity (Oi, 1986).

The combination of markets plus uncertainty provides the typical setting for the growth of clientelism and the formation of patron-client relations as the primary means of reducing transactions costs (Eisenstadt & Roniger, 1984:205). This will simply transform an earlier system of clientelist ties engendered by uncertainty in the political arena (Oi, 1985). The persistence of clientelism encouraged by the uncertainties of control of assets will in fact provide incentives for the maintenance of the patrimonial type of state administration.

A vicious circle emerges. State officials (cadres) will be concerned to maximize and preserve the advantages of their patronage. They will seek to keep as broad a domain for their influence as possible, and therefore resist the strict delimitation of their powers and responsibilities in law. For their part, the clients will conspire with their patrons to expand the degree of protection afforded by their particularistic relationship, resisting the rationalization of the state also, contributing to the blurring of functional divisions of state administration by their own protection-seeking behavior. State cadres thereby will perform the same functions for the Chinese that the cacique does in Mexico and in other parts of Latin America (Cornelius, Schmidt, Scott, Lande, & Guasti 1977:337-353).

Indeed, it may not be too farfetched to speak of the "Mexicanization" of the Chinese state in the context of the economic reforms. Political domination of state and society of a single political party, which uses clientelism to maintain its power and to distribute favors and effectively "trumps" the legal institutions of the state, but which nevertheless fosters a market, may be seen as China's future as well. Again, not only can the market coexist with such a semipatrimonial system, it can grow--only it may not exhibit all the efficiencies of capitalism, nor will it entail the distributional benefits of socialism, as the particularistic protection provided by patronage can mean protection for gross inequality.

The combination of a strong state with the market would entail an effective movement to secure property rights from below with the desire of the state to constitutionalize legal powers from above. This was the pattern that brought about the liberal revolution in England. More typically, however, as is often the case in the Third World, clientelism weakens the state, and by providing an alternative guarantee to exchange relations entrenches elites within the state and preempts the development of legal-rational procedures.

Conclusion

The Chinese reforms challenge us to probe the relationship between the state and the market. Economic mechanisms are not independent of the historical form of the state, nor will they function outside a favorable political framework. The Chinese are not unaware of this, and the calls for "political reform" and "the rule of law" are not only responses to Maoist forms of tyranny in social and political life, but are for some also important measures to rationalize the arbitrariness hindering the development of markets. Deng Xiaoping may have served notice that he is not himself a laissez-faire liberal, but in continuing to trumpet the advantages of market reforms, he is paving the way for future generations to call for "bourgeois liberalization" corresponding to the facts of socioeconomic life, rather than as an epithet for ideological miscreants. Some day, a nascent bourgeoisie may yet raise its own political demands in China, but that day is still far off. As one spokesman for political reform put it:

> It is wrong to delude oneself by the thought that as long as the reform of the economic structure is done well, the reform of the political and other structures will be naturally accomplished. Without the coordinated and synchronized development of political restructuring, economic restructuring will not succeed (Li, 1986:11).

Already, some of China's leading economists have raised the issue of property relations as "the crux of the reform" (Liu Guoguang, 1987:38). Chinese economists are beginning to call for the protection of property on grounds very similar to those pointed to by Lindblom: the encouragement of private investment for public ends. Whatever attempts are made to show this to be consistent with socialism and Marxism, it seems unlikely to prove acceptable to CCP leadership in the short term. However, as we have seen there is another alternative to the entrenchment of property rights as a precondition for the growth of markets. Clientelist relationships are already well entrenched in China, and only need to be exploited to new ends. "Socialism with Chinese characteristics" may well turn out to have a very familiar face.

Notes

1. For a description of post-Mao reforms and the system they set out to replace see Perry and Wong 1985:1-27.

2. Here for the moment I shall ignore the differences between the argument of North (1981) and Polanyi. North criticises Polanyi for equating the market with a price-clearing market (1981:42). The point here is that the type of market favored, but so far not implemented by the Chinese reformers is precisely a price-clearing market. (Tidrick & Chen: 132-142)

3. Since then, the Party has decided to remove the Discipline Inspection Commission form areas which are properly those of law enforcement agencies. See RMRB September 1987.

4. Williamson's argument treats the relationship of production costs to production costs in a market economy. In a situation when virtually every transaction may require an administrative intermediary—hiring, finance, the provision of inputs and marketing output—there is no way to accurately predict operations or production costs--a lesson many partners of joint ventures in China have had to learn at great expense. Clearly these businessmen, who have some experience with production costs outside China see no clear tradeoff between lower production costs and the high transactions costs in China. See for example, "Chinese's Business Practices Hard on Foreign Investors" *The Globe and Mail* (Toronto) July 7, 1987.

5. In fact, there are some recent moves which suggest at least a partial relaxation in that regard. See the author's "Political Reform in China: The End of Nomenklatura Leninism?" Unpublished MS. Regional Seminar in Chinese Studies, Berkeley 1988.

6. Tidrick (Tidrick & Chen 1987:180) asserts that there is no real planning at all in China, since everything is negotiable. Rather it would be more accurate to characterise China as a political economy of administrative bargaining.

References

Bennett, D., and Sharpe, K. (1985). *Transnational corporations versus the state.* Princeton, NJ: Princeton University Press.

Chang, T. (1987). The east is in the red. *China Business Review,* (March-April), 42-45.

Cohen, J. (1986). China adopts civil law principles. *China Business Review,* (September-October), 48-50.

Cornelius, Schmidt, S. W., Scott, J. C., Landé, C. H., & Guasti, L., et al. (Eds.). (1977) *Friends, followers and factions: A reader in political clientelism.* Berkeley: University of California Press.

Deng, X. (1984). *Selected works.* Beijing: Foreign Languages Press.

Documents of the Thirteenth National Congress of the Communist Party of China (1984). Beijing: Foreign Languages Press.

Eisenstadt, S. & Roniger (1984). *Patrons, clients, friends.* Cambridge: Cambridge University Press.

Eliasoph, E. (1986). Shedding light on Shanghai's laws. *China Business Review,* (May-June), 47-50.

Evans, P., Rueschemeyer, D. and Skocpol, T. (Eds.), (1985). *Bringing the state back in.* Cambridge: Cambridge University Press.

Hirschman, A. (1970). *Exit, voice and loyalty.* Cambridge, MA: Harvard University.

Hua, G. (1980). Report on the work of the government. *Beijing Review, 38* (September 22), 12-29.

Johnson, C. (1982). *MITI and the Japanese miracle.* Stanford, CA: Stanford University Press.

Jowitt, K. (1974). An organizational approach to the study of political culture in Leninist regimes. *American Political Science Review, 68,* 3, 1171-1191.

Jowitt, K. (1978). *The Leninist response to national dependency.* Berkeley: Institute of International Studies.

Jowitt, K. (1983). Soviet neotraditionalism: The political corruption of a Leninist regime. *Soviet Studies, 35,* 3 (July), 28.

Kornai, J. (1980). *The Economics of Shortage.* Amsterdam: North Holland.

Li, K. (1986). China's political restructuring and the development of political science. *Social Sciences in China, 3* (September), 9-24.

Li, T. and Lin, Q. (1987). Hunian Tongjiling. (Arrest warrant of the year of the tiger) *Dongxiang, 36* (March), 57-99.

Lichtenstein, N. (1987). Law and the enterprise. *China Business Review* (March-April), 34-42.

Lindblom, C. (1977). *Politics and markets.* New York: Basic.

Liu, G. (1987). Jinyibu fazhan shangpin jingjide jige wenti (Some questions on further developing the commodity economy). *Winhua Wenzhai, 97* (January), 38-44.

March, J., & Olsen, J. (1984). The new institutionalism: Organizational factors in political life. *American Political Science Review, 78*, 3, 734-749.

Mitnick, B. (1980). Myths of creation and fables of administration: Explanation of the strategic use of regulation. *Public Administration Review* (May-June), 275-276.

North, D. (1974). *Growth and welfare in the American past: A new economic history.* Engelwood Cliffs, NJ: Prentice-Hall.

North, D. (1981). *Structure and change in economic history.* New York: Norton.

Nove, A. (1983). *The economics of feasible socialism.* London: Allen & Unwin.

OI, J. (1985). Communism and clientelism: Rural politics in China. *World Politics, 38*, 2, 238-266.

OI, J. (1986). Commercializing China's rural cadres. *Problems of Communism, 5*, 1-15.

Perry, E., & Wong, C. (Eds.) (1985). *The political economy of reform in post-Mao China.* Cambridge, MA: Harvard University.

Polanyi, K. (1957). *The great transformation.* Boston: Beacon Hill.

Poulantzas, N. (1973). *Political power and social classes.* London: Sheed & Ward.

Qiao, S. (1986). Shenru zhashide kaizhan pufa gongzuo (Penetratingly and concretely develop the work of popularizing law). *Zhongguo Fazhibao*, (December 22).

Rigby, T. (1964). Traditional, market and organizational societies and the USSR. *World Politics, 16* (July 1964), 539-557.

Rigby, T. (1976). Politics in the mono-organizational society. In A. Janos, *Authoritarian politics in communist Europe.* Berkeley, CA: Institute of International Studies, 31-80.

Rigby, T., Brown, A. & Reddaway, P. (Eds.) (1980). *Authority power and policy in the USSR.* London: MacMillan.

Skocpol, T. (1979). *States and social revolutions.* Cambridge: Cambridge University.

Skorownek, S. (1982). *Building a new American state.* Cambridge: Cambridge University.

The decision on economic structural reform. (1984) *Beijing Review 44* (October 29): I-XVI.

Tidrick, G. & Chen, J. (Eds.). (1987). *China's industrial reform.* Oxford: Oxford University.

Walder, A. (1983). Organized dependency: Cultures of authority in Chinese industry. *Journal of Asian Studies, 43*, 1 (November), 51-76.

Walder, A. (1986). *Communist neotraditionalism: Work and authority in Chinese industry.* Berkeley, CA: University of California.

Weber, M. (1964). *The religion of China.* New York: Macmillan.

Weber, M. (1969). *Economy and society.* Glencoe, IL: Free Press.

Weber, M. (1947). *The theory of social and economic organization.* Glencoe, IL: Free Press.

Williamson, O. (1975). *Markets and hierarchies.* New York: Free Press.

Xia, S. (1985). *Xingzhengguanlixue.* Taiyuan: Shanxi Renminchubanshe.

Yeung, W. (1986). China's troubling mercantilist bent. *Asian Wall Street Journal* (May 12), 12.

Zhongong Haerbinshi Nangangquwei Zuzhibu Wenjian. (1985) Jianli jianquan gangwei zerenzhi, shixing mubiao guanli shixing fang'an. (Build a healthy system of post responsibility: Put into practice the experimental program of management by objectives.

Index

About the Contributors

James A. Caporaso is Virginia and Prentice Bloedel Professor of Political Science in the Department of Political Science of the University of Washington. He previously taught on the faculties of Northwestern University and the University of Denver and served as visiting professor at Carleton University (Canada) and Harvard University.

He is the editor of *Comparative Political Studies* (Sage Publications) and has served on the Editorial Board of *International Organization*. He has published in many journals, including the *American Political Science Review, International Organization, International Studies Quarterly,* and *Annals of the American Academy of Political and Social Science.*

Professor Caporaso's current interests and research are in the development of the theoretical foundations of political economy, international political economy, and theories of the state. He is currently working on a book with David Levine, an economist from the University of Denver, on theories of political economy and another coauthored book on international political economy, with W. Ladd Hollist from Brigham Young University.

Ted Robert Gurr is Professor of Government and Political Science and Distinguished Fellow at the Center for International Development and Conflict Management at the University of Maryland, College Park. He has written more than a dozen books and monographs on political conflict, criminal justice, and other public policy issues, including *Why Men Rebel* (winner of the Woodrow Wilson Prize as best book in political science of 1970); *Rogues, Rebels, and Reformers: A Political History of Urban Crime and Conflict* (1976); and *The State and the City* (with Desmond S. King, 1987). A new edition of his *Violence in America: Historical and Comparative Perspectives* (1969, with Hugh Davis Graham) was published as a two volume set (1989). One of his current research projects is a global analysis of communal groups in conflict; another is the historical analysis of the relations between war, revolution, and the growth of coercive states in Western societies.

Andrew Kirby is currently Associate Professor in the Department of Geography and Regional Development at the University of Arizona, following regular and visiting appointments at the Universities of Reading,

283

England; Colorado at Boulder; Berkeley; and Stanford. He is Review Editor of the journal *Political Geography Quarterly* and Editor of the *Routledge Series in Political Geography*. He has published in a number of journals, including *Comparative Political Studies, Policy and Politics, Policy Studies Journal, Urban Affairs Quarterly,* and *Government and Policy*. Author of *Politics of Location* (Methuen, 1982), he is currently completing a book on the state apparatus and local politics entitled *A State of Chaos*.

Stephen D. Krasner is Professor of Political Science at Stanford University. He is the author of *Defending the National Interest* (Princeton University Press, 1978), *Structural Conflict* (University of California Press, 1985), and *Asymmetries in Japanese American Trade* (Berkeley: Institute for International Studies, 1987) as well as articles in a number of scholarly journals.

Gregg O. Kvistad is an Assistant Professor in the Department of Political Science at the University of Denver. He held an SSRC fellowship during 1987-1988 at the Free University, West Berlin, and is now completing a book manuscript on the idea of the state and the politics of the German civil service. He has published on West German politics and on social theory in *West European Politics, Comparative Political Studies, Social Concept,* and *Worldview*.

Jeremy T. Paltiel is Assistant Professor of Political Science at the University of Alberta in Edmonton, Canada. He received his Ph.D. (1984) and M.A. (1979) from the University of California, Berkeley and B.A. in East Asian Studies from the University of Toronto in 1974 after which he spent two years as an exchange student in Beijing, China. His dissertation analysed the system of leadership in China and the Soviet Union in order to explain the conjunction of successions with major periods of social economic and political reforms. He has written and published articles in the area of comparative communism and political reform in China.

Bert A. Rockman is Professor of Political Science and Research Professor in the University Center for International Studies at the University of Pittsburgh. Among other works, he is coauthor of *Bureaucrats and Politicians in Western Democracies* (1981) and author of *The Leadership Question: The Presidency and the American System* (1984). Presently, he is engaged (along with Joel D. Aberbach) in a study of change in the United States Federal Executive, which is part of a cross-national project.

James N. Rosenau is the Director of the Institute for Transnational Studies at the University of Southern California as well as Professor of Political Science and International Relations. He is a past President of the International Studies Association and has also been a member of the faculties of Rutgers University (New Brunswick, New Jersey) and Ohio State University. He has published many books on the scientific study of foreign policy, global interdependence and political adaptation, including most recently coauthorship of *American Leadership in World Affairs* and coeditorship of *World Systems Structure: Continuity and Change,* and *New Directions in the Comparative Study of Foreign Policy.*

Janice E. Thomson is an Assistant Professor in the Department of Political Science at the University of Washington. An article that she coauthored with Stephen D. Krasner, entitled "Global Transactions and the Consolidation of Sovereignty," has been published in Ernst-Otto Czempiel and James N. Rosenau (eds.), *Global Changes and Theoretical Challenges: Approaches to World Politics for the 1990s* (Lexington, MA: Lexington Books, 1989).

David Wilsford (Ph.D., University of California, San Diego) is assistant professor of political science at the University of Oklahoma. He also holds degrees in French and in history from the University of South Carolina and from the Ecole des Hautes Etudes en Sciences Sociales in Paris, France. Recent publications include "Pouvoir médical, pouvoir politique et crise économique en France et aux Etats-Unis" (*Revue Française des Affaires Sociales,* 1986) and "Physicians and the State in France" (in Giorgio Freddi and James W. Björkman, Eds., *The Comparative Politics of Health Governance,* Sage, 1988).

NOTES